THE CIVILIZATION OF ANGKOR

THE CIVILIZATION OF

ANGKOR

Madeleine Giteau

RIZZOLI
NEW YORK

Translated from the French, *Angkor: Un Peuple – Un Art*,
by Katherine Watson.

French-language edition:
© 1976 by Office du Livre Fribourg

English translation published 1976
in the United States of America by:

*R*IZZOLI *INTERNATIONAL PUBLICATIONS, INC.*
712 Fifth Avenue / New York 10019

Library of Congress Catalog Card Number: 76-11250
ISBN: 0-8478-0040-7

Printed in Switzerland

CONTENTS

FOREWORD 9
INTRODUCTION 13

Part one: LIFE IN THE PROVINCES
LIFE IN THE TOWNS AND VILLAGES 31
THE SOCIAL AND ADMINISTRATIVE ORGANIZATION OF THE PROVINCES 64
JOURNEYS ACROSS THE PROVINCES 71
THE GREAT PROVINCIAL SANCTUARIES 81

Part two: LIFE IN ANGKOR
STAGES IN THE BUILDING OF ANGKOR 99
ACTIVITIES OF THE PEOPLE 148
ARISTOCRATIC DWELLINGS 161
THE SIGHTS OF THE CITY STREETS 169
THE WALLED CITY 173

Part three: LIFE IN THE PALACE
THE FUNCTION OF ROYALTY 191
KING AND COURT 201
JAYAVARMAN VII AND THE REORGANIZATION OF THE KINGDOM . . 213

Part four: LIFE IN THE TEMPLES AND CEREMONIALS
ASCETICS IN THE FOREST 219
LIFE IN TEMPLES AND MONASTERIES 223
THE CULTURAL ROLE OF TEMPLES AND MONASTERIES 231
THE TEMPLE AS A REFUGE FOR THE UNFORTUNATE AND THE SICK . 234
THE FEASTS OF THE YEAR 236

ROYAL CEREMONIAL 241
THE REVIVAL OF ANGKOR IN THE SIXTEENTH CENTURY 245

CONCLUSION 249
FOOTNOTES 252

APPENDIXES
BRAHMAN AND BUDDHIST ICONOGRAPHY 257
ŚIVA 257
VISHNU 260
BRAHMA 264
BUDDHIST ICONOGRAPHY 264
GLOSSARY 268
MAPS AND PLANS 269
BIBLIOGRAPHY 276
INDEX 277

IN MEMORY OF HENRI MARCHAL

CURATOR OF ANGKOR
(Paris 1876—Siem Reap 1970)

FOREWORD

"Since we are at present in this region and have spoken of the Kingdom of Camboja, we think it good to give here an account of a very fine city discovered in its forests... and which may be considered one of the wonders of the world."[1] Thus wrote a Portuguese traveler of the sixteenth century, Diego do Couto, when sending home a report on the death of a Khmer king at Angkor. He added: "In addition to the town being of great majesty in its arrangement, it was by reason of its site one of the best in this world, for the region is of the most pleasing, with groves, rivers and excellent springs of water." The travelers of the sixteenth century were able to see a resuscitated Angkor; visitors in the following centuries did not have this privilege, and could do no more than admire a dead city and wonder what might have been the life that once animated the crumbling monuments. It is true that the monasteries established in Angkor Wat maintained a life of religion in the great temple, but every temporal undertaking had abandoned the ruined capital. And yet the life of the Khmers of those times is not wholly lost. Inscriptions and carvings in stone perpetuate the memory of the days from the tenth to the fifteenth century when the capital was at Angkor and was called Yaśodharapura, from the name of its founder, King Yaśovarman I.

1 Face tower, Ta Som, west gate. Colossal images of guardian deities, these face towers protect the entrance of certain Angkorian temples, their eyes fixed on the four points of the compass. At the little shrine of Ta Som, one of the four faces of the west gate is almost smothered in dry twisted roots.

The Khmer temples provide an extraordinary wealth of documentation on the civilization of Angkor.
From late in the tenth century, and for as long as sovereigns and dignitaries built monuments in Cambodia, sculptors were bringing alive the old myths and epic scenes in the Khmer palaces or in the villages and towns of the countryside. On the pediments and gallery walls of the temples the kings preside in their palaces, converse with the high dignitaries of their court or watch the intricate ballets of their dancers; princes set off on pilgrimages at the head of brilliant retinues, to prostrate themselves at the feet of some deity or anchorite famous for his holiness. Hermits meditate in forests or busy themselves with the cares of their ascetic lives. Buildings, furnishings and utensils appear in the bas-reliefs carved on the walls. In the very center of Angkor, on a wall in the temple of the Bayon, there is an immense relief devoted to the narrative of a battle on land and water; its lower part reveals to us in all its immediacy the bustle of a town some thousand years ago, with its inhabitants, its houses, its market and its diversions.
In those crumbling galleries, there in the heart of a city reverting to forest, the visitor can single out all the varied activities of the life that enlivened the capital at that time, and other towns and cities as well; it is a life that did not disappear completely with the abandonment of Angkor. Passing through modern villages he will see in the hands of the country people the very pots and baskets he knows from the reliefs, and the people too resemble the Khmers of times gone by. The designs on the traditional clothing will remind him of the admirable zigzag motifs

9

that decorate the costumes of the lovely *devatá* of Angkor Wat. There has been no break in the daily round of the Khmer villagers since the time when that of their ancestors was carved in stone.

And while the scenes carved on the monuments show us the doings of the Khmers in the Middle Ages, the inscriptions engraved on stelae and walls lay bare the religious culture, the philosophy, the laws, the political and administrative organization, even the historical events of Cambodia in the period of Angkor.

As we set out on our excursion around the Khmer Kingdom in the period of Angkor we need as a basic guide to sketch for ourselves a picture of Cambodian civilization as it appears in the carvings and written documents, though we must take care that our interpretation does not go beyond our evidence. We have chosen for this journey the beginning of the thirteenth century, in preference to any other moment in the five centuries of the Angkor period. At that time Jayavarman VII was reigning in Cambodia. He had come to the throne in 1181 after delivering the country from foreign occupation, and he had finished the restoration of his capital, modern Angkor Thom, building new holy places on a religious plan designed to ensure that his kingdom would be completely inviolable. This project had been to a large extent completed by the early years of the thirteenth century. All the great Khmer monuments whose ruins we admire today were already built by this propitious time. Religious ceremonies were enacted both in the temples founded by the reigning monarch and in the sanctuaries erected by the kings who had governed Cambodia in the preceding centuries. The city was then at the zenith of its greatness. No other period provides such generous documentation for a study of Angkorian civilization. The epigraphy of Jayavarman VII is unusually abundant. The reliefs covering the pediments and walls of the monuments founded by this king and his predecessors represent, side by side, episodes of myth and epic and scenes inspired by the life of every day, not only of the princes but of the people. To evoke this period we can also use the documents of an earlier time, for there was certainly little change in customs between the beginning of the tenth century and the period with which we are concerned, nor did the civilization of Angkor alter during the thirteenth century; what a Chinese traveler, Chou Ta-kuan, who came to Angkor in 1296, reports on the life of the Khmers can very well be applied to the Cambodia of Jayavarman VII.

We will set out, then, to understand the Cambodia of that time, bearing in mind the observation noted by the Chinese Chronicler as he begins his description of the city of Angkor: "Doubtless the customs and affairs of this country cannot be known completely, but the main features are discernible." Limiting our ambitions, like him, we will report what we have seen, and what we have learnt from the inscriptions and travelers of those times.

2   *Devatā*, Banteay Chhmar. Forest has engulfed the holy place, but beneath the green moss the *devatā* have not ceased serving the gods who were once worshiped within the shrines.

3 Ships and market scenes, the Bayon, relief on the outer
south gallery. On the right, arranged in registers, long ships
laden with warriors are preparing for battle. On the left, on a
pleasure boat, the captain gives his orders to the sailors while
on deck men are dancing or drinking from a large jar. Round
them fishermen throw out their nets. The lower register shows
a village market by the river bank.

INTRODUCTION

Our knowledge of the civilization of Angkor is arrived at from the study of a variety of documents, some written, some pictured in stone, some native, some foreign. Each adds something to the others, but even so there are certain aspects of Khmer life which remain in shadow while others are more brightly lit. Nor will these sources, varied as they are, be able to bring the atmosphere of Cambodia in the Angkor period to life for us unless they are placed in the context of the geography, history and religion of the Khmer Middle Ages.

THE SOURCES

The scenes carved in relief on stone illustrate the life of the different classes of Khmer society in great variety, for the sculptors enjoyed portraying the daily round no less than religious ceremonies, court festivals or the drama of the battlefield. We have in them, therefore, a priceless record of the activities of the Khmers in every walk of life.

A study of the temples themselves, of the arrangement of the plans, of the iconography, brings us close to the religious life of our period, yet for a proper understanding of the spiritual life of Angkorian Cambodia we have to turn to the Indian texts, for it was India that gave its religious conceptions to southeast Asia. Features of the layout of Indian temples were often preserved by Khmer architects, and the peculiarity of a sanctuary can sometimes only be explained in terms of the interpretation of an Indian treatise.

The circumstances presiding over the erection of monuments are often described by the founders in the numerous inscriptions engraved on stelae or more simply on the jambs of the doors that give access to the halls of passage or to the sanctuaries themselves. Khmer inscriptions are an essential source for our study. They are lacking, of course, in the anecdotal charm of the figured carvings, but they contain an untold wealth of documentation on the history, the beliefs, the social and political arrangements of Angkorian Cambodia. The Khmers were consummate stone-carvers. The script they engraved on stone, a script originating from that of South India, is of great beauty. Often it is possible to tell, simply from the form of the writing, when an inscription was written, even when it is undated. The broadly drawn characters of pre-Angkorian stelae are followed in the tenth century by a smaller but still elegant hand. In the twelfth and thirteenth centuries the style is drier, but executed with no less perfect care.

The language used is either Sanskrit or Old Khmer. Sanskrit is reserved for the nobler texts: stanzas of homage to divine beings, panegyrics of kings or high dignitaries. When juridical decisions are drawn up in *fig. 4* Sanskrit they are usually repeated in Old Khmer. Inscriptions recording foundations, gifts of land to a temple, or grants by a sovereign to his followers needed to be understood by everyone; to avoid any subsequent disputes it was necessary to perpetuate them in the language understood by all the king's subjects. There is no need to dwell on the importance of these inscriptions for understanding the religion and history, the social and legal structures of the kingdom. Invocations to deities sometimes reveal the tendencies of different sects; panegyrics of the king will often tell of historical events; the legal proclamations give us insight into the juridical system, into customs and the organization of magistrates, and into social relations.

The other sources to which we can refer for our study of Angkorian civilization are from outside Cambodia; they are largely of Chinese origin. Cambodia maintained relations with almost all the states of southern and eastern Asia, from India and Ceylon to China. In the *Mahavamsa* we learn that in the tenth century King Parakrama Bahu sent a Singhalese princess to Cambodia. But the Indian and Singhalese texts give very little information on the great southeast Asian kingdom, whereas the Chinese Annals are a rich source of documentation.

Well before the foundation of Angkor the slowly developing Khmer monarchy exchanged embassies with the Chinese empire. As early as the seventh century Chinese envoys were reporting any events they thought of importance and noting down their observations on the life of the people of the kingdom they called Chenla. Throughout the following centuries, mentions of these exchanges of embassies were consigned to the Chinese Annals at more or less regular intervals, each time recording the gifts by which the King of Cambodia had rendered homage to the Emperor of China. In these texts Cambodia appears as a land of legendary riches. Towards the end of the thirteenth century the reports deteriorate. Cambodia refused to send the customary gifts that smacked of a kind of tribute. In 1195 the Emperor ordered an embassy to proceed to Cambodia to remedy this state of affairs and put an end to the strained relations between the two countries. The envoys left in the following year; among them was one Chou Ta-kuan. Besides sending in his findings on the mission, which he deemed a success, he composed a *Memoir on the Customs of the Cambodians* in which he reported all he had seen and heard during his travels. He allows us to follow him as he strolls the streets, visits people's homes, comments on how the Khmer people of the thirteenth century lived; we are even present with him at scenes that we can recognize on the reliefs of some of the temples; we are taken through the doors into Angkor Thom, nay more, we are admitted with him to a royal audience.

After scrutinizing the reliefs and reading the inscriptions, after following the Chinese on their journeys, we can no longer think of Angkor as a city of mystery, dead and gone. We should not forget however that this documentation, rich as it is, does not illustrate every single aspect of Cambodian civilization. Numbers of questions remain unanswered: as we visit the temples we are provoked to ask in what way and to what extent the requirements of the cult dictated the highly complex plans; to what use were put the multiple halls that must sometimes be traversed before arriving at the central sanctuary. What was the form of worship practiced in these holy places? Such questions are but inadequately answered by the carvings, even by the inscriptions. The religious buildings of modern times correspond to other concepts and are of little help, for the temples of Angkor were dedicated to the Hindu or Buddhist cults of Mahāyāna, the Greater Vehicle (of progress towards salvation), whereas for the past six centuries Cambodia has been converted to the Buddhism of the Theravāda, the "Doctrine of the Ancients," often scornfully termed Hīnayāna, the "Lesser Vehicle." A study of the Indian texts is the only means of elucidating some of these problems; in this work therefore we shall often have to turn to the experts on India.

In the texts of the inscriptions and even in the accounts of the Chinese annalists we can glean much information about the society and political, administrative and juridical systems of the Kingdom of Angkor. Yet upon undertaking such a study we can see that quite a few gaps remain in our documentation. We are still unable to work out the hierarchy of a section of the civil service, or draw up the articles of a legal code. After all, the inscriptions were not carved to instruct posterity in the history and institutions of the period. The legal decisions they confirm, the historical events they refer to, the careers of the dignitaries they recount are always represented in a religious light; all these occasions appear to us, as G. Coedès observed, in a "distorting mirror." We

4 Fragment of a text engraved on a stele. The script of Khmer writing comes from southern India. It was used to engraved texts in Sanskrit and Old Khmer. The stone carvers of pre-Angkorian and Angkorian times were highly skilled. Their calligraphy is beautiful because it is precise without being dry, and the curves are full and harmonious.

must then, as far as is possible, place ourselves within the religious context of the period if we are to draw valid conclusions about the organization of the Khmer state of Angkor from what is offered by epigraphy.

The inscriptions, written for princes, for dignitaries or at least for the notabilities, are little concerned with minor folk who only appear as slaves or as peasants owing labour dues or portions of their crops to the temple. Yet it is the life of these villagers that we can most easily imagine, in our own days, without fear of distortion. Until very recently one had only to go into the countryside in Cambodia to understand that despite the centuries that have passed the life of humble people had preserved the same activities as before. One could identify the cauldron set over the clay hearth as the one that figures in the reliefs of the Bayon, notice in some country marketplace a woman frying fish or bananas over a charcoal brazier with exactly the same movements and gestures as the villagers of those far-off days. The ox-carts on the roads have kept the elegant lines and raised shaft they had in the eleventh and twelfth centuries; plowmen drive their furrows with the same plow that was brandished like a weapon by Balarāma (brother of Krishna and himself also an incarnation of Vishnu) on a tenth century pediment of Banteay Srei. Thus modern peasant life is far from negligeable as a source of information to supplement the ancient documentation.

GEOGRAPHY

The basin of the Great Lake and the Plain of the Mekong, up-river from the Mekong delta, form the vital part of modern Cambodia, which stretches out to the Dangrek Plateau, to the Gulf of Siam and the highlands of Ratanakiri, covering an area of 180,000 square kilometers. In the early thirteenth century the Khmer kingdom was much larger: it comprised all the low-lying plain and delta of the Mekong, the south of Laos as far as the neighborhood of Vientiane, the provinces of southeast Thailand and even part of the Menam plain.

The sparsely populated mountainous regions, the

5 Angkor Wat at sunrise, taken from the air. Across the sea of forest, the sun rises on Angkor Wat, while the most honorable approaches to this western-oriented temple remain plunged in shadow. The light shows up in silhouette the multiple stories of the tower-shrines, clings to the roof ridges and is already beginning to invade the interior courtyards.

Cardamom chain or eastern plateau, lay outside the civilization of Angkor, whose activity was concentrated in the plains of the Mekong and Menam and above all in the region of the Great Lake. In these vast expanses of flat countryside the population was almost exclusively involved in agriculture; this has remained until today the principle resource of the country. The life of the villages and towns took its rhythm from the alternation of dry and rainy seasons.

In the thirteenth century kingdom of the Khmer, Angkor was in the heartland of the country and not on the remote periphery as it is today. The situation of Angkor lent great importance to the transversal northwest/southeast axis created by the Plain of the Great Lake and its outlet, the Tonle Sap; while the valley of the Mekong formed the north-south axis of the land. These two great waterways drain the waters carried into them by tributaries, some of them great rivers in their own right, like the Srepok that joins the Mekong in front of the modern town of Stung Treng. Large water courses feed the Great Lake, which is like an inland sea; some are fine rivers that irrigate the sites of Angkor. The Stung Sangker flows near the hills of Banon and Wat Ek Phnom, the Stung Sen waters the region of the old seventh century capital, Sambor Prei Kuk, and above all the Stung Siem Reap, though the smallest, is the river of Angkor.

The Mekong system dominates the whole vital area of Cambodia with its hydrography. When in spate, fed by the melting of the Tibetan snows and the precipitations of the rainy season, the flooding waters turn the marshy arms of the river into a veritable sea and flow up into the Tonle Sap; the waters wash back from the Mekong into the Great Lake. When in autumn the Tibetan snows begin to freeze and the winter monsoons dry up the rain, the Tonle Sap changes direction as it no longer receives the mass of water from the Mekong, and starts once more to drain the Great Lake. Gradually the flooded lands emerge again.

Since the far-off days of the kingdom of Funan, which probably had its capital near the Gulf of Siam, the problem of draining the lowlands has pressed on the inhabitants of the Cambodian plain. This preoccupation is apparent even in the epigraphy: the stele of Prāsāt Pram Loveng speaks of "a domain conquered from the mud"; it plays its part in one of the legends of the origins of the Khmer monarchy, which recounts how a king of the *nāga* wanted to make a kingdom for his son-in-law, the brahman Kaundinya, and drank all the water covering the lower plain of Cambodia. The first kingdom known to have been established in Khmer country, Funan, was maritime and commercial, and faced the sea. It was supplanted in the seventh century by a state that had been its vassal, Chenla, which was much less open to maritime influence, a land of agriculturalists which was to be inherited by the kingdom of Angkor. Limited at first like Chenla to the plains of the lower Mekong and the Great Lake, the Khmer kingdom became in the course of the eleventh and twelfth centuries the greatest state of southeast Asia. This expansion could only happen at a cost; internally the annexed regions made difficulties by sporadic bids for independence, externally, and even more serious, were the fights against neighbouring countries: the Mon states of the Menam, the Dai Viet of Tonking, the Champa kingdom further south from the Cloud Pass to the Mekong delta.

HISTORY

It would be hopeless to attempt to understand Khmer civilization of the thirteenth century without some acquaintance with the political and historical climate in which it developed. This civilization expanded under a monarchy which had been created long before the foundation of Angkor. The first organized

6   The temple of Bakong (late ninth century). In Hariharālaya, which was the capital before Angkor, King Indravarman I had the temple of Bakong built. This earliest of Khmer monuments, raised on a high pyramidal base, was inaugurated in 881. Between two wall tracts of a sandstone shrine the remains of a group of deities is still standing: Śiva "entwined in the liana arms" of his consorts, Umā and Gangā.

monarchy of which we have any knowledge in the land of the Khmers goes back to the first centuries of the Christian era, to the period when Indian influence penetrated throughout southeast Asia. Khmer epigraphy, and the Chinese Annals likewise, give evidence of the existence of little principalities over which sovereigns tried at intervals to establish domination, without ever succeeding completely. Early in the ninth century a king, Jayavarman II, managed to impose his authority on a whole area of Cambodia. A ceremony celebrated on the Phnom Kulen, north of the region of Angkor, consecrated the independence of the kingdom, making a rejection in form of the sovereignty which Java had apparently imposed on Cambodia in the preceding century. Henceforth all the Khmer sovereigns sought recognition as *chakravartin* kings, that is to say universal monarchs according to the Indian ideal. King Indravarman, the second successor of Jayavarman II, continued the work of unification begun by the latter, and brought most of Cambodia under his rule, meanwhile building impressive sanctuaries in his capital, Hariharālaya, on the site of modern Roluos. His son came to the throne as Yaśovarman I in 889, and it was he who founded the new and more glorious capital, Yaśodharapura, on the site of Angkor.

fig. 6

The city of Yaśodharapura as it was built for Yaśovarman did not occupy the exact site of Angkor Thom, which corresponds to the capital of Jayavarman VII. Its center was a temple built on a natural hill, Phnom Bakheng, slightly south of the present walls of Angkor Thom. Yaśovarman's aim was to found the ideal capital of a *chakravartin* king, a truly divine world on earth in the center of his kingdom, so that the city should become an inviolable dwelling to equal the dwelling of the gods.

fig. 57

After the apparently rather sombre reigns of the two sons of Yaśovarman the crown was lost to his line, and at the same time Angkor was abandoned by royalty. Jayavarman IV, the brother-in-law of Yaśovarman, once he had mounted the throne went to reign some hundred kilometers northeast of Angkor on the site of Koh Ker, and here he founded a capital full of grandiose monuments. For two decades until 944 the center of the kingdom was Koh Ker. After

fig. 51

the death of Jayavarman IV in 942 his son, a young child, became king but disappeared after two years. The extinction of Jayavarman's succession and the accession of Yaśovarman's nephew Rājendravarman II brought the monarchy back to Yaśodharapura.

Royalty was not to leave the site of Angkor again, virtually speaking, until the end of the fourteenth century. Yaśodharapura was the coveted prize in a series of wars of succession between rival claimants. After the reign of Jayavarman V (968–1001) and the death of the infant king Udayādityavarman there were two rivals who aspired to the throne. Jayavīravarman installed himself at Angkor but was eliminated by Sūryavarman I whose dynasty then ruled the land throughout the eleventh century. The beginning of the twelfth century saw another dynastic crisis which culminated in the brilliant reign of Sūryavarman II, founder of Angkor Wat.

Despite these troubles the monarchy itself was firmly established, supported on a strongly structured administrative system. Yaśodharapura remained the one true capital and its possession seems always to have ensured the success of a claimant, at times when there were disputes about the succession. In spite of the evident gravity of these rivalries they never put in question the principle of monarchy, for it alone was capable of presiding over the destinies of an organized state, nor did they ever constitute a threat to the independence of the kingdom. Indeed the monarchy emerged fortified from the two most serious crises. The government of Sūryavarman I (1002–1050) saw a strengthening of administrative and legal institutions. The reign of Sūryavarman II (1113–c. 1155) took luster from a brilliant foreign policy, at least in its early years, and from the construction of numer-

7 Battle between Khmers and Cham, the Bayon, outer gallery. Throughout the twelfth century there was seldom any long peace between the Khmers and the Cham. Here, under standards that float in the wind, Khmers with close-cropped hair fight Cham who wear strange helmets shaped like upturned flowers. A Khmer horseman is throwing his spear as one of his adversaries, apparently smitten to death, falls from his horse as it rears. The slain are lying on the ground.

ous monuments, some of which are numbered among the masterpieces of Khmer art. At no time was Yaśodharapura threatened by interference from her neighbors. The protection of religion, instituted by Yaśovarman and consolidated by his successors, seemed to be completely effective. But in the second half of the twelfth century a series of dramatic events followed by a foreign invasion were to destroy all these protective arrangements and place the Khmer monarchy itself in peril.

No document has so far come to light that mentions the date and conditions of the disappearance of Sūryavarman II. It seems that this king suffered military and diplomatic setbacks towards the end of his reign, when he was fighting in the west against the Mon of the north and of modern Thailand, and in the east against the Cham and the Dai Viet of Tonking. He was probably succeeded by Yaśovarman II. Of the history of this king we know little apart from the rebellion of a personage referred to in the epigraphy as Bharata Rahu, recalling the legend of the *asura* Rahu who tries during an eclipse to devour the sun and the moon. Yaśovarman II came to a tragic end. In 1165 he was overthrown by a noble who put him to death and, taking the name of Tribhuvanādityavarman, had himself recognized as king. The usurper reigned until 1177, in which year Angkor was taken by the Cham, the darkest moment in its history.

The pretext of the Cham intervention is not known. Perhaps King Jaya Indravarman IV who had taken the Champa throne by force had dynastic rights by virtue of matrimonial alliances, or else he was merely pursuing his ambitions. The epigraphy says nothing on that score; it tells us that "Jaya Indravarman, King of the Cham, as presumptuous as Ravana, transporting his army on chariots, came to fight the god-like land of Kambu."² After a vain attempt to attack Cambodia overland, Jaya Indravarman decided to use the sea route. Guided by a shipwrecked Chinese mariner who knew the route, the Cham army, embarked "on a powerful fleet," reached Angkor. The city was taken and sacked and king Tribhuvanādityavarman perished in the fighting. The Cham became masters of Cambodia. Angkor, the divine city, had not been protected. This spelt the collapse of the whole political and religious system of the Angkor monarchy. The Khmer kingdom faced being reduced to the state of a vassal principality of the Cham king who, says the Chinese Chronicler Ma Tuan-lin, "would listen to no peace proposals."

The resurgence of Angkorian Cambodia seems the more spectacular for the dimensions of the disaster. Just when the country seemed doomed to being submerged "in a sea of affliction," its wealth and sovereign lost, its faith in an all-powerful religious protection destroyed; a prince, the future Jayavarman VII, was to return it to prosperity and bring it to the greatest glory it had ever known. By building a wondrous system of religious protection he endeavored to ensure for it whatever stability and invulnerability can be hoped for in this transitory world. The work of Jayavarman VII was tremendous. The Cham, defeated and pursued onto their own territory, were forced in their turn to experience foreign domination and bend to Khmer suzerainty. In Cambodia the traces of the invasion were wiped out: life resumed its rhythms in the farms and villages, and Jayavarman VII was consecrated king in 1181, in his restored capital.

RELIGION

Jayavarman VII was a Buddhist, whereas his predecessors had been Hindu. Nevertheless, the Hindu temples continued their worship without interruption. A true Buddhist should never stand in the way of other religions, for they too are a Way of progression along the path of salvation. Moreover, the Buddhist texts do not reject the gods of Brahmanism, who have their place in the Buddhist cosmology. While the king built Buddhist temples, the restored Hindu sanctuaries were able to witness the celebration of ceremonies in honor of their gods.

In the great temples built in previous centuries by earlier sovereigns, the god venerated in the central sanctuary was generally Śiva, singled out as the favorite divinity of the founders. The image in which Śiva came to reside was rarely anthropomorphic; the god was most usually figured in the aspect of a phallic *lingam*, the symbol of his creative power. Round the main sanctuary were subsidiary sanctuaries dedicated to different divinities, primarily to Vishnu and Brahma, the two other members of the Trimūrti. No great Vishnuite temples were consecrated in the tenth and eleventh centuries, but in the twelfth century arose Angkor Wat in which Vishnu, the god preferred by Sūryavarman II, was worshiped.

fig. 5

We learn from inscriptions that some sanctuaries contain statues representing a dead man, a relative of the founder, worshiped as a divinity. The sovereigns attached importance to the erection of temples to the memory of their ancestors and predecessors. We see Yaśovarman I constructing the temple of Lolei and Rājendravarman II the temple of the Eastern Mebon to the memory of their ancestors.

The inner walls of the cells generally had no sculptured decoration, but on the pediments and lintels and, from the eleventh century, on the walls of the galleries and halls of passage, the decorators carved innumerable reliefs with scenes from the myths of

fig. 42 Śiva and Vishnu, from episodes of Indian epic,

8   *Lingam*, Preah Pithu. In the center of the crumbled shrine the *lingam* has remained standing, covered in moss. The phallic symbol of the creative potency of Śiva, it also represents the Trimūrti: its square base is Brahma, the middle octagonal part is Vishnu and the summit, which is circular in section, is Śiva himself.

9   Fight scene. Banteay Srei, lintel decoration (third quarter of the tenth century). In the center of the lintel, under an arcade of foliage, two people are fighting. Both have their hair tied back, which is the style of very young men. The victor, wearing heavy jewelery, has thrown his adversary who is strangely shown with three feet; it is quite unusual in Khmer art to see people with an uneven number of limbs. The meaning of this scene is not known. In Indian iconography Agni may be represented with three feet.

10   Group of Śiva and Umā, Prāsāt Muang Tam (Thailand). Seated on the bull Nandin, Śiva sits with his left arm round his wife Umā. He holds in his right hand his principal attribute, the trident. Only rarely has the divine couple been carved with such charming naivety. Beneath the hoofs of Nandin appears the monstrous head that is often carved at the base of lintels, to guard the entrance to sanctuaries against all maleficent beings.

especially the Rāmāyana and Mahābharata. The scenes on the reliefs were familiar to the faithful who came to render homage to the divinities. Indian culture had been imported during the first centuries of our era and had entered deeply into the soul of the Cambodians. As they looked at the carvings they could immediately identify the manifestations of Śiva or the *avatars* of Vishnu, the "descents" of the god to our world. Among these incarnations of Vishnu

the most popular were certainly Krishna and Rāma, *fig. 26* and their exploits inspired the sculptors with splendid compositions.

When Buddhism became the religion of the sovereign there was no cessation in the carving of Brahmanical subjects. At the Bayon, the great Buddhist temple erected by Jayavarman VII in the center of his capital, the walls of the galleries display numerous representations of Hindu myths, while at the same time on the highest terrace the Buddha was worshiped in the central sanctuary. In Cambodia the introduction of Buddhism in its Mahāyāna form, that is to say the form of the "great Way of progression" to salvation, goes back to the beginnings of Hinduisation. Nonetheless, though it had a considerable number of adepts, Buddhism does not seem to have been the religion of the sovereigns until the late twelfth century. Jayavarman VII had received from his parents his faith in Mahāyāna Buddhism. When he became king he multiplied the foundation of temples and monasteries in which the images of Buddha and of certain *Bodhisattvas* were venerated, especially Avalo- *fig. 44* kiteśvara. When the politico-religious system of his Śivaite predecessors crumbled, he sought in a Buddhist ideal the means to render the monarchy he had restored indestructible for the whole duration of the present *kalpa*, the cosmic period of our time.

At the beginning of the thirteenth century the organization of the Khmer kingdom seemed to have reached perfection. Jayavarman VII had definitively

11 Hevajra, Angkor, Banteay Kdei, Phnom Penh, National Museum (late twelfth-early thirteenth century). The eight-headed god with sixteen arms is represented dancing on a demon.

12 Buddha on *nāga*, Banon, central shrine. After his Enlightenment the Buddha remained in the same place for several weeks in order to meditate the truths of which he had become aware. During the sixth week it deluged with rain. Then the *nāga* snake Muchilinda came to the Blessed One to protect him by making him a seat of his coils and stretching over him the hoods of seven heads. At the temple of Banon, built on the top of a hill, the faithful have set up this fine thirteenth century image in the central shrine.

thrown off the threat from the Cham. He fortified Cambodia with a series of religious foundations that would prevent forever a catastrophe like that of 1177. From the capital that he raised from its ruins and set up anew, his power radiated throughout the land. Governors carried out his orders in the provinces; roads connected Angkor with the farthest regions of the kingdom. For some years the Khmers enjoyed their new-found peace. Never perhaps had the civilization of Angkor been so brilliant. By the time Chou Ta-kuan came to Cambodia in 1295 the confidence of the Khmer kingdom in its future had been somewhat shaken by a difficult succession and by a foreign war against the Thais, new and warlike neighbors. We shall, therefore, anticipate Chou Ta-kuan by some eighty years in our exploration of Angkorian Cambodia: seeing the life of its inhabitants, entering through the gateways of Angkor, and penetrating at last the Royal Palace and the sanctuaries of the temples.

Part one:
LIFE IN THE PROVINCES

LIFE IN THE TOWNS AND VILLAGES

The stranger arriving in Cambodia after a hard sea voyage had still a long journey ahead of him across the kingdom before he reached the capital. The landscape that first met his eyes was the waste and marshy region of the Mekong delta. Chou Ta-kuan has left us a description of it: "Whichever way one looks there is nothing but long rattans, old trees, yellow sand, white reeds; at first sight it is not easy to see one's way, and the sailors find even the discovery of the mouth [of the river] a delicate task".[3] Having found the only branch of the Mekong that will allow the passage of a large ship, the pilot sails up river with the tide. Then the aspect of the landscape changes: "on every side are great thickets of low forest; the wide estuaries of the great river stretch over hundreds of *li;* everywhere deep glades, the luxuriant foliage of old trees and long rattans. They are alive with the cries of animals. Half way up the river one has the first sight of the immense plain, without a stick of wood. As far as the eye can see are cereals in abundance." After two weeks the ship came to a stop in a port that was perhaps situated at the confluence of four rivers where Phnom Penh now stands, or perhaps some hundred kilometers upriver on the Tonle Sap where the port of Kompong Chhnang was then built. They had to re-embark on smaller boats and the flotilla prepared to cross the "Fresh water sea," the Tonle Sap that we call the Great Lake.

Throughout this journey the strangers went through villages, stopped in towns, observed the Cambodians living in their houses, working in their fields or making their way along the roads to some provincial center or place of pilgrimage. They gradually became acquainted with this life of the provinces as they slowly approached the capital. We too, who are making the same journey in our imaginations in search of the vanished civilization that slumbers in the ruins, shall also see how life went on in the Cambodian provinces among the peasants and notables who lived there seven centuries ago.

Angkorian villages were probably little different from those scattered today about the Khmer countryside, huddled deep under their trees. This is how they appear in the Angkor reliefs, especially on those of the Bayon temple.

Village Houses

In the flat denuded countryside of the rice fields the villages appear among clusters of trees and palms. The villages of Angkor look the same; coconuts and trees are shown behind the houses. No doubt each peasant had round his house a little area planted with fruit trees: pawpaws, coconuts, bananas. In this courtyard the woman pounded paddy and cooked meals on stones or a clay hearth. Often the Cambodians quite simply "bury three stones to make the hearth." The reliefs show clearly that cooking is not done under a roof but in the open, or under the house if it is a large one built on piles.

Today typical Cambodian village dwellings are built of wood, raised on piles and covered with a roof of tiles. Poor houses have a roof and sometimes walls of bundles of straw. The village dwellings we see on the reliefs, particularly on the exterior south gallery of the Bayon, do not seem to be on piles. On the other hand they have no walls. The roof rests on pillars; raised or knotted curtains seem to serve as partitions. It is obvious that if the sculptor wanted to represent a scene inside a house this would have to be wide open. Cambodian houses almost all comprise a sort of wide open veranda in front of the dwelling part, with the roof supported by wooden columns. Curtains hung between the columns shade the veranda from the sun; they are raised when it is cool. It seems to us therefore, that the sculptor has often portrayed his scenes as taking place on the veranda and has not thought it necessary to put in the dwelling part of the house which is of no interest for the illustration of his story. It is probably also because he systematically avoided crowding his composition with what seemed unnecessary to him; he only carved the story that served as background to his scene, and left out the piles. However, in some large build-

fig. 100 ings a crowd of servants is busied on a lower floor among the piles, under the room in which the master is entertaining his guests. The oldest Chinese texts referring to Cambodia mention that the common people live "in raised dwellings." Chou Ta-kuan stresses the fact that slaves "are only allowed to sit and lie down on the ground floor."

All the texts mention that houses are made of wood: "they cut down trees to build their houses" and "the common people only roof with thatch and would not dare to use tiles." In fact this roofing would not always be of real thatch but often of dried leaves. Very simple houses have a roof of double pitch with no decoration. Village houses of more careful construction have a roof decorated with a carved pediment above the entrance, and on the roof ridge a row of spikes.

On the most elegant houses, and on little pavilions the roof is higher in the middle and lowered on each side to make one, or two, angles. On the middle part which is square in plan, one section of roofing corresponds to the meeting of two roofs perpendicular one to the other. Each of the four gables of this cross-plan roof has a carved pediment. The same arrange-

ment, found in the stone roofs of the Khmer monuments, has survived to the present day on buildings in light materials.

The Villagers

The reliefs represent a whole village population about their tasks and occupations. They are surely the ancestors of the Cambodian peasants one meets today in the fields, in the houses or in the market place. Muscular and sturdily built, both men and women are square of face and straight eyed. This latter feature, possessed by none of the Mongoloid race, seems to have impressed the Chinese. As a result of a faulty transcription, a Chinese commentator of the ninth century, giving a fantastic etymology for the word *Cambodia*, explains the word by the name of a fruit, the *kan-p'ou*, which is round, white and red, and marked by three transverse lines; this fruit, he adds, resembles the faces of Cambodian women. The three lines would evidently correspond to the lines of the eyebrows, eyes and mouth which the Cambodians have broad and fleshy. The etymology is not of course to be entertained for a moment but the noting of the straight eyes is characteristic. The other physical traits that attracted the attention of the Chinese are the dark skin and curly hair: the Cambodians "are coarse and very dark. Whether they live in the remote island villages or in the most frequented streets they are all the same." Long before this the Chinese Annals had recorded: "the men are all ugly, and dark; their hair is curly."[4] The Chinese have

13 Krishna the butter thief, Banteay Samre (mid-twelfth century). The child Krishna was brought up among villagers. One day when he had stolen some butter from his foster-mother she got angry and tied him to a heavy stone mortar; but the child, endowed with divine strength, dragged the mortar behind him. It hit and uprooted two trees, thus freeing two individuals who had been magically imprisoned in them.
On this half-gable at Banteay Samre the silhouette of Krishna dragging the mortar can only just be made out in front of his foster-mother and another village woman, while the two liberated individuals fly off.

never thought a bronzed complexion beautiful. In his description of the character of the Cambodians, the same chronicler recognized that "they have a simple nature and are not at all thievish"; but this is not perhaps a compliment. Is the simplicity not a naivety which the author rather despises? There is more admiration to be felt in a slightly later passage of the Annals that describes the inhabitants as "cunning and astute."

Hair Styles, Dress and Ornament

Some modern Cambodians have wavy hair, but all who are more or less pure strain and not partly Chinese have straight eyes and a dark skin. On the reliefs very few Cambodians are to be seen with curly hair; it is true that the men of common rank are close-cropped. The women did their hair less austerely. In this chapter we will not describe the very elaborate arrangements of the *devatā* and court ladies seen carved on the temple walls; but even among the humble village women there were some who took the trouble to be elegant. The reliefs have much to tell on this topic. For going to market to sell fish or fruit, the matrons were content to draw their hair back and roll it into a tight uncompromising bun, but the young women plaited their hair or rolled it up and knotted it and sometimes decked it with flowers. Peasant women have no other ornaments. "The women of common rank wear a bun but have no hairpins or combs or other ornament." The legend of Krishna provided the sculptors with country scenes, for the young prince, an incarnation of Vishnu, was brought up in a village. More than once, notably at Angkor Wat and Banteay Samre, the Khmer sculptors represented the episode where the infant Krishna is attached to a heavy mortar as a punishment for stealing butter from his foster-mother. She together with another village woman is contemplating the child who is *fig. 13* crawling on all fours, dragging the heavy stone mortar behind him. These young women are always portrayed as very simply dressed, but elegant in their sobriety; their hair is carried on the top of the head in two large buns. The hair of the infant Krishna is

33

generally divided into three locks that are knotted over his head. Whether this was how it was worn by all children or only by young nobles we do not know. Sometimes Krishna's hair is not divided in strands but simply held together in one big knot. The custom of leaving at least one lock of a child's hair to grow has remained in the villages until modern times. Early in the present century the cutting of this lock was the occasion of an important ceremony in rich families. We have no means of telling whether this custom existed in the countryside in the Angkorian period.

fig. 16   The men of humble rank, whether in country or town, dressed very simply: a length of cloth, like a large scarf, surrounds the hips; the two ends are knotted in front and taken behind between the legs to be fixed at the back under the belt. This is the short *sampot* still worn by the peasants for certain kinds of work and for bathing. On the reliefs there are costumes even more exiguous, though the tying is less simple; a very long cloth no wider than a belt is wound once or twice round the hips; the ends are knotted before being taken between the legs, and then raised to the waist and let hang down to the knees. This is precisely the costume worn today by the mountain-dwellers of the eastern plateaux in Cambodia. The *sampot*, made of a rich cloth and tied with greater elaboration, was the garment of the well-to-do and even of princes and gods. Probably this elegant costume was worn over a small under-*sampot*. "They simply wind a piece of cloth round their hips. When they go out, they add a wide length of cloth that they drape over the small one." The male costume leaves the chest bare; under certain circumstances, particularly when travelling, they take a rather thick scarf, twisted into a thick rope; they carry it round their necks and crossed over the chest. This is not an ornament but an additional garment the traveler or soldier can unwind and use as a wrap if the evenings are cool.

fig. 14   The female garment also leaves the chest bare. It appears to be a sort of skirt made of a wide piece of cloth wrapped round the body from the waist to the ankles and held above the hips with a belt or simply a knot. It corresponds to the modern *sarong*. We shall see later how the fine ladies used richly decorated cloths and draped this skirt according to fashion. We gather from the reliefs that the village women had shorter sarongs than well-to-do ladies; they used plainer cloth though they still draped it to leave a loose floating end. Complicated arrangements would have been unsuitable to peasant women who had their many tasks to attend to throughout the day.

Household Activities

The household activities of the villagers were of little inspiration to the sculptors of Angkor. We can imagine that the women were concerned with the house and its garden. The rooms were small; sweeping was an affair of running a bundle of twigs over the planks of the more or less well jointed floor; the dust and smaller rubbish fell through the cracks. The job was then begun again beneath the house and in the yard, and the sweepings thrown outside the fence. Care of the children is naturally the essential household role of the women. A charming scene carved on the south gallery of the Bayon shows a woman seated on the ground with a baby on her lap while a slightly older child comes to share her caress. On a relief in Angkor Wat a woman bends tenderly over a little boy. The   fig. 14 gentle upbringing the Cambodians give their children is seen again in a scene in the southwest pavilion of Angkor Wat, where a father is carrying one of his children against his shoulder. Family feeling is very strong among the Khmers; a father is always proud to take one of his children out with him.

The preparation of meals is not exclusively a feminine occupation; on a very small relief at the base of a pilaster in Ta Prohm, two women are grinding rice in mortars, but on the walls of the Bayon it is men who are cooking rice or plunging a whole pig into a cauldron. Cooking is done on little clay stoves which are exactly like those made today in the region of Kompong Chhnang. They are very rudimentary stoves. Some are fire-pots of which the upper part is   fig. 35 a tripod. This type is also found in Vietnam and throughout southeast Asia; it is well attested on the reliefs of the Bayon. Another variety of stove more

particularly Cambodian, is a kind of large oblong dish of which one end is narrower and hollower and forms the hearth; the edge of this dish is raised in three teeth to form a tripod; the other end is wider and flatter and here are placed the embers that are gradually slid into the hearth. This second type seems also to have been depicted at the Bayon. Chou Ta-kuan speaks only of a hearth made with three stones sunk in the ground.

Meals

Food is cooked in clay vessels. On the great relief of the exterior south gallery of the Bayon a man is pouring grains, probably rice, into a wide bellied vase. *fig. 92* The pig is being cooked in a huge cauldron, vaguely hemispherical with a rounded rim. Large cauldrons of the same type, some hemispherical, some cylindrical, appear in the scenes of Hell. At Banteay Chhmar the damned are being boiled in them. Chou Ta-kuan *fig. 15* mentions these clay vessels:

"For cooking rice they use a clay cooking pot, for preparing the sauce they have a clay pan…for serving rice they use Chinese plates of clay or copper. For the sauce they use the leaves of certain trees from which they make little cups, which do not leak although full of gravy. They also make out of leaves… little spoons to take up the juice and bring it to the mouth; when they have finished they throw them away." They "use a coconut as a ladle." Modern Cambodians serve from their dishes with ladles the cup of which is cut out of the hard shell of a coconut and joined by a thong to a wooden handle. Ladles of this kind, elegant in their simplicity, are sold in all the markets of southeast Asia. It is amusing to note that they were already using Chinese plates of coarse pottery.

In Cambodia leaves are no longer used for holding sauces, whereas this custom has persisted in some parts of India where they have always used pieces of banana leaf as plates. The Cambodians seem not to have adopted the ancient Indian custom of breaking one's plate after a meal, for they surely would not wantonly break plates imported from so far away, and

14 Women and children, Angkor Wat, southwest pavilion (first half of the twelfth century). On the lower register of a mythical relief a few women have met together. Their clothing is exiguous, but their costume is elegantly draped and their hair carefully arranged. One of them bends affectionately over a little boy, responding to his impetuous appeal.

there was certainly no question of only using copper plates once, for a single meal. Cambodian families passed down from generation to generation their plates, and specially bowls, of copper and bronze. Bowls of *samrit*, a bronze alloy containing some gold and silver, were considered to have the property of keeping the food in it fresh.

Vegetables were part of the diet: "onions, mustard, leeks, aubergines, watermelon, pumpkin," and also gourds and taro. The Cambodians raised chicken, ducks, pigs, sheep and even geese of whom it is said: "Previously there were no geese; they have these now, thanks to sailors who brought them from China." Their Indian culture probably forbad them *fig. 34* to eat beef. "Oxen are everywhere. They are ridden when alive, but when dead they are neither eaten nor flayed. They are left to rot, for the reason that they spent their strength in the service of man." Here the Chinese attributed a purely Chinese way of thinking to the Cambodians.

It seems likely that in the period of Angkor as now, *fig. 29* fish, both those of the Great Lake and from the sea, was an important part of the diet. The Cambodians also ate crayfish "that weigh a pound and more," bivalves and cephalopods. Shellfish were important from pre-historic times as an article of food. At the site of Samrong Sen, to the north of the Tonle Sap in the province of Kompong Chhnang, enormous mounds of bivalve shells have been found that represent the remains of the meals of the inhabitants. Water creatures provided other dishes for the Cambodians. Chou Ta-kuan mentions tortoise feet and even the "very crisp" belly of crocodile. We are however surprised to learn from him: "one sees no crabs. I think there are some but the people do not eat them." There are plenty of crabs in Cambodia at the present time, of the kind that live on both land and sea. When the *beng*, the marshy hollows, dry out in the hot season, the crabs emigrate to the rivers; they can often be seen crossing the roads.

For seasoning the Cambodians had sea salt. "In Cambodia there is no control on the preparation of salt." At the seaside "it is evaporated by boiling. In the mountains there is also a mineral with a flavor superior to that of salt." For acid flavor "the people do not know about making vinegar; when they want to make a liquid acid they use leaves of the *hsien-p'ing* tree. If the tree is in bud they use the buds. If it has seeds they use the seeds." It is not known what the *hsien-p'ing* tree is. Today for acid flavor the Cambodians use plant products, especially the fleshy berries extracted from tamarind. These fruit give a more delicate aroma to Cambodian soups than would vinegar. No Chinese source mentions *prahoc*, the fermented fish paste that supplies, in modern Cambodian cooking, both seasoning and a rich source of protein. It has probably been introduced more recently into Cambodia.

We observe that the culinary habits of Angkorian Cambodia were much closer to Indian habits than to Chinese. At no time were the people of Cambodia vegetarian. The Chinese chronicler Ma Tuan-lin mentions "cakes eaten soaked in meat gravy," and the Bayon reliefs have several pictures of animals being cooked. Chou Ta-kuan does not speak of milk-based foods, but the earlier text of Ma Tuan-lin records that the Cambodians of the first centuries of our era ate butter and curds.[5] Now, unlike the Chinese, who have a repugnance for milk products, the Indians make much use of milk, curd and butter in their diet. It may be that Indian-type food of the seventh century was abandoned during the following centuries. There are no representations, as far as we know, of cows being milked on the reliefs, whereas in India such scenes appear among illustrations of the Krishna legend. At the Baphuon, however, there are scenes of hermits shown using a churn, which implies that they made butter. It is an Indian type of churn activated by a cord wound round a pivot. An inscription of the late eleventh century refers to a person who had adhered to the Vaishnava sect of the Pañcharātra, and states that he lived on melted butter. Therefore

15 Tortures of the damned, Banteay Chhmar (late twelfth-early thirteenth century). In the foreground the executioners are throwing the damned into a cauldron placed over the flames, a cauldron resembling that used by the cooks to boil or scald a whole animal. Behind can be seen the thorny trees up which, say the texts, those guilty of adultery have to climb, chased by dogs.

it is certain that in the eleventh century the consumption of milk products, at any rate by ascetics, had not yet ceased.

The normal drink of the Cambodians was obviously water, but there were also alcoholic drinks. "They have four kinds of wine. The first is called *honey wine* by the Chinese; they use a ferment and make the wine of half honey, half water;" the second kind was made by macerating the leaves of trees, an ancient method since it was already in use in the seventh century. The third kind is made "of raw rice or the remains of cooked rice.... The last kind is sugar wine...; it is made with cane sugar. In addition, when you go up the river and follow its tributary, there is wine from the juice of the *kiao*. There is a kind of *kiao* that grows beside the water, and its juice can be fermented." It is difficult to guess what plant is meant by the word *kiao*. It is interesting that nowadays the sugar palm, *borassus*, provides the Cambodians both with leaves for thatching roofs and a juice that can be fermented, and which is mostly used for manufacturing palm sugar.

fig. 22

The reliefs rarely show people at table. There are, however, at the eastern end of the market scene on the Bayon, two fellows installed away from the crowd, intent on enjoying their lunch. One is joyously drinking the contents of a kind of gourd, the other bent over a well-filled plate, is raising a mouthful to his lips with his fingers. In southeast Asia, it is interesting to notice even today the distinction between the peoples who eat with chopsticks under Chinese influence and those who, having received their culture from India, eat with their fingers. Nowadays the Cambodians, while they have adopted the fork and spoon, are also able to eat with their fingers, but very rarely use chopsticks. Ma Tuan-lin already observed that they "regard the right hand as pure and the left as impure." This distinction is Indian; the right hand takes food, the left serves to wash the soiled parts of the body. Furthermore, "they also have beside them a tin or clay bowl full of water for rinsing their hands; they only use their fingers for taking rice and this sticks to the fingers and would not be got rid of without this water." Frequent hand washing was ritually obligatory.

fig. 16

Hygiene

After eating: "They repeat their ablutions before the meal, use their tooth picks of poplar wood immediately after, and then recite prayers."[6]

The Cambodians' concern with cleanliness aroused the astonishment and indeed the disapproval of Chou Ta-kuan. In his view "the people are often ill, which is to a great extent due to their too frequent baths and incessant hair washing." Half amused, half shocked, he describes the baths: "Each family has a pool, or two or three families have one in common, in which they all, men and women, bathe naked. Only when the father, mother or older people are in the pool do their sons and daughters or young people stay out. Or if the young ones are in the pool, the older people keep away. But if they are the same age there is no obstacle. They hide their sex with the left hand while going into the water and that is all." Let us note in passing that it is the left hand, the impure one, that hides the sex. There is no doubt that care of the body had a religious character. "They perform ablutions each morning, clean their teeth with little pieces of poplar wood and never fail to read or recite their prayers." In fact the poplar does not grow in Cambodia, but in the forest there is a tree, the *daem ulok*, whose wood, which is used to make fine sticks, resembles that of poplar. While still suspicious of the dangers to health of frequent bathing, Chou Ta-kuan recognizes the necessity of baths, for the country "is terribly hot, and one could not spend a day without bathing several times. Even at night one has to do it once or twice." It is evident that these baths were indispensible to the villagers who were working all day in the fields.

16 A little snack, the Bayon, outer south gallery (late twelfth-early thirteenth century). A little apart from the market—for no one likes eating in public—two men are eating a hasty meal. One of them has raised a flask and is pouring the liquid down his throat; the other has taken a ball of rice from the dish in his fingers and is bringing it to his mouth. Both wear a simple loin-cloth with the ends tucked into the belt, a very exiguous garment which has remained that of the mountain-dwellers.

The Great Events of Village Life

In Angkorian Cambodia life ran in rhythm with the seasonal work, and the monotony was only interrupted by the events that mark the existence of every individual. It is the solemn moments, joyous or sad, that punctuate the life of each one and give the family cause to celebrate and suspend all labor. The carvings on the temple walls pay no attention to the personal life of humble people. As for Chou Ta-kuan, he was no doubt unable to attend the religious ceremonies, so he limits himself to recounting what he saw or what he was told by his compatriots who were established in Cambodia. Thus he tells us: "in the family where I lodged, a daughter gave birth to a baby, and I was able to find out [that] the next day, carrying the child in her arms, she went to wash in the river; it really is extraordinary." He also explains why she was up so quickly: "the recently confined girl cooks rice, rolls it in salt and applies it to her sexual parts. After a day and a night she removes it. This prevents any troubles after the birth, and she remains like a young girl."

On the relief of the exterior south gallery of the Bayon is a figure in a house, half seated, half lying, with bent legs and hand pressed in pain on the belly, her chest raised on the lap of another person. She has been identified as a woman in labor, and a third figure, seated in front of the group, is the midwife. She certainly has an air of matronly authority, but is it really a scene of childbirth that the sculptor wanted to portray? Is this person, clearly wracked by pain, a woman giving birth to a child or a sick woman with terrible stomach pains? It is hard to tell, but one cannot look at this scene and remain unmoved by the patient lying in the lap of a relative, who supports her with great tenderness and raises a hand to her eyes to wipe away tears of compassion.

After the birth, the most important moment was certainly the name-giving. "For many they make a personal name of the name of the day on which they are born." It is interesting that this custom still survives today.

What was the education of these young villagers? Several times the reliefs show women bending over children and speaking tenderly to them. Elsewhere children are shown going about with groups of adults. They accompany their parents, and if the journey is too long, the father takes the youngest on his shoulders. The children seem to enjoy an unconstrained education, close to nature, which the young Cambodians have continued to receive, living among the grown ups, joining in their activities and contributing to the work in the fields.

The texts hardly mention education except when it applies to a prince. Chou Ta-kuan gives a detailed account of a strange defloration custom for young girls, the *chen-t'an*. Perhaps this ritual was part of rural life as well, though the Chinese chronicler relates it as an event of urban life:

"Parents with a daughter generally make this prayer: 'May you be desired by men! May a hundred and a thousand husbands ask you in marriage.'" According to Chou Ta-kuan, the marriage that followed the *chen-t'an* gave little occasion for festivities: "for weddings they have the custom of giving presents of cloth, but it's a formality without great importance. Many men marry a woman they have first had as a mistress; this causes no surprise or shame." In fact after the *chen-t'an* the girl who previously slept under the same roof as her parents "is shut out of the dwelling and goes where she wants without constraint or surveillance."

This minimal importance given to marriage ceremonies contradicts the account of Ma Tuan-lin: "A man who wants to marry first sends gifts to the girl; then the girl's family itself chooses a propitious day to conduct the bride to the house of the groom, guarded by a broker. When the wedding ceremony is over, the husband receives a portion of the goods of his parents and goes to set up in a house of his own." These customs described by Ma Tuan-lin anticipate

17 Scene of childbirth (?), the Bayon, outer south gallery (late twelfth–early thirteenth century). One person lies with a hand pressing on his/her belly and is twisted as though in pain. His/her head rests on the knees of a helper who weeps with a hand over his/her eyes. It may represent a woman about to give birth while a midwife seated in front of her gives advice.

some of the arrangements of a modern Cambodian marriage.[7]

The family life of a village couple was only marked by such festive events as the birth of a child, and an exceptional harvest; or bad ones like bad weather, the passage of an army in an area of contention during a dynastic war, the illness or death of a member of the family. The reliefs of the Bayon show people who are ill being tended by their relatives. On the *fig. 19* inner south gallery a very young man is being cared for by a number of attentive people; one of them, probably a doctor, touches his brow and seems to be dictating a prescription that a scribe is noting behind him, while another assistant is conveying his instructions. Chou Ta-kuan attributes illness mainly to the Cambodians excessive concern for cleanliness: "The people are often ill, which is in large measure due to their over frequent baths and incessant hair washing. Often they recover by themselves. There are many lepers standing by the roadside, and though they eat and sleep alongside them, the people do not catch the disease. It's an illness to which they are accustomed in this country, they say. Once a king was infected; he was not scorned for it. In my humble opinion it is their amatory excesses and the abuse of bathing that causes this disease in them." There was already a pharmacopoeia that was perhaps peculiar to southeast Asia: "drugs are sold on the market, but very different from those of China.... There is also a kind of sorcerer who practices on these people and is quite ridiculous." One of the most lethal diseases was clearly dysentery: "About eight or nine out of ten people who catch dysentery die of it." Leprosy, dysentery and cholera, on the wane since the introduction of modern cures, were until recently the great scourges. We should of

18 The Vessantarajātaka, relief fragment, National Museum, Phnom Penh (late twelfth century). Prince Vessantara, the last incarnation of the Buddha before his ultimate birth, was of inexhaustible charity. After giving away all his possessions he granted as gifts the people who were most dear to him. In the right section of the relief he gives his children to a Brahman who has asked for them as his slaves. On the left, pouring water over the hand of a hermit, he makes him the gift of his wife. However, the hermit was Indra and the prince and his family were soon reunited.

course also add malaria which is perhaps what the patient on the Bayon relief is suffering from, since she evidently has a fever.

There are, apparently, no funeral scenes on the reliefs, although the Chinese chroniclers all recount with astonishment and many details the customs surrounding a death. "They have no coffins for their dead but only a kind of basketry. They cover them with a cloth. In the funeral procession they too use flags, banners and musical instruments. They shed two *pan* of fried rice along the route. Having arrived outside the town in some remote and uninhabited spot, they leave the body and depart. They wait for the vultures and dogs to consume it. If this happens quickly they say that their dead had merit and have obtained this reward; if the animals will not eat them or only partially eat them they say this is a result of some fault in life. Now, there are also some people who make some effort to burn their dead; these are all descendants of Chinese." The early Annals already enumerate the different types of ceremony: "For the dead there are four kinds of 'burial': 'burial by water' which consists in throwing (the corpse) into the river current; 'burial by fire' which consists in reducing it to ashes; 'burial by the earth' which consists in burying it in a ditch; 'burial by the birds' which consists in leaving it in the countryside." Later the annalists added: "When they are ill they make a vow to be 'buried by the birds.' With songs and dances they are led out of the city, and there are birds that devour them. The remaining bones are burnt and put in a jar that is thrown into the sea. If the birds do not eat them they are put in a basket."[8] As for 'burial by fire,' the only one mentioned by Ma Tuan-lin, "the funeral is conducted as follows: the children of the dead spend a week without eating, shave their heads in mourning and cry out loudly. The relatives assemble with the priests and priestesses of *Fu* or the monks of the *Tao*, who accompany the dead with singing and playing on various musical instruments. The body is burnt on a pyre formed of every kind of aromatic wood; the ashes are collected in an urn of gold or silver and thrown into deep water. The poor use an earthenware urn painted with different colors."

It is not known if exposure to wild animals and throwing corpses into water was frequent. Burial in the ground was certainly only practiced in exceptional cases; no cemeteries have been found. Nowadays incineration is the usual method, and it seems to have been adopted some centuries ago. This is proven by the discovery of a necropolis between the temple of Banteay Kdei and the Srah Srang reservoir and the numerous finds of little urns of an ancient type containing ashes, placed in the temples of Angkor.

The death of a relative was followed by a period of mourning. "When one of their parents dies, the children do not wear mourning clothes, but the sons shave their heads and the daughters cut some hair from their foreheads, about the size of a cash; this is their sign of filial piety." Nowadays after the death of a father or mother one of the sons who is put in charge of the mourning shaves his head and may enter a monastery for a short time.

Chou Ta-kuan mentions death by illness, and also violent death by murder of passion or ritual murder, and reports on the strange custom of gall collecting: "In olden times, in the eight month, they collected gall bladders because every year the king of the Champa demanded a jar full of human gall bladders containing thousands. At night, they posted men in many places in the towns and villages; when they met people abroad at night, they covered their heads with a hood tied by a cord, and with a little knife removed the gall bladder at the bottom of the diaphragm on the right side. They waited until there were enough to present them to the king of the Champa. But they do not take gall bladders of Chinese people. One year they took the gall bladder of a Chinese and put it with the others; then all the gall bladders in the jar went rotten, and they could not be used. Recently

19 The sickbed, the Bayon, inner south gallery (late twelfth-early thirteenth century). A man lies propped up on cushions. His relatives are busy round about him. One of them, perhaps a doctor, feels his brow; another helper gives orders. The carving of the Bayon reliefs is often lacking in skill, but the poses and expression of the faces are generally very life-like. Here they achieve a deeply human emotion.

this custom has been abolished, but there is still the official of the gall bladder 'harvest' who lives in the city, near the northern gate."

This tribute to the king of Champa perhaps recalls the time, between 1177 and 1181, when Champa imposed its yoke on Cambodia, before the revenge of Jayavarman VII. However, if the official in charge of the gall bladder 'harvest' was still living in the time of Chou Ta-kuan, more than a hundred years after the Cham defeat, we must conclude that the custom had not disappeared before the mid-thirteenth century. This barbarous practice continued in the Far East and was rampant, until recently, especially in Champa. In Cambodia it was formally prohibited in the nineteenth century by King Ang Duong; after this time it would only appear again as an exception. It was of course in total opposition to Buddhist doctrine, which teaches a careful respect of life, and to all the religious principles of Cambodia.

Agricultural Work

Cultivation of the land, fishing, gathering the products of the forest and hunting, these were the tasks of the villagers. The little information we can glean from the texts or read in the reliefs allows us to conclude that the methods of work and the rhythm of peasant life had changed very little between the end of the Angkorian period and the beginning of the twentieth century.

The earliest Chinese travelers who came to Cambodia reported that the inhabitants "are concerned with agriculture" and that they "sow one year and harvest for three." This note is in Annals of the fourth and then of the seventh century. It seems unlikely that sowing was only done one year in three. The Chinese must have misinterpreted the fertility of the soil and the rapid growth of plants that was also observed by Chou Ta-kuan. "Generally they have three or four crops a year in this country."

As nowadays, the work of the fields followed the rhythm of the seasons. "There white frost and snow are unknown. For half the year it rains; for half the year it never rains. From the fourth to the ninth month it rains every afternoon. From the tenth to the third month not a drop falls... the peasants calculate the moment when the rice is ripe, the time of the flood, the limits it will reach, and according to what land they have, they sow. For plowing they do not use oxen. Their plows, scythes and hoes are of the same kind as ours, but made differently."

The plow is the characteristic attribute of Krishna's brother, Balarāma; it is often illustrated in the hands *fig. 20* of this hero.[9] Unfortunately there do not seem to be any scenes of plowing carved on the reliefs. Plows were certainly drawn by animals, oxen or buffalo, otherwise the very long wooden shaft would be inexplicable. The handle of the plow was also of wood. Only the share was either forged iron or wood encased in iron, as it still was in the nintheenth century. This very simple plow was all that was needed to dig furrows in the friable soil of the Cambodian plains. With it the sovereign himself, or one of his high dignitaries, who represented him, performed the "opening of the first furrow" every year until quite recently, during the Feast of the Royal Plowing, when the first rains had softened the earth.

In April the rainy season is heralded by a heavy atmosphere. Once or twice a week a storm breaks, and rain falls in fierce showers. A pediment of the temple of Banteay Srei shows one of these diluvian *fig. 21* rains falling perpendicularly on the forest, welcomed with joy by two figures surrounded by wild animals. Soon all the vegetation is green and the sowing can begin. All over the lowlands water covers the ricefields, and during July the peasants, both men and women, replant the rice. In October the rains subside and as the dry season settles throughout the country; the grain ripens in the fields. After the grey days of the rainy season the landscape bursts into color. The villages, which had gone quiet during the rainy season, begin to bustle with activity.

Cultivated Plants

While the plains "are nothing but abundant cereals," the peasants grow vegetables and fruit trees all along the river banks, in village gardens. "Pomegranate, sugar cane, lotus flowers and roots, taro, peach and banana... are the only crops they share with China. Lychee and oranges are the same shape, but sour. None of their other plants is known in China.... As vegetables, they have onions, mustard, leek, aubergine, watermelon, pumpkin... but no turnips, nor lettuce, endives or spinach. They have gourds from the beginning of the year. Gourd stems last several years. The cotton trees grow higher than the houses and last more than ten years. There are many vegetables I have never heard of, and there are also some edible water plants." It seems that the Cambodians have always enjoyed growing decorative plants, and these figure in their architectural decoration. As well as pink and blue lotus there are the different kinds of jasmin, and *champa* flowers that cover some of the walls of Angkor Wat with their long petals carved in delicate lacey relief.

fig. 23

Banana trees grow by the houses, and in quiet pools flower the lotus whose stems are still prepared as a vegetable today. On one wall of the southwest pavilion of Angkor Wat, men are scaling the trunks of palm trees, coconut palms or areca. At another place mangoes hang from the branches of a leafy tree. The village houses are surrounded by trees, or even small orchards. Vegetables would have to be grown near springs and on the banks of the water courses where the soil could be easily irrigated and enriched by river deposits, for the Khmers never fertilized their soil. Cambodian peasants refused to use manure: "To nourish their land and grow vegetables they never use animal manure; they scorn it as unclean. The Chinese who live there never mention it, and I think they would be disgusted by the methods of the Chinese." The use of human manure would have been inconceivable to a Cambodian. He was content to let the soil lie fallow, and satisfied with the crops thus obtained. It would have been quite easy for them to get animal manure, as they raised domestic animals.

Stock Raising

Here a buffalo cow is suckling her calf, there humped oxen are drawing a cart. Both at Angkor Wat and at the Bayon groups of gamblers are standing round the splendid fighting cocks. But chicken were certainly not only raised to provide for sport. Farm animals lived round the houses: chicken, ducks, horses, pigs and sheep. The horses are all very small. Oxen are numerous.

fig. 31

One mythological scene, carved many times over, provides an opportunity to depict herds of cattle. This is the episode of Krishna Govardhanaswami, Lord of Mount Govardhana.[10] The god Krishna stands with his arm raised, holding Mount Govardhana. He has uprooted it to protect the villagers, threatened by a storm unleashed by the anger of Indra. The Khmer sculptors reproduced this scene as they imagined it, remembering seeing herds seeking shelter under trees or overhanging rocks during a thunderstorm. Generally Mount Govardhana only protects the cowherds and their charges.

Hardly a sheep is to be seen on the reliefs. Apparently they have never been raised in any quantity in Cambodia, though there is mention, in an inscription of the eleventh century engraved on the stele of the Sdok Kak Thom,[11] of a hundred rams and a hundred pigs. The Cambodian pig is small and black; the ridge of its back has a concave profile and its belly drags on the ground. It is this profile that distinguishes it from the wild boar, for they both have a crest of hard bristles along the back. Most often it is the wild boar that is depicted on the reliefs. It is a more noble animal: it was one of the *avatars* of

20 Krishna and Balarāma, detail of a gable pediment at Banteay Srei (tenth century). Near a scene of battle between two heroes of the Mahābhārata stand the brothers Krishna and Balarāma, both *avatar* of Vishnu. Krishna, the major incarnation, is shown with the god's four arms; Balarāma is easily identified because of his attribute, the plow, which he holds by the shaft. It is interesting to note that this type of tenth century plow is still used today.

21 The rain of Indra, pediment of Banteay Srei (second quarter of the tenth century). Riding his three-headed elephant, Indra scatters the celestial waters that fall in heavy rain on the forest. The animals of the woods show their joy at the rain which brings coolness. Birds fly in the sky. The rain is shown as parallel lines in the midst of which rises a *nāga*, a water deity.

Vishnu when the god took on an incarnation to rescue the goddess of Earth when she was imprisoned at the bottom of the sea. The sculptors were particularly interested in animals in a mythological context. Thus we see splendid carvings of *Nandin*, proudly bearing Śiva and his consort Umā, horses drawing the chariot of Sūrya, Skanda riding on a peacock and the *hamsa*, Brahma's sacred bird, shown as a duck crowned with a diadem. Horses are seen but rarely in village scenes; they are shown marching in an army or harnessed to the chariot of a deity. The reliefs show no elephants serving as draft animals in the countryside. Domesticated elephants are for riding, on journeys, for war or for ceremonies; on the fa- *fig. 106* mous Elephant Terrace at Angkor Thom some are participating in the big game hunt.

Forest Gathering and Hunting

Forests are still abundant in Cambodia, and in the Angkorian period they must have covered vast areas. The Khmers have always made use of the plant and animal resources of the forest. It is difficult to tell how important some of the forest plants were to them in a period that is already remote. Little red lychees called *kulen* still grew then in April on Phnom Kulen; the villagers of the plateau gather them on their branches and make bunches to sell at the market in town.

Among the forest harvest: "the *kiang-chen* grows in the deep forests. The barbarians are at great pains to cut them; it is the heart of a tree and round it there are up to nine or ten inches of sapwood; even the little trees have at least four or five inches." What can this tree be? Clearly it was exploited for the hardness of its wood, but the Cambodian forests contain several varieties of hardwoods. "The *hua-huang* is the resin of a tree. The Cambodians cut the tree a year ahead. They leave the resin to ooze and only collect it the following year." P. Pelliot, who translated the text of Chou Ta-kuan, suggests that this resin may possibly be identified as gamboge. It is true that there is a gamboge tree in Cambodia, the *dom rong*, but there are many different trees in the forests that give resin. One of the commonest is the *chhoeu-teal* of which the "oleoresin serves among other things to make a mastic for caulking boats." Chou Ta-kuan also mentions "*ta-feng-tzu* oil" which "is derived

22 Palm grove, Angkor Wat, southwest pavilion (first half of the twelfth century). In the palm grove men are scaling the trunks to get coconuts. On other reliefs sugar palms and arec palms can be identified. At Angkor Wat the sculptors were fond of showing the trees of the villages and forests, noting the peculiarities of each species.

23 Lotus, relief of Banteay Chhmar (late twelfth-early thirteenth century). In a pond crossed by fish, all kinds of water plants are growing. Lotus rise above the water: blue lotus with thin pointed petals, pink lotus opening in clusters among their broad leaves. They are often stylized into decorative motifs, but here are shown quite simply, just as the artist might have seen them.

from the seed of a large tree. The fruit is like a coco-nut, and contains dozens of seeds." This may be the *doem-krabau* tree whose fruit is full of seeds from which an oil used for lighting is extracted.

Forest gathering was the resource of the mountain peoples who were regarded as savages. "There are two kinds of savage. One kind understands the current language, and it is they who are sold as slaves in the towns. The others do not respond to civilization and do not understand the language. This kind does not live in houses in families but roams the mountains, carrying clay jars on their heads. If they meet a wild animal, they bring it down with an arrow or hunting spear, strike fire from a stone, cook the creature and all gather round to eat it, then they move on. They are wild by nature and their poisons are very dangerous. They often kill each other, even within their own bands. Recently there are some who have begun to cultivate cardamum and cotton and weave cloth. But this is very coarse and the designs are very irregular." For the Cambodians these primitive peoples were as formidable as wild beasts and their relations with them were probably restricted to exchanging a few products for cardamums. Cardamum grows wild, but it has to be kept clear of plant parasites. The seeds are used as spice, but are primarily valued as a medicament. They are mentioned in inscriptions as one of the medical ingredients that must be supplied to hospitals.

Pepper, which has long since been cultivated in plantations was then apparently a forest plant. In the Angkorian period "it grows round the rattan and twines like green grass. The blue-green one is the most bitter."

Together with the gathering of forest plants went the collection of wild honey and beeswax: "Beeswax is found in the rotten trees of the villages. It is produced by winged insects with narrow waists like ants. The Cambodians take it from them. Every boat can carry two or three thousand cakes; a large cake weighs 30 or 40 lb.; a small one, not less than 18 or 19 lb." Today honey is still a forest product and the bees, which are very small, make their combs in hollow tree trunks.

Myriads of insects infest the Cambodian forest, playing their part in making it formidable to the peasants who hardly venture there except to gather its fruits or to hunt. There has been a certain amount of cultivation and reclamation round about Angkor since the beginning of this century, but further afield it remains as it must have been in the great period of the Khmer kingdom. It fascinated the authors who visited it in the nineteenth century. Their descriptions and engravings envelop us in an atmosphere that is entirely that of the dense forests that figure in the Bayon and Banteay Chhmar reliefs. We will quote a description from Moura, published in 1883:

"In the evening, once the sun has set, everything comes to life, and on every hand you hear startling cries, of which till then there was no sign: here are trees creaking from the irresistible pushing of hordes of elephants; there you hear a dull bellowing that heralds a herd of wild buffalo; then piercing cries come from all the small creatures disturbed by this tumult; deer bark, and amidst this concert of diverse and discordant noises you can single out at last the sharp yapping of tigers on the prowl."[12]

The Forest Animals

Since time immemorial animals large and small, mammals, birds and reptiles have been hunted by the Cambodians. The reliefs give perfect illustrations of the texts of the Chinese Annals that enumerate the forest animals. "As animals they have the rhinoceros, *fig. 25* the elephant, the wild ox and the 'mountain horse' which are not known in China. There are large numbers of tigers, panthers, bears, boar, deer, red and fallow, musk deer, gibbon, foxes; there are only few lions, *sing-sing* and camels." The lion has totally disappeared from Cambodia, probably for some centuries. It is possible that there were still some in the mid-ninth century, since we learn from an inscription that king Jayavarman III was passionately fond of lion-hunting. Certainly they no longer roamed the forests in the Angkorian period; the lions figured in the temples, on the staircases, are purely conventional types. It is clear that the sculptors had never seen any.

24 Kirātārjuna, Prāsāt Sen Kev (second half of the eleventh century). Śiva, dressed as a *kirāta*, a Himalayan hunter, and Arjuna, one of the heroes of the Mahābhārata, simultaneously let fly an arrow at an *asura* which had taken the form of a boar.

Both arrows hit their mark, but the archers started fighting. Arjuna did not know who his adversary was until he recognized him by his irresistible strength, and did obeisance. Śiva, thus gratified, gave him a miraculous weapon.

54

25 Agni, Banteay Samre, pilaster base (first half of the twelfth century). Agni, god of fire, is shown on his mount, the rhinoceros. He holds a lotus in his hand. His head is shaded by a parasol and at his sides two women wave palm-leaf fans. Agni is a very ancient Vedic deity who should be represented with two faces. Only one is visible, of course, on a relief. In India Agni is represented differently: his mount is a goat, he has two visible heads and he may, on late images, be shown with three legs.

26 Rāma killing the golden hind, Angkor Wat, southwest pavilion (first half of the twelfth century). In the midst of the forest peopled with hermits, whither he had been exiled with his wife Sītā and his brother Lakshmana, Rāma pursues a golden hind into which the *rākshasa* Marīcha had transformed himself, at Rāvana's command. Rāma has just let fly an arrow and the hind is wounded; as he dies, Marīcha imitates the voice of Rāma calling to his brother for help, so that Rāvana can carry off Sītā, once she is left alone.

The Chinese chronicler himself speaks of a lion skin "as a royal object."

It seems unlikely that there ever had been camels in Cambodia. As for the *sing-sing*, P. Pelliot says it is "a kind of large monkey to which the Chinese attribute magical powers, and which devours humans. It is not known what animal gave rise to these legends."

"In the mountains there are many strange woods. Where there are no woods rhinoceros and elephants assemble and live. There are countless rare birds and curious animals." Outside the cultivated plain and the marshy regions, the land was covered with forest, dense near the rivers and on the reliefs, more sparse on the arid plains. Thin forest or glades are the favorite haunts of the large wild beasts, where sparse trees dominate tall grasses and bushes.

Both woods and marshes shelter populations of birds: "Among the birds, the peacock, kingfisher and parrot are unknown in China. All the others, such as falcon, crow, egret, sparrow, cormorant, stork, crane, wild duck, canary, we have." To this list can be added blackbirds, vultures, hornbill and pelican, as well as eagles, among them the fisher eagle. Some of these are highly picturesque: heavy hornbill with their enormous yellow beaks, squawking in the trees, the ox-pecker with its white plumage perched on the backs of oxen and buffalo. Most splendid is the kingfisher with his bright blue feathers, gleaming like a jewel with green lights.

In every period the Khmers enjoyed representing the forest and its animals. On the pediments of Banteay Srei, on the small reliefs of the Baphuon and the great ones of Angkor Wat, the Bayon and Banteay

fig. 27

Chhmar there are always wild animals disporting themselves, usually in luxuriant vegetation, while hunters and armies on the march are crossing zones of parkland with fewer trees.

Among the creatures frolicking in the undergrowth we can recognize squirrel, hare, deer, monkeys and large felines who often cannot be more precisely identified; now and then however the artist has engraved the stripes of the tiger or the speckled coat of the panther. Monkeys and squirrels venture close to the villages in the trees outlined behind the houses. Animals play in the forest round a hermitage, near a temple or along the banks of a river full of fish. Predators chase hinds and sometimes a man; more than once we are shown, with a certain eye for the *fig. 133* comical, a hermit climbing a tree to escape, just in time, from the claws of a great feline. Birds fly overhead or perch on branches; not all can be identified, but here and there we can recognize a parrakeet, a wild cock, a wader, or a peacock whose decorative silhouette is a constant inspiration to the sculptors, especially at Angkor Wat.

Hunting

It might seem surprising that in a country with an Indian religion there should be so many hunting scenes on the reliefs. In fact the Cambodians do hunt the animals that are dangerous for them and their crops. So we see, in the south gallery of the Bayon, a man being eaten by a tiger, just outside a village. Game also is hunted for food; it is eaten either grilled or dried. The principal weapons of the hunter are *fig. 24* the bow and cross-bow. On the *gopura* East II of the Baphuon is a relief in three registers which shows a series of men, each fighting single-handed against a great feline, and trying to thrust a long hunting spear down the animal's throat. One episode frequently *fig. 26* repeated is from the *Rāmāyana:* Rāma doing to death the *rākshasa* Marīcha who has appeared to him in the form of a golden hind. It provides the sculptor with a splendid subject; a magnificent archer letting fly an arrow at a fleeing hind appears again and again on wall reliefs, pediments, lintels and even in foliage scrolls.

Some peasants use blow-pipes to shoot birds. In one little scene, carved on the base of a pillar in the Bayon, a man is aiming his blow-pipe at some birds perched on a tree, while his companion is holding three by the leg that have already been brought down; indifferent to their sorry fate, a squirrel is climbing up the tree trunk.

On another Bayon relief a hunter aims his cross-bow at a hind.[13] He is wearing a headdress in the form of a deer's head, with its neck fitting over his own head. It has been suggested that this huntsman had donned this strange headdress as a disguise to put his quarry off the scent, but this is not an easy thing to do with a wild animal. The huntsman's headdress is in fact the one worn in the royal ballets by the actor who impersonates Marīcha; it also appears in the so-called "Trott" animal dance. This folk dance figuring a hunter chasing deer must originally have had magical significance. Perhaps the curious headdress affected by the Bayon hunter is connected with some lost ritual.

Whether the villagers hunted and killed snakes is not known. The myth of the infant Krishna putting the monster snake Kalya to death gives rise to an illustration of the young god performing a dance on the body of the defeated reptile. Perhaps there were already snake charmers to make the creatures innocuous. According to Buddhist legend the mythical bird *Garuda* was in possession of a charm to tame *nāga*. The snake certainly seems to have been both feared and venerated. *Nāga* are water-dwelling deities, sometimes benevolent, and regarded as guardians of treasure hoards. This is why stone *nāga* raise their multiple heads along the roads leading to the sanctuaries, and the *nāga* Muchilinda is represented over and over again protecting the Buddha during his meditation. The Cambodians may therefore have hesitated to kill

27 Animals in the forest, the Bayon, outer south gallery (late twelfth-early thirteenth century). The scene is shown above the floor of the forest, in the branches of the trees. Perched among the leaves, two peacocks seem to be conversing, while monkeys jump from one tree to another, birds fly past and a squirrel climbs along a branch. The silhouettes of the peacocks are most elegant; the neck movement of the one on the right, bending to its neighbor, is rendered with great verisimilitude.

these creatures, especially as they thought they had the power to assume human form and seemed to them more like spirits than animals.

Hunting, then, was a matter of self-defence for the villagers, and it provided a supplement to their diet, but in addition they obtained by its means a number of precious materials that could be profitably traded. They sought the kingfisher for its brilliant plumage, the rhinoceros for the horn on its snout and the elephant for its ivory tusks. "The kingfisher is rather difficult to catch: hidden in the foliage, the Cambodian crouches by the water side. He has a female in a cage to attract the male, and holds a little net in his hand. He waits for the bird to come, and catches it in the net. Some days he catches three or five, on other days none at all the whole day long." The kingfishers thus taken have a luminous blue plumage which the villagers removed and exported, particularly to China. The Chinese used them to adorn their most sumptuous clothing. P. Pelliot notes that kingfisher feathers formed part of the decoration of "those very iridescent jewels with enamel luster, manufactured in Canton by sticking the minute feathers of kingfishers onto metal."[14]

Rhinoceros horn is used in the Chinese pharmacopoeia, and curative and aphrodisiac properties are ascribed to it. Some rhinoceros must have been captured alive. According to a tradition handed down by Moura, "rhinoceros were raised in the countryside round the capital and brought in to fight on certain feast days of the year, in front of the king's palace."[15]

"Ivory is procured by the mountain people. Each elephant killed provides two tusks. It used to be said that the elephant sheds his tusks every year, this is not so. Ivory from an animal killed by the spear is the best. Next comes that found soon after the creature has died from natural causes. The least valued is when it is found in the mountains."

Diego do Couto described the capture of wild elephants which must have been going on in exactly the same way for centuries: "They make a kraal in thick wood which can only be entered by one door that is shut with a heavy portcullis. They let out one or two already trained and tamed females in the places where the wild males come to graze. As soon as the females see them they start running off towards the kraal and the elephants, seeing them, follow them and go in through the door. Then the hunters who are up above drop the portcullis straight away. And there are the elephants, shut up in a small kraal, where they are subdued by the effects of hunger and thirst. And when they are ready to be trained, they are taken out and placed between two domesticated elephants, and led off to the stables where they are kept."[16]

Every representation of an army on the march has processions of elephants, carrying the king or some high nobleman. On the Royal Terrace of Angkor Thom, on a relief on the inner wall which has as its centerpiece a five-headed horse, a war elephant has seized a soldier in its trunk and is about to fling him in the air while the victim shouts in terror. The outer walls of the two wings of the same terrace, specially named the "Elephant Terrace," are covered with *fig. 112* hunting scenes showing these animals fighting forest beasts: large felines, deer, wild ox. Although the reliefs are eroded, the two long friezes are extremely impressive; such is the majesty of the composition and the implacable power of this elephant march, each creature led by its mahout.

Fishing

Meat from hunting certainly provided only a small part of the diet of the Cambodians who have always been great fish eaters. The waters of Cambodia, still and running alike, are all full of fish. Towards the end of the rainy season the catch is little short of miraculous. As the waters retreat the fish that had been feeding in the flooded forests move towards the

28 Fishermen, the Bayon, outer south gallery (late twelfth-early thirteenth century). Three fishermen are crouched in a long boat. At the bow, one of them flings a cast-net; amidships, the second hits a fish against the side. At the stern, the third is steering with a paddle as a rudder. Above them another fisherman holds a dip-net in which trapped fish are jumping about.

Great Lake. The is the time for the great fishing season on the Tonle Sap to begin. It is particularly fruitful during the full moons of December and January; no more need be done than throw out a net and bring it in, weighed down with fish. Every little pool, even the rice fields, gives a yield at this time. Gradually the water dries out and the fish that are not caught are liable to die in the hardening mud. There is a Cambodian saying: "It is the rainy season, the fish eat the ants" in the flooded forest; "it is the

dry season, the ants eat the fish" in the dried up pools.

"Of fish and tortoise the black carp is the most abundant, and very abundant too are bastard carp, the

29 A river bank, the Bayon, outer south gallery (late twelfth-early thirteenth century). Fish are swimming in the water near a bank. Near them paddles a turtle. The sculptors of the reliefs have carefully shown the different kinds of fish by the shapes of their bodies and their scales. Here the movements of the turtle are particularly well observed.

ts'ao-yu. There are 'spitting fish;' the big ones weigh at least two pounds. Many fish exist of which I do not know the names. All these are found in the Great Lake; but there are also many sea fish of every kind, eels, and congers. The Cambodians do not eat frogs, so that at night they are all over the roads. Tortoise and iguana are as large as *ho-ch'u*, and even tortoise with *liao-tsang* are eaten. The prawns of Ch'a-nan weigh a pound and more. The legs of Chen-p'u tortoise are up to eight or nine inches long. There are crocodiles as large as ships, they have four legs and look exactly like dragons, but they have no horns; their belly is very crisp. In the Great Lake you can catch bivalves and octopus." The chronicler has rather exaggeraged the size of the crocodiles. He doubtless saw some, and must also have looked at representations of the *makara*, the mythical animal like a crocodile that resembles the Chinese dragon.

The sculptors have frequently shown fish, either in pools covered with lotus, or in rivers running between banks, sometimes in the sea. The best drawings of fish are carved in the East gallery of Angkor Wat in the scene of the Churning of the Sea of Milk, and on the rim of the Reservoir of the Royal Palace of Angkor Thom. In both these scenes real and imaginary water creatures appear together. Beside the wierd sea monsters swim eels, smooth-skinned fish—some round, others long—and large scaly fish that look like carp. At Angkor Wat they crowd in terror, caught up and even slashed and cut by the whirl of the churning. In the Royal Palace Reservoir, they glide in calmer waters. Fish are not the only inhabitants of the water depicted on the reliefs: *nāga*, great snakes with multiple heads, coil there in rings, crocodiles pounce on their prey, tortoise swim with all their strength and, in the Royal Palace Reservoir, a crab is seen crawling between two mythical creatures.

On the outer south gallery of the Bayon a fishing boat *fig. 28* winds among junks. Three men are on board; one, crouched at the stern, is manipulating the steering oar; at the prow a fisherman is throwing a net which is a replica of the cast-net used today; the third member of the crew is sitting amidships and has a fish in his left hand that he is about to knock out against the

side. Nearby another fisherman is bringing a square dip-net, full of leaping fish, out of the water. The same scene is depicted at Banteay Chhmar. On this latter relief there is another fishing device lying in a boat, a lobster pot, unfortunately partly hidden by the gunwale.

Basket fishing is still practiced today in pools and on the riverside. The basket is shaped like a funnel. The fisherman holds his arm in the narrow opening and glides the basket along the bottom to catch the fish prisoner. Other questions arise: did the villagers of Angkorian times use the large nets that are dragged along in open water? Did they build barrages of bamboo wattle across the little streams? There are no answers to these questions. In the modern period the fishermen are often Vietnamese or Cham in origin; they have perhaps brought some new techniques with them from their homelands. It is certain however that the Cambodians have always given fishing a large place in their activities, and given fish a large place in their diet.

Sanctuaries of Villages and Country Towns

The reliefs never show villagers participating in a ceremony in a temple. On the same reliefs we can recognize the nobles and even the monarch making their way on a pilgrimage to a great temple buried in the forest. We cannot deduce from that that there was no religious life in the countryside. "Every village has a temple or a stupa." There is no doubting the importance of the village sanctuaries, for there are little temples, more or less ruined, scattered throughout the countryside.

Many of these monuments contain inscriptions referring to their foundation. We learn in this way that they were put up by local dignitaries. The sanctuary was the dwelling of the god, built at the order of the founder; the latter, responsible for its construction, also saw to its upkeep and guaranteed subsistance for the ministrants, providing them with rice and other food and with cloth for making their clothes. Rich proprietors bestowed on their foundations the resources they drew from certain of their villages. It has to be remembered that the merit of the gift was acquired by the founder and not by the humble folk who provided the materials.

It would be impossible here to study all the monuments standing now where there used to be a village. fig. 30 At Tang Kauk on the road from Phnom Penh to Siem Reap there is a laterite temple, built of rough material but enchanting to the sight, for the beauty of its lines and proportions and the warm color of its stone. A broad enceinte encloses an imposing shrine and its annexed buildings.[17]

Some little towns had several temples. At about twenty-one kilometers from Battambang the little village of Sneng[18] is famous for its two monuments, Prāsāt Sneng East and Prāsāt Sneng West. The first comprises three fine towers of red brick. The second is a single shrine of sandstone; its superstructures have fallen to the ground, but the lintels of its doors, carved with naive images of very fine workmanship, prove that the founders were able to choose artists of talent for building and decorating a monument, even in a village far from any large town.

The sculptors commissioned with decorating a temple had not only to embellish the dwelling of a god and recall the myths relating to his different manifestations, but they had to include decorative elements that ensured the prosperity and protection of the sanctuary: thus the scrolls of foliage that twine round the pilasters evoke the creeper that grants wishes. A protective role is assigned to the guardian figures framing the door and even to the monstrous head that often appears in the center of the lintel.

One or two ministrants were employed in the attentions necessary to the sacred image. They saw to the cleaning of the *cella*, presented the offerings, and most important of all, carried out the *pūjā*, the rite of homage to the god manifested in the image. The villagers' way of participating in the cult was to bring offerings and, on feast days, to carry out rites, notably circum-ambulation of the sanctuary, *prādākshina*, in the auspicious direction, according to which the worshiper always keeps the sanctuary on his right. Thus honored the god gave his protection to the village.

Unfortunately we know very little about village feasts. Certain ceremonies were celebrated every year, and with great solemnity if the founder was a man of high standing. In the early eleventh century we have a record of the spiritual advisor of King Sūryavarman II, the famous Divākarapandita, proceeding to a great ceremony at Phnom Sandak. On this occasion "he covered with cloth all the towers, the courts and the avenue as far as the place where they burn the paddy every year."[19] The rite of "burning the paddy" has continued until the present time. It was the occasion of an important ceremony in the Royal Palace, but it was also celebrated in the villages. E. Porée-Maspéro describes it thus: "This feast is called by different names in different localities. The most usual are 'the fire offering' or 'piling the paddy' or 'burning the paddy'.... Each family brings to the appointed place a basket full of fresh paddy [rice in the husk] which is poured onto a mat.... The heaps of paddy have to form five 'hills.' Nearby, priests have been invited under a specially built barn.... After prayers the master of ceremonies shoots his arrows to the eight points of the compass. Then he breaks the bow and throws the pieces on a fire lit near the barn. Then the bonzes... go to the great jars of water collected by the faithful who douche them before they go to dry by the fire. Formerly the paddy that had been heaped by the faithful was burnt; nowadays the proceeds of its sale go to the pagoda."[20]

In this ceremony of "burning the paddy" at the end of the harvest we can discover evidence of one of the feasts that took place year by year and to which the great solemnities of the Royal Palace were devoted. The royal rites had to correspond to the Earth rites organized in the countryside. In a country where agriculture formed the principal source of prosperity, the sovereign had the duty of celebrating the great occasions of peasant life. The ties that bound the king with the provinces, where a hierarchy of nobles and officials represented him, were very close.

30 The temple of Kuk Nokor at Tang Kauk (twelfth century). The lines of this small-town temple are in no way inferior to those of the great sanctuaries; the materials, however, are not so noble: only the framing of the bays—lintels, jambs and colonettes—are of sandstone. The main building is of laterite, a coarse material, but of a lovely reddish color.

THE SOCIAL AND ADMINISTRATIVE ORGANIZATION OF THE PROVINCES

A hierarchical society, dominated by an aristocracy of officials, is what emerges from the inscriptions commemorating the foundation of temples in the provinces. Attracted as they were by the capital, the Chinese travelers had few contacts with provincial Khmer society, which was organized in the Indian fashion, very different from what they knew; nor do they give us much information about the administration. To find out what social life was like and how administration was organized in the provinces, our major source is the inscriptions.

Provincial Society

There are large numbers of epigraphic texts mentioning the division of society into four casts, on the Indian model: Brahmans, *kshatriya*, *vaiśya* and *śudra*. These castes corresponded in fact to two social levels: the first two formed a small aristocracy, the others probably comprised the mass of the people, except for the slaves and the untouchables. The members of the first caste boasted descent from Brahmans who had come from India, either in groups at the beginning of the Indianization of southeast Asia, or individually during the following centuries. The *kshatriya* belonged to families that had ruled ancient principalities and often married into the Angkorian dynasty. These two castes occupied all the high offices in the provinces, either by family right, or by virtue of a royal mandate. Their influence was considerable. More than once during a civil war their secession would amputate a portion of territory from

the kingdom, and conversely their support could bring success to a claimant; occasionally an alliance with the descendants of an ancient dynasty allowed them to press the rights of their families and rise to the throne.

The two upper castes provided all the higher personnel for religious and civil administration in the provinces. On the whole the lower *vaiśya*, agriculturalist, and *śudra*, servant and especially artisan, castes, populated the villages and country towns. No doubt among the individuals in these subordinate castes there were some who managed to get rich and rise to a social level higher than their birth, but these were only exceptional cases; the mass remained attached to the work to which they were born and their relations with the administration were confined to labour dues for the construction of a bridge, for making a road or even for building a sanctuary. In addition they had to pay rents to the owners of the great estates or to the religious foundations that owned their villages.

The primitive peoples, for the most part mountain folk, lived on the fringes of society. "For servants, you buy savages to do the work. Those who have many have more than a hundred; those who have few have from ten to twenty; only the poorest have none at all. Savages come from the mountainous wastes. They form a race apart, which is called *Ch'uang*, thieves. When they are brought into town, they do not dare to show themselves abroad. If someone is called *Ch'uang* in a quarrel he feels hatred rise in him right to the marrow of his bones, so far below the human race are they regarded." Country slaves, those whom the inscriptions describe as slaves "for doing" the ricefields seem to have been the lowliest of all, inferior even to the house slaves, and certainly to those employed in the service of a temple. One has only to read the names of some slaves to see how they were despised. In inscriptions giving slave lists, we even find names like "Dog," "Detestable" and "Stinking."

All the evidence confirms that the families of slaves had no recognition. Inscriptions enroll women slaves in the service of a temple with their small children, but they never mention the family as a whole; of course it is not impossible that the husbands of these women were among the group of men enrolled at the same time as the women.

Whereas we are richly documented on the daily life of the peasantry, only very little light is thrown on their social condition, their liberties, their rights on the land they cultivated, their opportunities for acquiring wealth and improving their situation. All of this escapes us. They were too ordinary to interest the Chinese chroniclers. Inscriptions with attributions to sanctuaries of the dues owed by villages, give grounds for thinking that there were peasants, more or less bound to the land they worked; but who, after having handed over the portion stipulated, were probably free of any further obligations.

It is not known whether there were the same divisions into sub-castes in the provinces as are shown by the inscriptions to have existed in urban society; these mention how the king created sub-castes to correspond to certain functions. Probably sub-castes would have only secondary importance amid the peasantry, whereas they would tend to create a hierarchy among the officials concerned with administration.

Provincial Administration

Here and there in the temple inscriptions one chances upon the titles of officials whose careers it is sometimes possible to follow. We can thus glean a few isolated details, but it would presumptuous to expect to be able deduce a general view of the administration from them. The texts of the inscriptions have much to say of the duties incumbent on dignitaries in the capital, but give only fleeting reference to their functions in the provinces. Cambodia was divided into provinces, called at different periods *praman* or *vishaya*, and these were subdivided into *sruk*. At first sight this division seems simple enough, but there appears to have been another division into four groups over and above it. G. Coedès noticed long since that the numbers one, two, three and four were associated with the titles of certain classes of officials. In a study made in collaboration with P. Dupont he added: "Rather than signifying grades, these four numbers seem to correspond to peculiarities of the Cambodian administration until the time of King Norodom. The whole territory was divided into four apanages; that of the king, of the *yuvarāja*, of the *upayuvarāja* and of the queen mother or first queen; numbered from one to four. The great majority of the provinces were included in the first apanage, that of the king. However, each apanage had its own autonomous administrative apparatus: ministers, justices, mandarins etc.... This rather strange institution was studied at a time when it no longer was in operation and when the division of the provinces had undergone frequent rearrangements. It appears, however, that it was in full force in Angkorian Cambodia, and inscriptions dealing with questions of real estate mention officials who presumably belong to these apanages."[21]

There is no lack of examples of the nomination of high officials, but they provide no information about the methods of recruitment. The king apparently chose the people who enjoyed his greatest confidence. The categories from which the elite of these officials were chosen probably did not correspond to any definite specializations; officials with the title of *sanjak* might equally well be charged with the government of a province, a diplomatic mission or a military command. Doubtless the king entrusted them with responsibilities according to the needs of the government and their personal qualities, by reason of the confidence he had in them. Sometimes the king chose one of his familiars. One inscription follows the rise of Simhadatta, "physician to the glorious lion of kings, to the victorious Jayavarman;" the king, "having seen that he was the right man, established him with honour in the government of this town of Adhyapura."[22]

Governors had to administer the territory and "ward off dangers." They were also responsible for supervising religious foundations in the province. They chose their own subordinates who worked under their orders. Their powers were extensive since they were representatives of the king in their provinces.

There is no way of discovering what were the relations between the royal officials and the great families of the aristocracy. The latter certainly played a very important part in provincial society. Some were descended from princely families that had been subjected to the sovereign of Angkor and were generally linked to the royal family by marriage; others had received great estates from the king as a reward for their fidelity. Some families were even invested with a hereditary right to high offices.

Land Holding

There are many mentions in the epigraphy of allocations of land conceded by the sovereign to those who had served him loyally. Some lines thus received considerable grants which were transmitted through a number of generations. An interesting example is the family of the Brahman Śivakaivalya who worked in the service of Jayavarman II. It was showered with gifts. According to the stele of Sdok Kak Thom this great personage "having obtained from the king an estate in the eastern district, founded a town called Kutī and installed his family there. Having obtained from the sovereign an estate in the neighbourhood of Amarendrapura, he founded a town called Bhavālaya and erected a *lingam* there." The successors of Jayavarman II made further contributions to the wealth of this house. Jayavarman III gave a mountain "in the district of 'Piedmont'" to the brother of Śivakaivalya. Under Yaśovarman, the king's guru, Vāmaśiva, a member of the same family "received the estate of Jayapattanī as a gracious gift from the king. On this estate the king founded a town called Bhadrapattana and erected in it, in favour of his guru,

a *lingam* of Iśvara. He gave him household furniture: cups, ewers, etc. abundant riches: cows, etc., two hundred men and women servants." The younger brother of Vāmaśiva received from the king an estate called Vamśahrada. Throughout the tenth century the family continued its rise. In the reign of Sūryavarman I the head of the family, Sadāśiva, returned to secular life. King Sūryavarman saw to his entry into the position of head of the household according to the rite and gave him as wife the sister of queen Vīralakshmī "in presence of the fire and the Brahmans." Henceforth Sadāśiva became a "Holder of great powers" in the region of Bhadrayogi and elsewhere, and "at Indrapuri and elsewhere he carried out as a fruitful work of piety towards the gods established there, ponds and other works.... At Bhadrapattana he erected according to the rite a *lingam* and two statues.... He built a dyke and a reservoir for the prosperity of the region.... At Vamśahrada... he built a moat, a dyke and a reservoir for prosperity [of the land]."[23] Every text that is concerned with gifts of land from the king to his followers gives the list of the properties thus granted, and the new owners never fail to mention the pious works they have carried out in their new domain: the setting up of images and public works, for the common good.

Among ways of acquiring property the inscriptions give evidence not only of royal gifts, inheritance and purchase. The rules of succession seem to have been very complex and remain obscure on a number of points. Women's rights of inheritance seem clearly attested; often a man's estate goes to the descendants

31 Detail of a relief, Angkor Thom (late twelfth-early thirteenth century). In the north part of the Royal Terrace some large reliefs have been cleared. The center of each of these compositions is occupied by a five-headed horse. Round this miraculous animal step forward military looking personages, brandishing weapons and wearing the tall top-knot encased in metal work. Some poor, frightened people beg their protection. Like these individuals, royal officials were invested with intimidating power, but they had a duty to protect the people.

of his sisters; but this is far from an absolute rule. In the inscription of Tūol Prāsāt the property of a personage called Gavya has been inherited by his own progeny. It is probable that the rules of succession were much influenced by local usages which do not appear clearly in the epigraphy.

On the acquisition of property by purchase the documentation is extensive. Some inscriptions consist entirely of a series of records of sales. The first thing to be noticed on reading these texts is that the price of a piece of land or any other property is never indicated by a money value. The sale is always in fact an act of barter. Land is exchanged against heads of cattle or a certain number of objects. Here are a few examples: in the tenth century we see that a piece of land of unspecified size has been sold for five buffalo and five oxen; for another piece the price is sixty measures of paddy, a silver bowl and some clothing. The transaction generally contains the precise delimitation of the land and the names of the witnesses to the operation. If the limits of the property were uncertain an investigation was usually set up. At the end of the ninth century we find that "a royal order required Mratan Śrī Vikramāyudha... to go and interrogate under oath the inhabitants of the four [surrounding] districts on the dimensions of the estate of Tamvon and to set up boundary posts."[24]

Some records of sales reveal a whole legal procedure. The stele of Wat Baset sanctions two sales of land, one in 1036, the other in 1042.[25] The first concerns a transaction over land belonging to five different proprietors; the text gives the areas and measurements, the objects given in exchange, the names of the witnesses to the operation and the names of the members of the court who marked the boundaries. The sale of 1042 gave rise to more detailed procedure. It concerns a group of properties belonging to fifteen vendors; the lands were in fact to be assigned to a deity. The author of the inscription has carefully noted down the list of objects given in exchange, the names of the vendors and witnesses, then he speaks of beating of the bounds; witnesses including a judge and a reciter of the Dharmachāstra "went the rounds of this land and planted boundary marks in the eight directions, following the length and width marked

in the register." Lastly another personage "took away [a clod] of earth from this land, proceeded once more to the god's ablution, offered [the earth] to the god."

These transactions in land did not always go uncontested, sometimes with some violence. The stele of Tūol Prāsāt dated 1003, which we have already quoted, refers to an affair of this kind.[26] One Gavya, the great-grandfather of the author of the inscription, "devoted all he had to buy the lands that were offered him and that met his desires... having bought these lands in the regular manner, with his titles in order and without lacunae, he then asked for them from king Rājendravarman. Then this king, protector of the land, graciously gave these lands to the above-named Gavya who asked them from him. The king charged an agreed emissary to set out the boundary marks and to declare: 'These [lands] have been given to this man.' When this man died, three men named Hī, Pū and Ke, desiring to take over these lands by force, declared 'This land is ours.' The man named Hem ordered the man named Pū to remove the efficacious boundary marks placed on these lands by order of the king. The descendent of this [Gavya], Sahadeva, informed king Jayavarman in writing of all the violations committed by these people. The action of Pū and his consorts was the subject of a thorough investigation by the ministers, counselors in the king's court, and was recognized as being manifestly an offence. 'Let the lips, and let the hands of the man named Hem and the man named Pū be cut off, in punishment of their crime,' this was the king's order. Then the men named Pan, Ap ...and the woman named Ayak made another claim on these lands. Although they had seen and heard the misfortune that had befallen those who had tried to seize these lands, they had the folly to try and seize them. The man named Sahadeva denounced these rebels to the supreme king Śrī Jayavīravarman. ...Having heard his declaration on this matter, the king examined the action [of the accused] with the minister and the court counselors and recognized it as an offence. By order of the king, they had their feet and their heads squeezed; the man named Ap suffered from it and the man named Pan died of it. As for the woman named Ayak, she also had her head squeezed, and her relatives were so alarmed they suddenly fled in all directions to hide. 'All these lands, as they have been bought, then given by the kings, are the property of Sahadeva,' this was the king's order."

In all these proceedings the king appears as the supreme judge. He has to sanction all the sales for them to be valid, for he is in effect the ultimate proprietor of all the lands in his kingdom. Judging from the texts we have quoted, it seems that disputes arose when there had been a change of reign. Those who made the second attempt on the lands of Sahadeva thought to win the ear of the new king, Jayavīravarman, whose accession to the throne seems to have been irregular; but a king, even if he was a usurper, owed it to himself to respect and confirm the grants made by his predecessors. In a family successive generations transmitted to one another the titles to property sanctioned by royal grant. For this reason the texts of the inscriptions recite all the grants and all the purchases that lay at the origin of the domains, and have these arrangements confirmed by the king, whose power thus radiates over the whole kingdom.

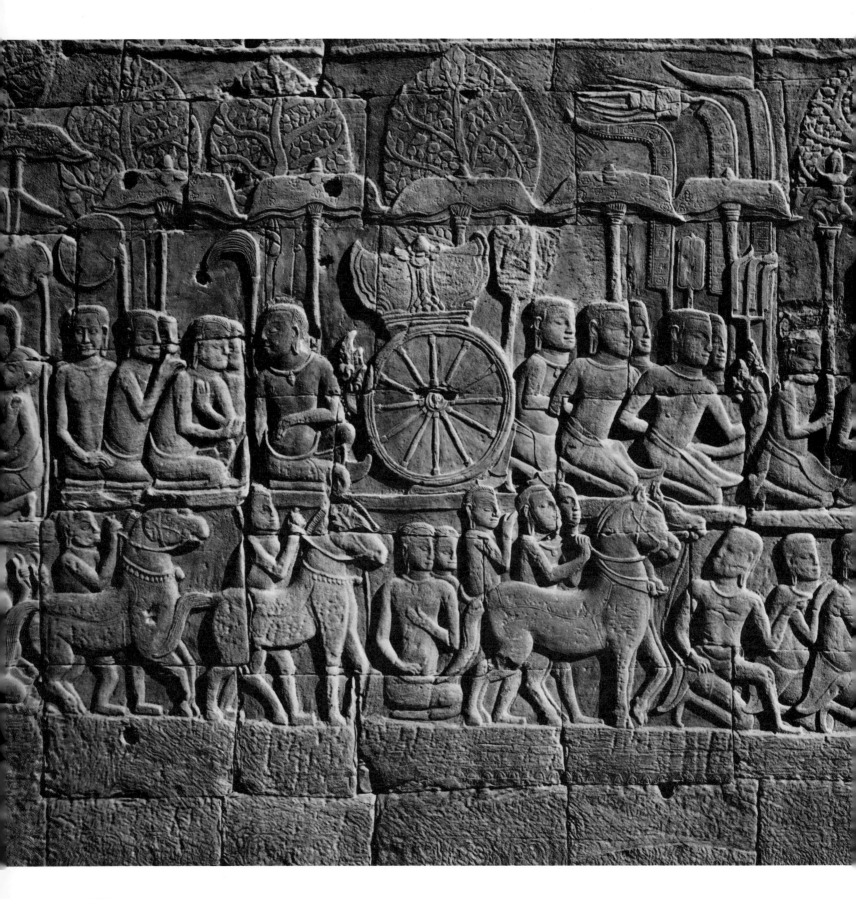

JOURNEYS ACROSS THE PROVINCES

If we question the reliefs or follow Chou Ta-kuan it is clear that the Khmers of the thirteenth century, like those of the present day, enjoyed traveling to exchange merchandise, to visit members of their families or to go on pilgrimages.

Roads

The Khmer kingdom was covered with a network of roads joining Angkor with the principal towns and connecting the provincial cities one with another. Listing the stopping places along the roads built by Jayavarman VII the stele of Preah Khan[27] mentions the existence of roads radiating round Angkor towards the Champa capital, towards Phimai, Jayavatī, Jayasimhavatī, Jayavīravatī, Jayarājagiri and Śrī Suvīrapuri, and lastly towards Śrī Sūryaparvata, that is Phnom Chisor. Traces of sections of Angkorian roads can be found in the ground. Some modern roads run in places along several kilometers of medieval roadways; indeed they still use the old bridges, like the Spean Praptos in the village of Kompong Kdei on the road running to the north of the

Great Lake between Siem Reap and Kompong Thom. Further north a road joins Angkor to Beng Mealea, after which it divides into two branches, one running to the Preah Khan of Kompong Svay, the other to Koh Ker and Wat Phu. The Angkor-Phimai road has also been rediscovered for a long time. Aerial research has confirmed and supplemented the epigraphic and archaeological data. M. Déricourt has made very interesting aerial observations on the northeast quadrant of the Khmer kingdom and into the south of Laos. This pilot has revealed the existence of an enormous ancient network. He has discovered in particular a road from Sambor Prei Kuk to the confluence of the Srepok and the Mekong, near the modern town of Stung Treng. Stretches of road are visible all over lower Laos, especially in the region of Wat Phu and Champassak. An important route leaves Wat Phu and runs into the plain of Vientiane towards the old center of Ban Thalat in which vestiges of Mōn culture have been discovered. Apart from the main roads there were certainly tracks of less precise alignment, skirting obstacles; for in the forests when a tree falls across the road there is no question of clearing it: a new bit of track goes round it instead.

The main roads were very wide. Those recognized reach widths of about forty meters. They run straight for kilometers on end, crossing the forests with sunken tracks and rising on causeways where the rainy season forms marshes. M. Déricourt makes an interesting observation on how rivers were crossed: "These roads are for the most part formed of stretches of straight lines ending in curves approaching the

32 Arrival of a high-ranking traveler, the Bayon, inner gallery (late twelfth-early thirteenth century). A grandee and his escort have reached the end of their journey. In the lower register, servants are leading off the horses from the carriage. In the upper register, which represents a second plane, set further back, the members of the escort are sitting round the carriage, an elegant vehicle with large wheels and a long shaft rising at the end with a finial of bronze in the form of a *nāga*.

rivers at an angle suitable for establishing a ford or a bridge," or building a point of embarcation. "Generally the embarcation point is sited so that the current facilitates the crossing for a traveler going north. This would seem to show that travelers went northward by road at a time when the currents of the rivers they crossed were strong; when the waters are low currents are easier to mount. It may be also that the return was made entirely by water."[28]

The bridges of which traces remain are built of laterite on corbeled arches. One of the finest, the Spean Praptos, measures eighty meters in length and fourteen in width. It comprises eighteen arches which only have a span of two meters for a height of rise of five meters, and rest on pillars one meter thirty wide. The roadway of the bridge is flanked by sandstone parapets in the form of *nāga* with heads raised at the ends, sheltering images of the Buddha. It is a remarkable work of art, both because of its imposing size and because of the contrast of the grey-green sandstone with the warm colors of the laterite.

fig. 33 (margin, left of "Praptos")

Traveling by Road

The dry season will have been the great time for traveling. As they wound along the interminable burning roads of the plains, or across the zones of sparse forest where the trees, having lost their dried-up leaves, offer no relief from the glare of the day, the travelers must have longed to arrive in some shady village nestling in its trees and palms. The road was most frequented in the cool hours of the morning and when the sun began to set.

The reliefs allow us to imagine the look of these roads when peopled with pedestrians, vehicles and animals. Early in the morning long lines of villagers set out for the little market towns, carrying the produce they were going to sell. We see them, particularly the women, carrying jars and baskets full of fruit on their heads; the men balance yokes on their shoulders at the ends of which hang baskets with produce, attached by a kind of framework of rattan.

The center of the road is for vehicles. "To travel far, they ride on elephants, or horses, or in carriages. The carriages are like those of other countries." The reliefs show heavily-laden ox carts progressing slowly along the roads. They are covered with a roof of basket-work or straw, the shaft raised in a well defined curve whose elegant line has survived to our own day. Even the spacing of the wheels has not changed. The grooves worn in the paving of the carriage gates of the temples correspond exactly to the ruts made by modern carts.[29] Cart builders in the Angkorian period were already putting a slightly curved horizontal bar on either side outside the wheels so that when a wheel got stuck in a deep rut the cart could glide on these bars like a sledge.

fig. 34 (margin, right)

Perhaps the roads of Angkorian times would see the same long lines of carts as move up today from the country to bring the newly harvested paddy to barter for fish from the Great Lake. There was no need to hurry over the journey. If there was an accident the cart could be mended on the spot, for it was held together entirely with ropes of rattan. The driver never traveled alone. On a Bayon relief there is a whole family accompanying a cart drawn by humped oxen. Following the cart, the father carries the youngest child on his shoulder, while a small boy trots beside him; the wife walks behind. The driver stands on the shaft to guide the beasts; there is even a dog loping along between the wheels. Sometimes the load is so heavy a man has to push the cart from behind. When night fell the travelers turned in. The driver unyoked the oxen, the family camped down beside the cart and everyone began preparing the meal. An amusing detail on a Bayon relief is the figure of a man kneeling flat on the ground and blowing with all his might to get the fire going in one of the little baked clay stoves that are still made by the potters of Kompong Chhnang.

fig. 35 (margin, right)

33 The bridge of Kompong Kdei (late twelfth-early thirteenth century). The road from Phnom Penh to Siem Reap still crosses the Spean Praptos, the laterite bridge of the village of Kompong Kdei, built in the Angkorian period, and one of the most beautiful on the Khmer roadways. The arches of the bridge are built by corbeling, and are narrow and very tall. On the sides of the apron it has been possible to reconstruct the *nāga* whose heads, lifted up at the entrances to the bridge, sheltered images of the Buddha.

34 Ox cart, the Bayon, outer west gallery (late twelfth-early thirteenth century). Harnessed to two oxen, a cart goes along the road. It is heavily laden, and the owner is having to push it to help the oxen along. With its roof of basketwork and sides of split bamboo, it is like the carts that can still be seen up and down the roads of Cambodia. Outside the wheel can be seen the long piece of curved wood that prevents the vehicle from sticking in deep ruts by sliding along the sides of the track like the runners of a sledge.

The heavy peasant convoys were always being overtaken by faster carriages, some drawn by horses, others by oxen—for we must remember that oxen were used for racing chariots up to a century ago. These light vehicles are of the same type as the carts, though they have finer lines and the shaft is decorated with a finial in the form of a *nāga*, while the rails are carved. Finds are not infrequently made of the bronze mounts that decorated shafts and frames. They were generally fashioned in the form of a *nāga* and are among the masterpieces of Khmer bronze working.

Now and then carriages and carts would have to make way for some noble traveler borne on a palanquin. "Their palanquin are made of a plank of wood *fig. 96* that is curved in the middle and rises at each end. Motifs of flowers are carved on it, and it is plated with gold and silver: this is what are called gold and silver palanquin supports. A hook is fixed at about a foot from each end, and a large piece of cloth several times folded is attached to the two hooks by ropes. You sit on this cloth and two men carry the palanquin." There are many reliefs at Angkor Wat, the

35 A halt on the journey, the Bayon, outer west gallery (late twelfth-early thirteenth century). With a child on her hip and a kind of saddle bag over her shoulder, and a parcel on her head, a woman follows her husband who is pushing the cart. Near them one of their fellow travelers has stopped; he has unharnessed his oxen and is blowing up the fire, in a little clay stove, to cook his meal. Behind the cart, quite relaxed, two men are drinking from a jar with straws.

Bayon and Banteay Chhmar with representations of these palanquin. On some very plain ones, the sick and wounded are carried away from a battlefield; others are richly decorated with carving and bronze ornaments and carry elegant young ladies. In the Historical Gallery of Angkor Wat the sculptors have portrayed the princesses of Sūryavarman II's court seated in splendid palanquin, protected from the sun by a little roof.

Still at Angkor Wat, in the Gallery of Heaven and Hell, the just are being carried to a paradise on sedan chairs. These ceremonial vehicles were only to be used for royal processions and could still be seen on grand occasions at the court of Phnom Penh. In addition there were probably litters like those portrayed on an inner gallery of the Bayon. One of them is an immense carriage resting on six wheels, shaped like a little pavilion and closed in with hangings; it is not occupied, but a figure is kneeling at the front to draw back the curtains. It seems unlikely that this litter could have been pulled by animals; perhaps it was set in motion by attendants, like the funeral

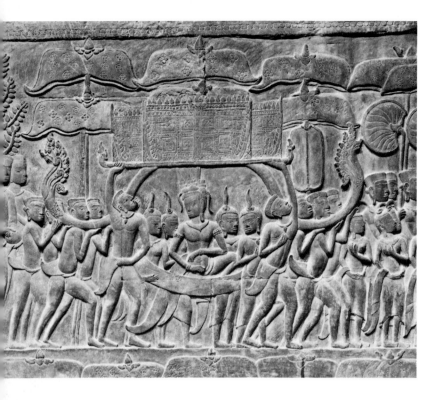

36 A noble lady in a litter, Angkor Wat, Historical Gallery (first half of the twelfth century). Surrounded by her followers, a richly adorned lady is seated on a palanquin shaped like a hammock. Six men carry on their shoulders the triple curved shafts which end with bronze finials in the form of *nāga* heads. Other servants hold up the roof at arm's length. Round this group can be seen parasols and fans of palm leaves, or of cloth stretched between two frames of rattan.

carts used until recently—though there are no grounds for thinking that the litters of the Bayon were for funerals.

Threading their way quickly among all this heavy traffic are a few horsemen. As was noted by Chou Ta-kuan, the horses have no saddles. The Chinese chronicler also says that the elephants "have no benches for sitting on." The reliefs do show elephants saddled, however. Sometimes the seat is covered with a roof, often it is simply a double bench with the rails forming a richly decorated balustrade. Under the angles of this seat were heavy thick hooks, probably encased in bronze. To saddle the elephant the mahout knotted ropes onto these brackets and attached them to the saddle girth, crupper and breast band of the animal. Bronze bells were also hung on chains from these hooks.

To judge from the reliefs all the travelers were full of jollity and animation. We note the gilt bronze and carved decoration of the vehicles, probably all painted in bright colors. The villagers call and wave to each other from group to group; cart drivers converse together and no doubt sing as they have continued to do to the present day, while the tinkle of little bells marks the regular step of the elephants, and the trotting horses and oxen make their harness jingle.

Traveling by Boat

When Chou Ta-kuan crossed Cambodia to reach Angkor, he did not use the kingdom-wide road network; as we have seen, he came to the capital by boat. Cambodia has a very fine system of waterways. At this period quite a large fleet must have been sailing the Mekong, the Tonle Sap, the Great Lake and the rivers feeding it. The Chinese chronicler made a distinction between boats made from a single tree trunk and those built of planks. There are many carvings of the slender long ships which are similar to the racing canoes that used to compete in the *fig. 3* Water Festival each year at Phnom Penh. "Their small boats are made from large trees that they hollow out like a trough; it is softened by fire and stretched with wooden bracers, so that these boats are wide in the center and pointed at the ends. They have no sail and can carry several people; they are simply steered by rowing." The long vessels that feature in the naval battles at the Bayon or at Banteay Chhmar are of this kind. The river fleet was composed of these monoxylous craft, as is borne out by the fact that the fish, shellfish and reptiles swimming round them are all river creatures. The oarsmen row facing astern, with lance or leaf-shaped blades. They provide the motive force while a sailor seated astern steers with a long steering oar. The prow of these boats rises to a *garuda* head, or sometimes a *nāga* head issuing from the mouth of a *makara;* the stern post forms the animal's tail. As early as the Funan period the Chinese annalists had noted their zoomorphic

37 Large junk, the Bayon, outer south gallery (late twelfth-early thirteenth century). The junk, built of planks, has stopped. A sailor is dropping the anchor by letting the rope run over a winch. Topmen are pulling ropes to manipulate the sails which are made of matting. The helmsman gives orders, standing by the rudder. At the mast top a kind of basket for the look-outs can be seen. Flags float in the wind, birds fly round the masts, and two men play chess on deck.

aspect: "They make boats eight or nine *ch'ang* long, and carve them to a width of six or seven feet. The bow and stern are like the head and tail of a fish."[30] These craft could not have been used for long stints. At night they tied up to the bank, as can be seen on one of the naval battle reliefs of the Bayon.

For long voyages there were ships built of planks. "Their large ships are made of planks of hard wood. The carpenters have no saws and work entirely with axes. Thus each plank requires much wood and much time, and if anyone has to fashion anything in wood, he only has a chisel.... For boats they still use iron nails, and cover the vessels with *kiao* leaves held in place by slats of areca palm. A boat of this kind is called a *sin-na;* it is propeled by rowing. For caulking they use fish oils mixed with mineral lime." P. Paris has made a special study of a sailing boat constructed from planks in an article on the boats seen on Khmer reliefs. It is true that the rigging is not very skillfully shown. It is possible to make out the sails made of matting, however, and there may be half-tops like baskets up the masts. P. Paris thinks that "the need for raised look-outs could be explained by their having to find navigable channels in the Great Lake at low water, or in the flooded forests in times of flood."[31] The hull is carefully carved; the planking is clearly marked; a sailor is pulling an anchor with a winch. This type of craft is probably of Sino-Vietnamese origin, but the presence on the deck of a little Khmer-type structure makes it likely that the ship is of Cambodian manufacture; Chou Ta-kuan indeed stated that plank-built ships were constructed there.

Royal processions were performed with monoxylous vessels. Like the fighting ships they have neither stem posts nor rudder posts. P. Paris notes that on the royal ships "the oarsmen row facing forwards, on other they face astern like the Europeans." The curve of the deck on these ceremonial ships is much more pronounced than on other monoxylous craft; the decoration of prow and stern also is represented as richer and is more carefully executed. In the center among the flywhisks, parasols and oriflammes a sort of canopy shelters the noble company. In these processions some boats often carry dancers or entertainers. Pleasure boats were often used by princes to

go from place to place, and of course for nautical festivals; but they also, as we learn from a Bayon relief, might carry people on longer journeys to places of pilgrimage.

Pilgrimages

The practice of pilgrimage finds mention in Khmer epigraphy. The inscription of Phnom Preah Vihear relates how a poet called Vidyāpushpa set off to visit divers places of pilgrimage, "sanctuaries and mountains." We know that after his coronation Sūryavarman II sent his spiritual advisor, Divākarapandita, to make offerings in his name at a number of the great sanctuaries of the kingdom: "So the venerable lord Guru Śrī Divākarapandita carried out a pilgrimage to offer gifts at all the temples, beginning with Kamraten jagat Bhadreśvara, according to the holy stanza that His Majesty Śrī Sūryavarmadeva has composed to be engraved on all the golden palanquin and all the riches listed above, destined to be offered to all the temples in all places."[82]

Indian tradition required that the *chakravartin* monarch, lord of the universe, should beat the bounds of his states to take possession. J. Boisselier suggested that king Jayavarman II's changes of capital, mentioned in the inscription of Sdok Kak Thom, correspond to this act of sovereignty over the country. The circuit was completed at the Phnom Kulen, where the ceremony of consecration was celebrated. Though there is no information on the itinary of royal pilgrimages, there is no grounds for doubting that when circumstances permitted the kings went to the holy places throughout their kingdom to offer homage to the deities venerated there.

One relief of the inner north galleries of the Bayon certainly seems to represent the journey of two high-ranking pilgrims. At the left of the scene, two boats, richly decorated, each carry a personage with a train of followers among whom some are holding offerings. Each wears his hair knotted in a bun in the fashion of an ascetic, and wears a *triśūla*, making it possible to identify them both as high Brahman dignitaries. A third boat carries men in strange costume who are

fig. 37

fig. 38

38 Royal pilgrim worshiping an image of Vishnu, the Bayon, inner south gallery (late twelfth-early thirteenth century). A king has come on pilgrimage to a shrine of Vishnu's, built beside a lotus-covered basin. The king has prostrated himself to make an offering to the god. Vishnu holds his usual attributes; but he wears the hermit's hair-bun and his garment is a long skirt. It has been thought that this long skirt represents the carapace of the tortoise *avatār*; the identification is doubtful. We are in the presence of an image of Vishnu as a hermit.

dancing, and drinking with straws from a jar. Behind the flotilla we can recognize a forest inhabited by hermits from which apparently the convoy has come. In the right part of the composition, the two Brahmans and their suite have disembarked and are approaching a sanctuary built in the middle of a forest on the side of a mountain which has at its peak a *lingam* wrapped in a filigree veil. A mountain topped by a *lingam* evokes the Lingaparvata, the mountain of Wat Phu, and indeed the sanctuary half way up it, figured on the relief, is not unrelated to the façade of the temple of Wat Phu.

In the scene of the north gallery the sculptor has not portrayed the pilgrim paying homage to the god of the holy place. On the other hand, still at the Bayon, a relief on the inner south gallery shows two scenes of statues being worshiped, one of Śiva, the other Vishnu. On each panel the king, wearing a diadem, is lying prostrate to present to the god an unidentifiable offering, while round him his followers kneel with their hands raised in *añjali*.

The reliefs give no rendering of the pilgrimages of simple people. These acts of piety were nonetheless widespread, as they still are in India. While the Angkorian period has left us nothing about the pilgrimages of humbler folk, there are many later inscriptions carved in the sixteenth and seventeenth centuries, that relate how people came from the villages alone or in groups to pay their respects to the old Khmer temples. It can be allowed that in our period the great provinical sanctuaries received such visits from pilgrims of every walk of life.

Halting Places

The roads listed on the stele of Preah Khan, and which have been in part identified either on the ground or by air reconnaissance, were certainly important from the political and economic point of view, but their primary *raison d'être* was to link Angkor with the old religious centers of the kingdom. They were basically pilgrimage routes. When Jayavarman VII had hostels and shelters built at the halting places along these roads, he was intent on providing places where travelers, and most especially pilgrims, could rest.[33]

The stele of Preah Khan tells us that this king established 121 "houses with hearths." There were 17 on the Phimai road, 57 between Yaśodharapura and the Champa capital, in the central part of modern Vietnam. These posting houses were not located at regular intervals, but the average distance between them was about fifteen kilometers. The inscription describes them as "houses with hearths," so travelers were able to rest there and prepare their meals. Chou Ta-kuan saw them and noted, "On the main roads there are resting places like our posting stations." This custom of providing shelter for travelers has still not disappeared; along the roads of modern Cambodia there are little huts raised on wooden stilts, called *sālā*, some very simple, with a thatched roof, others more elegant in line; often, at the side of the *sālā*, there is a jar full of water so that the passer-by can slake his thirst. Thus when the pilgrim was tired he rested at a halting place, if he was ill he found succour in one of the 102 hospitals that Jayavarman VII had built at various points in the kingdom, in particular in most of the great temples.

THE GREAT PROVINCIAL SANCTUARIES

After many long days traveling from one halting-place to another, whether coming on foot or carried in palanquin and surrounded by servants, the travelers at last reached the goal of their pilgrimage, one of the great temples which bore witness to the four cardinal points of the piety of the sovereigns and the universality of their power.

Wat Phu

Situated half-way up the Lingaparvata, the "Mountain of the *lingam*," the temple of Wat Phu[34] is indubitably the most ancient and the most holy of all the provincial foundations. An enormous rock crowns the summit; its vaguely phallic shape recalls a gigantic *lingam*, the manifestation of the creative power of Śiva. To the pilgrim approaching Wat Phu, the rocky peak outlined against the sky appeared like a *lingam* projected from the sky itself by the will of the god.

fig. 39

Raised on this sacred mountain, the temple of Wat Phu was the traditional holy center of the Khmer dynasty and its origins. The kings reigning at Angkor remembered the time when their remote ancestors in the early seventh century, the princes of Chenla, had extended their power over Cambodia, starting from their March of the middle Mekong in the neighborhood of Wat Phu. A few vestiges of this far-off time survive, primarily a brick *cella*. In the following centuries dynastic endowments gave rise to a vast complex, dedicated to Bhadreśvara, that was erected in front of the original sanctuary.

Angkorian temples are usually enclosed within a series of concentric surrounding walls and give access to the visitor only after he has passed through numbers of monumental gateways. At Wat Phu the whole monument can be taken in at a single glance. A majestic approach runs up to the first slopes, passing between two side buildings whose long halls enclose twin courtyards. A staircase, now dilapidated, climbs the mountain between two rows of red jasmine trees, up to a terrace edged with *nāga*. Brick sanctuaries were aligned on platforms to either side of this terrace. They disintegrated centuries ago, and are now no more than heaps of pink rubble, but in the Angkorian period they were faced with stucco and must have shone out brilliantly. Above the terrace the stairway climbs more steeply to reach the forecourt of the central sanctuary. In the twelfth century the modest brick *cella* was dwarfed by a new donation, a cruciform hall and a kind of broad three-naved vestibule erected in front of it.

While most provincial Khmer temples have ceased to be important cult-centers, Wat Phu has remained a sanctuary venerated by the Laotians. In the early eighteenth century they established the principality of Champassak in the area. In February of each year crowds climb the steps of the temple to pay homage to the statues of the Buddha that were erected in the cruciform hall after the adoption of Theravāda Buddhism. As they pass, the faithful lay an offering of flowers and candles at the feet of a statue of Vishnu riding on the shoulder of *Garuda*.

Minor temples sanctify the approaches of the mountain. No one knows in which of them the silver statue was worshiped, only its head has been found *fig. 139*

81

in the waters of a little stream, near the Lingaparvata. This exquisite piece is probably of eighth century date. The sumptuous material, the fine workmanship, the nobility of the features and more than all else the infinite sweetness of its smile make this image, sadly mutilated though it is, one of the most extraordinary masterpieces of southeast Asia. It bears witness to the piety and splendor of the princes of Chenla from whom all the Khmer kings were to proclaim their descent.

Wat Nokor

fig. 41 The second stage of the pilgrimage to the holy sites is the sanctuary of Wat Nokor,[35] in no way comparable to Wat Phu. It is a Buddhist temple built in the early thirteenth century and the largest in the eastern regions of Cambodia. It is very homogenous in style and quite well preserved, but its proportions are not the most elegant and its decoration tends to be monotonous. Nonetheless, on the outer eastern *gopura*, which is the main entrance to the monument, there are some very charming figures of *devatā;* one of the most attractive is posed most gracefully with a bird perched on her hand.

In the sixteenth century the whole aspect of the central zone was transformed by restorations to the superstructure. More recently two monasteries have been installed within its walls and perpetuate the cult of the Buddha in the temple.

Phnom Chisor

Continuing their journey southward, pilgrims reached Phnom Chisor,[36] in the Angkorian period called Sūryaparvata, the "Mountain of Sūrya." The stele of Preah Khan states that a road joined it to Yaśodharapura and that King Jayavarman VII had a halting place built there.

The temple of Phnom Chisor was raised by King Sūryavarman I in the first half of the eleventh century. It faces east at the top of the high hill that gives it its name, and is open to the light of the rising sun.

The faithful approached by a broad avenue which led from a pool which is now dried out to the foot of the monumental stairway. After climbing its many high steps the pilgrim passed through a gatehouse giving access to the interior courtyard. There the central sanctuary of brick rises, preceded by a vaulted hall. The decoration is sober. The sculptors of the eleventh century excelled in the composition of plant motifs to cover pediments, lintels and pilasters. Occasionally a figure appears among the scrolls. Here Krishna holds up Mount Govardhana; there gods and *asura* join together to churn the Sea of Milk from which they will extract the juice of immortality; further on, on a fragment of the pediment, Vishnu lies at rest on the surface of the primordial waters, reclining on the eternal serpent, Ananta, "He who has no end." The grey, faintly bluish tone of the sandstone contrasts delicately with the warm brick.

Up there the eye can rove over the vast plains away to the first ramparts of the Elephant Ridge. By their foundations on Phnom Chisor, Sūryaparvata, the Khmer kings sanctified the whole southern region of their kingdom.

The Sanctuaries of Southwest Cambodia

The pilgrimage continues for some three hundred kilometers from Phnom Chisor to the great temples of the modern region of Battambang, across the low bush, burnt dry during the dry season and sodden during the rains. Ancient monuments line the road: the sanctuaries of Phnom Udong[37] not yet at this time the site of royal sepulcher, the little brick temple of Phnom Basset,[38] built in the seventh century over a cave halfway up a hill; the towers of Kompong Prah,[39] also built in brick a century later.

39   The temple of Wat Phu (South Laos). A holy place venerated by the princes of Chenla, the ancestors of the Angkorian dynasties, the temple of Wat Phu was built over the centuries by the Khmer kings in front of a very ancient little brick shrine. The site, called "Mountain of the *lingam*" owes its name to the rock overtopping it which is considered to be a *lingam* "which arose by itself," by the will of the god Śiva.

Further on again near Stung Sangker, the western-most of the tributaries of the Great Lake, rises the rocky spike of Banon,[40] surely a holy place for centuries before but crowned in the time of Jayavarman VII with a temple sacred to the Buddha, to the *Bodhisattva* Lokeśvara and to the Prajñāpāramitā. A steep staircase climbs the sharp slope. The sanctuary is surrounded by a wall and guarded by delicate *devatā*. There are some very fine images of the Buddha that have been placed in the *cella* over the centuries, statues of wood eaten by termites, and effigies in

figs. 43, 127

fig. 12

stone of the Buddha meditating on the *nāga*, gilded by some devotee anxious to acquire merit.

Behind the temple lay a statue of a radiant Lokeśvara whose headdress is carved with a multitude of figures seated in meditation, representing all those who have been set on the path of Deliverance through the compassion of the *Bodhisattva*.

fig. 40

Wat Ek Phnom

A few dozen kilometers separate Banon from the little knoll of Wat Ek Phnom.[41] The fine sandstone monastery, erected there in the mid-eleventh century, was dedicated to Śiva. Here the plant ornament of the early eleventh century is enriched by a few reliefs with scenes. Thus over a passage between the *mandapa* and the sanctuary two episodes from Vishnuite legend came to be carved. On the lintel gods and *asura* are churning the Sea of Milk; on the pediment Sītā, in tears and closely guarded by *rākshasi*, is being comforted by the monkey Hanuman who has brought her her husband's ring and is urging her not to despair. This scene is often represented in Khmer art, but here it reaches an unusually touching degree of emotion. We see it bathed in light, under a vault that has partly collapsed; in the Angkorian period it was in deep shadow and it can hardly have been possible to make out the silhouettes of Sītā and Hanuman. The artist made no effort to have his work admired. It was enough that the image was there to glorify the divine epic.

fig. 42

40 Torso of Lokeśvara, in the ruins of the temple of Banon (late twelfth-early thirteenth century). Banon, a Mahāyānist Buddhist sanctuary, was built on a rocky peak dominating the region of Battambang. In one of the ruined buildings lie the fragments of a statue of a radiant Lokeśvara, or Avalokiteśvara. Multitudes of little figures seated in meditation cover the chest of the image, representing the beings whom the compassionate *Bodhisattva* has guided towards their salvation.

41 The temple of Wat Nokor (late twelfth-early thirteenth century). An avenue of sugar palms leads to the western entrance of the temple of Wat Nokor, a provincial sanctuary in the Bayon style. It was originally a Mahāyānist Buddhist temple, but was not abandoned at the end of the Angkorian period. It became a Theravāda Buddhist shrine, and was restored several times. In the sixteenth century some sculpture was added, while worshipers had the superstructures of the central shrine rebuilt in the form of a *stūpa*.

Banteay Chhmar

Situated at the northwest of the Great Lake in a zone of sparse forest, the temple of Banteay Chhmar[42] is one of the principal foundations of Jayavarman VII; he had it built in honor of his son Śrīndrakumāra and four of his companions-in-arms who saved the life of the young prince in a battle. *fig. 46*

As at Angkor Thom and Preah Khan, the temple was reached along an avenue flanked by stone giants. Now it is mostly in ruins, and to reach the central sanctuary you have to clamber over enormous blocks of fallen stone and find your way among the debris. The decoration is still admirable. The scenes on the pediments and lintels are harmoniously composed. A frieze runs all round a cruciform hall with *kinnarī* spreading their harpy wings. The walls of the gallery of the second enceinte are carved with huge reliefs. Their composition and style of carving recall the Bayon reliefs. On the eastern gallery there is even a rendering of a naval battle. Again as at the Bayon, we find the ships with their warriors, facing each other on the water and, dominating the battle, a majestic figure that may be Jayavarman VII himself. Many tracts of the wall have unfortunately crumbled, but the western galleries are almost all standing; to the north and south there are large fragments remaining in place. *fig. 45*

Scenes of daily life give these reliefs a picturesque note: musicians beat their long drums, porters heave together at a heavy burden, elsewhere a ballet mistress corrects the position of a young pupil. Like invocations in a litany evoking the different aspects of the *Bodhisattva*, great figures of Avalokiteśvara punctuate the southern relief of the western gallery. Here the *Bodhisattva* appears amid a retinue of *devatā*, there he receives the homage of a group of worshipers, *fig. 44*

42 Pediment and lintel, Wat Ek Phnom (mid-eleventh century). On the lintel, *deva* and *asura* are churning the Ocean of Milk to extract the elixir of immortality. Mount Mandara, the pivot of the churn, is shown as a column resting on the back of the tortoise into which Vishnu has incarnated himself. The god also appears in the center of the composition. On the pediment, Sītā, taken prisoner by Rāvana, is in despair; the gesture of her hand raised to her eyes denotes that she is weeping. Two *rākshasī* watch over her; but behind her the monkey Hanuman is approaching to give her the ring of her husband, Rāma.

43 *Devatā*, Banon (late twelfth-early thirteenth century). Only the lovely face with its hint of a smile was finished; the chiseling of the necklace and belt, and the brocaded decoration of the garment, have not been carved. Stones of different provenance were used for building the Banon; grey, yellowish or pink sandstones.

44 Avalokiteśvara, Banteay Chhmar, west gallery (late twelfth-early thirteenth century). Large images of Avalokiteśvara punctuate the composition of the mural relief on the west gallery. Showing various aspects of the compassionate *Bodhisattva*, they recur like the invocations of a litany. Here Avalokiteśvara is shown with a single head and eight arms; among his attributes the book, the rosary and the flask can be identified. Round him gather imploring worshipers, and divine messengers descending from the sky bring him lotus and garlands of flowers.

45 Rāma and Rāvana (?), Banteay Chhmar (late twelfth-early thirteenth century). The archer who has just killed with his arrow an individual with many heads and a demon-like aspect, may be Rāma beating Rāvana at the battle of Lanka. Rāvana, if he is represented here, is falling from his lion-drawn chariot. In spite of the worn state of the stone the relief on this pediment is still vigorous. The composition is beautifully balanced. The straight silhouette of the archer turning back is contrasted with the bent body of his enemy as he falls.

further on he announces salvation to the gods themselves, to Śiva and Parvatī, and to simple gods of the terrestial world who kneel at his feet to implore his help.

Phimai and the Temples of the Menam Plain

In the west the empire of Jayavarman VII extended as far as the Menam, over several provinces now in the heart of the kingdom of Thailand. In the regions of Korat, Lopburi and even of Sukhotaya, Khmer temples were built during the twelfth century. Some of these monuments still have original features that give them a distinctive aspect. In Cambodia the architects of the twelfth century used stone almost exclusively, and sandstone in particular. In the lands of the Menam they sometimes used brick covered with stucco decoration, which is a mode of construction proper to these regions, inherited from the ancient traditions of Dvāravatī art. J. Boisselier found traces on the walls of the Preah Prang Sam Yot in Lopburi[43] of decorative motifs characteristic of Bayon art, but executed in stucco, not in stone. Decoration of this kind needed constant upkeep because of its fragility. When the Siamese took over these monuments, they set about restoring and preserving them. They kept the motifs but interpreted them more and more in their own idiom. A small number of sandstone temples in these regions are counted among the finest examples of Khmer art. Among these are Phanom Rung and, the most famous of all, Phimai.

fig. 48 The central tower-sanctuary of Phimai dominates the galleries and minor buildings of the temple with sober majesty. The iconography of Phimai[44] is notable both for its fine workmanship and its originality. The subjects of some of the reliefs are unusual: Buddha

46 Banteay Chhmar, south gallery (late twelfth-early thirteenth century). The temple of Banteay Chhmar was built by King Jayavarman VII, in memory of a royal prince who was killed in the time of King Yaśovarman II during a battle against a rebel with the strange name of Bhārata-Rāhu. Two warriors who had defended the young prince were associated with his memory. The outer gallery, now partially ruined, was carved on the whole length of the wall with reliefs comparable to those of the Bayon.

47 Temple of Prāsāt Muang Tam (Thailand). This little temple, its shrines reflected in the waters of a moat, is one of the Khmer monuments of Thailand. The warm evening light gilds the pink tones of the brick. In these ancient Khmer provinces brick often replaced the sandstone that the architects found difficult to obtain in the Menam basin.

48   The temple of Phimai (early twelfth century). The temple of Phimai is one of the most beautiful Khmer sanctuaries built in the territory of modern Thailand. It was a Mahāyānist Buddhist shrine, probably belonging to a Tantric sect. Built in the style of Angkor Wat, the central shrine is reminiscent, in form, of the tower-shrines of the great temple of Sūryavarman I.

figures are given ornaments and garments hanging in folds; Mahāyāna deities are seated in the center of two of the lintels of the central sanctuary, Vajradhara holding the *vajra* and bell, Trailokyavijaya dancing on the skin of a monstrous elephant. Round the deities are throngs of musicians and dancers.

There are many fragments lying on the ground, and among them are some splendid pieces. One complete statue has even been found which seems to be one of the portraits of Jayavarman VII; unfortunately the face is damaged. This very beautiful image, now exhibited in the Bangkok Museum, must once have stood, therefore, in one of the most eminent sanctuaries of the kingdom.

Preah Vihear

fig. 49 Turning eastward, our pilgrimage round Cambodia brings us to the temple of Preah Vihear.[45] Its site is impressive. The monument rears up on a spur of the sandstone Dangrek plateau, dominating the Cambodian plain from a precipice more than four hundred meters high, but sloping away gently in the direction of Thailand. From the height of this gigantic cliff the land of the Khmer stretches out before our eyes; yet the designers of Preah Vihear put up no building to open onto this view; on the contrary, even the back façade of the temple is completely blind. It is on the northeast slope that the approach is made, up the *fig. 50* avenue and through the series of surrounding walls, to reach the central sanctuary.

The terraced arrangement of Preah Vihear is reminiscent of that of Wat Phu. Here again is the avenue

50 The ruined entrance pavilion, Preah Vihear (early eleventh century). The temple of Preah Vihear opens onto a slope that runs gently down into Thailand. There is an avenue lined with boundary stones, then with *nāga*, to be followed, before arriving at the entrance pavilion, now partially collapsed, which rears its splendid triangular pediments against the sky. After passing through several enclosing walls the visitor reaches the central shrine, to which Sūryavarman I magically transported the god Bhadreśvara, a manifestation of Śiva worshiped at Wat Phu.

49 Preah Vihear (eleventh century). At Preah Vihear the temple of Śikhareśvara, Śiva "Lord of the Summit" is built at the edge of a plateau which dominates the Cambodian plain from a vertical height of some five hundred meters. Yet there is not a single opening in the back wall of the temple to give onto this dizzying panorama that stretches, slightly veiled in mist, into the far distance.

flanked with stones, the series of brick sanctuaries and finally the sanctuary closed to the back. At Wat Phu the temple backs against the mountain side, at Preah Vihear it turns its back on the vertiginous drop from the edge of the plateau. This similarity of arrangement together with an interpretation of an inscription have allowed J. Boisselier to describe Preah Vihear as a "copy" of Wat Phu. Sūryavarman I transported hither "by magic" the deity of the old Chenla sanctuary.

Preah Vihear has kept its religious importance into modern times, for it is from the temple pool that the water must be taken that is poured over the king of Thailand at his coronation.

Koh Ker

Koh Ker, some fifty kilometers south of Preah Vihear, is one of the chief historical monuments of medieval Cambodia.[46] It is unlikely that it was ever a halting place for pilgrims, but it preserves the imposing ruins of a royal city that was the capital of king Jayavarman IV in the tenth century. The crown fell to this prince, brother-in-law of Yaśovarman, after the death of his two nephews. However, he had not waited for this double disappearance to establish a capital at Koh Ker.

Jayavarman IV had notions of grandeur. The monuments of Koh Ker impress by their well-nigh colossal proportions, so much so that the gateway to the principal temple, the Preah Thom, has been given its own name by local folk, Prāsāt Kraham, the "red tower sanctuary." It must be admitted that this immense brick tower has all the majesty of a temple. Beneath a lintel illustrating the myth of Vishnu as a lionman tearing out the entrails of an impious *asura*, a tall doorway discloses in the half dark the fragments of a huge statue of a dancing Śiva. The god is figured with five heads, in his aspect of Sadāśiva, the "Always Benevolent." He is performing a hieratic dance, his knees bent, his multiple arms spread in a fan around him. Now this marvelous statue lies broken and half buried in the soil of Prāsāt Kraham.

Paradoxically the center of the Prāsāt Thom does not contain a large shrine but nine chapels. Behind the temple rises a pyramid in seven tiers, thirty-five meters high, the Prang, on top of which the king had an enormous stone *lingam* set up. An inscription in Koh Ker celebrates this prodigious foundation by the king, "Rejoicing the hearts of men of good will, and reducing to nothing the pride of the proud, he erected an extremely heavy *lingam* of Ugra, placing it on nine times nine cubits."

fig. 51

Yet Koh Ker was not to outlive Jayavarman IV for long. When his son disappeared only two years after he had died, the capital was definitively abandoned.

Preah Khan of Kompong Svay

While Koh Ker saw its importance decline after the mid-tenth century, another town that was for long no more than a sizeable village grew two centuries later into a considerable city. It is known under the name of Preah Khan of Kompong Svay.[47] As has been suggested by P. Stern, the analogy between the name of this town and that of the Preah Khan of Angkor is certainly not fortuitous; there are features for comparison between the two groups of monuments.

The Preah Khan of Kompong Svay was a large town with an enceinte extending five kilometers on a side. No more than a bank of earth with a moat alongside, this enceinte was perhaps fortified with a rampart of tree trunks. All the urban installations disappeared centuries ago, and the whole town is submerged by forest growth; all that remains of the Preah

51 The *prang* of Koh Ker (second quarter of the tenth century). While his nephews were reigning at Yaśodharapura, the city of Angkor, Jayavarman IV founded a capital full of imposing monuments at Koh Ker. Behind the largest temple, Prāsāt Thom, he erected a stepped pyramid, the *prang*, in order to place on it a colossal stone *lingam*. When his nephews died Jayavarman IV become the legitimate king, but Koh Ker did not long remain the royal residence. After the ephemeral reign of Jayavarman IV's son, the new king Rājendravarman brought the capital back to Angkor.

Khan of Kompong Svay is a large religious complex comprising a main temple, the Preah Khan properly speaking, a little stepped pyramid; and two shrines, one, Preah Thkol, built in the middle of a pool and the other, Preah Stung, standing on the bank of this same large reservoir.

Almost everything inside the first surrounding wall of the Preah Khan is in ruins, but the central sanctuary, even so, is among the supreme examples of the last phase of the art of Angkor Wat. The *devatā* adorning its walls are very beautiful. The surrounding wall of the temple itself and several other buildings belong to the art of the Bayon. The layout is harmonious and dignified. North of the avenue leading to the east entrance stands the chapel of one of the travelers' lodges built at the order of Jayavarman VII.

At the east end of this avenue lay one of the reservoirs the Cambodians call *baray*. In the middle of the water a little island served as the base for the Preah Thkol whose sanctuary, flanked by two libraries, was built at the end of the twelfth century. In the reign of Jayavarman VII the town was further endowed, on the one hand with the Prāsāt Preah Stung crowned with one of the oldest "face" towers, and on the other with the pyramid of Preah Damrei, guarded at four corners by a stone elephant.

P. Stern has stressed the special interest that Jayavarman VII seems to have taken in this town; it may have been the residence of a member of his family.[48] About twenty years ago a splendid head of a statue thought to be of this king was discovered in the ruins of the main temple. The monarch's face is much younger than on the effigies of Phimai and Krol Romeas. The purity of the modeling and the expression of meditation make this piece one of the most remarkable of Bayon art. Its presence alone demonstrates how this town enjoyed the favor of Jayavarman VII, since he wished his image to reside there.

Beng Mealea

Following the road leading back to Angkor from the Preah Khan of Kompong Svay, the pilgrims could stop at Beng Mealea,[49] a large temple built in the purest Angkor Wat style. After crossing a great pool, now filled in, they reached the monument by a long stone-lined avenue and then by a terrace flanked by *nāga*. The *nāga* of Beng Mealea with their multiple heads haloed in a single diadem are among the most lovely mythical animals of Khmer art.

The plan of the temple is like that of Angkor Wat, except that here the monument is not erected on a stepped pyramid; its buildings are all on the same ground level. The sandstone masonry is so fine that the joints are scarcely visible. Beng Mealea has no great reliefs to correspond with those covering the walls of the third enceinte of Angkor Wat, but the decoration on pediments, lintels and even the bases of pilasters comprises skillfully composed scenes. On the walls elegant *devatā* figures keep guard over the shrine.

In the Angkorian period Beng Mealea must have been one of the loveliest temples in Cambodia, both for its layout and for the care taken in its construction and sculpture. Few monuments have suffered so *fig. 52* much. Some galleries are no more than heaps of collapsed blocks of stone, showing here and there among the debris a fragment of finely carved frieze, a pilaster scroll or the smile of a *devatā*.

Phnom Kulen

Though Wat Phu was the original shrine of the Khmer dynasty, it was at Phnom Kulen that the ceremony was enacted in the early ninth century that consecrated the independence and aspirations for unity of the country that was to become the kingdom of Angkor.[50]

52 Beng Mealea, gallery in ruins (first half of the twelfth century). Few monuments have suffered as much as Beng Mealea, a splendid temple built in the purest Angkor Wat style. The sandstone used in its construction is of the finest, and the blocks are so perfectly trimmed that the joints are scarcely visible. The decoration is refined and devoid of any excessive elaboration, harmonizing exquisitely with the architectural lines.

There are no great monuments on Phnom Kulen, the "lychee mountain," but numerous shrines dotted about on the sandstone plateau. All built of brick though of very varied aspect, these little temples stand in clearings in the heart of the forest. The tower of O Paong rises with its sober silhouette in a copse of lychees, in April covered with clusters of the small red fruit; the three shrines of Prāsāt Damrei Krap represent a purely Cham type of architecture in the center of Khmer country, bearing witness to the eclecticism of the art of Jayavarman II; Thma Dap, probably the most recent, preserves large fragments of decoration modeled in stucco on its walls.

In the Angkorian period Phnom Kulen was Mahendraparvata, the "Mountain of Mahendra," that is to say of Śiva. It is one of the holiest places in the kingdom. One of the sources of the river of Siem Reap rises on this plateau; its bed is carved with a multitude of *lingam*. Thus the waters that irrigate the region of Angkor have been sanctified by flowing over the holy images of the god; the whole course of this river is holy; one of its affluents, the "River of a Thousand *fig. 53* *Lingam*"[51] coming from a neighboring plateau, passes likewise over images of Vishnu recumbent and of Brahma that can be seen, hardly obscured at all by the shimmer of the moving water.

Hermits still inhabit the caves of Phnom Kulen and the faithful continue to come, sometimes from far off, to worship at Preah Thom the great Buddha reclining in Mahāparinirvāna, carved in the sixteenth century at the top of a great rock.

After leaving Phnom Kulen the pilgrimage to the great shrines brings us back to the religious center of Angkor, the capital whence royal power radiated throughout the kingdom.

At this time in the early thirteenth century, the one we have chosen for our journey round Angkorian Cambodia, the peace restored by Jayavarman VII had brought back the villages and towns to their traditional activities, following the rhythm of the seasons. But this peaceful life of the countryside could only be assured by a government in harmony with divine order. Represented by his officials even in the outermost provinces, supreme proprietor of all the land, the king was responsible for the prosperity of his

53 "The river of a thousand *lingam*." Like the river of Siem Reap, its tributary, the "river of a thousand *lingam*" flows over divine images. Thousands of *lingam* and other divine images are carved in its bed: Śiva and Umā riding on the bull Nandin, Vishnu lying on the snake Ananta.

kingdom. If, as Jayavarman VII proclaims in his Hospital stele, "the sorrow of the people makes the sorrow of kings," then the king had to make justice reign and multiply pious works, as he did by founding sanctuaries, creating lodges for travelers, and hospitals, and carrying out public works for religious ends. To guarantee its prosperity, the land needed an ideal capital at its center: a holy city, impregnable, to assure the permanence of the kingdom. It is with this aim in mind that the Khmer sovereigns built Angkor.

Part two:
LIFE IN ANGKOR

STAGES IN THE BUILDING OF ANGKOR

Among the foreigners, from the thirteenth century to the present day, who have had the good fortune to see Angkor, there are few who have been able to repress their enthusiasm at the discovery of such an imposing group of monuments. Rare indeed are the writers who have not felt a strong impact. The astonishment of one of the earliest travelers, the Portuguese Diego do Couto, is perhaps more moving than the romantic rapture of nineteenth century explorers: "This town was square and a league in length down each side. It had four main gates and one in addition that served the royal palaces. And on each face of the square there was a superb bastion. ...[The town] was surrounded by a moat a blunderbuss shot wide and [holding] three fathom of water without its ever getting lower. Over [the moat] there are five bridges corresponding to the five gates already mentioned; each of these is twelve feet wide... [they] have on either side their parapets of pierced stone like marble, with above them a beautiful well-made rail on which [there are] stone giants riding at regular intervals....The walls of the town are entirely of dressed stone, so perfect and well set that they seem to be all one single stone."[52] With its walls approximately square and more than 3,000 meters on each side, with its five gates opening onto avenues flanked by giants, Angkor Thom appears to us very like its description by Diego do Couto.

Our Western towns founded in the Middle Ages have been redesigned and reformed over the centuries, but no urban life has touched Angkor since the sixteenth century. Every temple, every building that rouses our admiration today was built between the end of the ninth and the middle of the thirteenth century. Since that time Angkor has kept all its architecture in durable material, among the trees of the living forest.

The city that we can see today and that all the texts, Chinese and Western, describe, is Angkor Thom, rebuilt on the initiative of Jayavarman VII. The site does however preserve monuments bequeathed by this king's predecessors that were occupied throughout the Angkorian period, for once a foundation existed it must never be abandoned. In the course of the four centuries during which the Angkorian monarchy lasted almost every reign saw new temples arise within the city or on its outskirts.

The Foundation of Angkor

In 889 Yaśovarman became king in Hariharālaya after the death of his father, Indravarman, the great artisan of Khmer unity. Hariharālaya, on the site of Roluos, was a large town near the Great Lake. Following his two predecessors, Jayavarman II and Jayavarman III, Indravarman had endowed it with imposing monuments, the temple of Bakong on a

54 Angkor Thom, south gate (late twelfth century). Five gates, each surmounted by four monumental heads, punctuate the square enceinte of Angkor Thom. Two of them, the Gate of the Dead and the Gate of Victory, open to the east. In front of each of these gates a causeway on a bank gives passage over the moat surrounding the ramparts, flanked by a guard of 108 stone giants carrying a *nāga*.

55 Roluos, temple of Preah Ko (late ninth century). In his capital of Hariharālaya, on the site of Roluos, King Indravarman had the six shrines of the brick temple of Preah Ko built in honor of his ancestors. The pink brick was then covered with stucco which was modeled with a very rich decoration.

fig. 55   high sandstone pyramid and the six brick sanctuaries of Preah Ko dedicated to the memory of his ancestors, to cite only his two principal foundations. He had had an enormous artifical pool constructed, called the Indratatāka after him. But Yaśovarman was soon to abandon this capital. After paying his respects to his ancestors by building the four brick towers of the temple of Lolei, on the central islet of the Indratatāka, he went off to found a new capital, some twenty kilometers from Hariharālaya, on the site of Angkor.

Why did the king abandon a flourishing capital to establish another residence so near the old one? It is true that the plain of Angkor offers excellent condi-

tions for the creation of a town. Situated outside the limits of the annual floods, it is still close to the magnificent waterway and to the incredible reserve of fish that is constituted by the Great Lake. The plain is irrigated by the Stung Siem Reap coming down from Phnom Kulen that shuts it off to the north with its sandstone rampart. Three hills, three *phnom*, break the monotony of this plain: the Phnom Nok to the north, Phnom Krom, near the Great Lake, and, right in the center, Phnom Bakheng. Yaśovarman crowned the two former with temples dedicated to the Tri-mūrti; the third, the lowest, he chose for the center of his town. While the plain has to be irrigated to bear crops, the banks of the Stung Siem Reap are naturally green. It cannot be doubted that these physical considerations weighed with Yaśovarman in his choice of the site, yet the intention presiding over the foundation of the new capital was essentially religious.

The epigraphy gives prominence to the personality of Yaśovarman, his beauty surpassing even that of Kāma, the god of Love; the perfection of his education as a prince during his "childhood without constraint,"[53] and above all the depth of his Śivaite faith. His religious formation was owed to his spiritual advisor Vāmaśiva, who had himself received it from a disciple of the Indian philosopher Chankārāchārya.[54] His reading of the Indian texts had taught him what a perfect capital should be, on the model of the divine world. Hariharālaya, already encumbered with monuments, could only answer partially to this ideal. It was impossible to remodel it. Therefore, Yaśovarman needed to create a new royal residence, not in any youthful thirst for glory; but in a desire to inaugurate in the center of the kingdom an abode for

56 Head of a benevolent giant, Angkor Thom, south gate (late twelfth century). Various groups of mythical beings, in charge of guarding the capital, are assembled at the gates of Angkor Thom. In the front rank of the city's defenders, the two rows of giants supporting *nāga* stand facing all possible aggression from outside. As one enters the city on the right there are ferocious giants, while there are kindly ones on the left. These latter wear the adornment of gods, while the former have the military headdress of the *asura*.

the gods, a surety for the prosperity of the land. He gave it his name, Yasodharapura.

The foundation of Angkor marks for Cambodia the beginning of a new era, celebrated in an inscription that salutes the accession of Yasovarman to the throne: "At his accession as [at the rising of the sun] the lotus stood erect once more... the brightness of the other stars was dispelled."[55]

The Beginnings of Yasodharapura

The center of the capital founded by Yasovarman, Phnom Bakheng, rises outside the town of Angkor Thom, to the south of its famous enceinte. The fact that the city shifted on its own site made some of the early research on Angkor confused and caused mistakes in the chronology of Khmer monuments.

From an airplane, or even from the top of Phnom Bakheng, the original moat of Yasodharapura is plainly visible to the southwest of the site; it was transformed into a rice swamp in the rainy season. To the east, the river of Siem Reap, diverted from its course, acted as a moat. A double bank of earth formed the ramparts. There remains no trace of any enceinte on the north of Yasovarman's city. Perhaps the rebuilding eliminated all vestiges of these ancient works, but more probably there was never either moat or bank on the north.

Nothing remains on the ground of the houses or structures of perishable materials. The royal residence has likewise disappeared. The religious buildings alone were built of stone or brick. Of the first Yasodharapura, we can still see the temple constructed on Phnom Bakheng, the great Western Baray, and some traces of the surrounding walls. The epigraphy mentions monasteries and describes the location of two of them.

There is no reason to doubt that the temple now crowning the top of Phnom Bakheng is the great foundation of Yasovarman himself; this is confirmed both by the epigraphy and by art history. Built on the summit of the hill and further raised up on a five-tiered pyramidal sandstone terrace thirteen meters high, the temple dominates the whole site with a majesty appropriate to the dwelling of the gods. On each axis of the pyramid a monumental staircase leads to the upper platform. On each of the five tiers of the tall base little chapels have been built in sandstone, in the corners and on either side of the stairways. The base of the terrace is surrounded by forty-four brick towers decorated in stucco.

The tall pyramid base surmounted by five tower-sanctuaries arranged in a square with one in the center is reminiscent of Mount Meru with its five peaks. In Indian cosmology the gods have their seat on Mount Meru, whence they survey the revolutions of the stars. The whole monument is laden with symbolism. On the highest terrace the main shrine rises higher than the others, just as Siva overtops all other gods. Below it are laid out 108 shrines. The number 108 is peculiarly beneficent since it comprises the auspicious numbers 1 and 8. The result of multiplying the number of lunar mansions, which is 27, by the number 4, which corresponds to the phases of the moon, is 108. In a study of the symbolism of Phnom Bakheng J. Filliozat[56] observed that when anyone looks at the temple on Phnom Bakheng as he is about to climb one of the stairways of the pyramid, he can only see thirty-three shrines, corresponding to the thirty-three gods who reside on Mount Meru. At the top he can only see three tower-sanctuaries, representing the three gods of the Trimūrti, Siva, Vishnu and Brahma; Siva, in the center, overtops the rest. Thus Phnom Bakheng appears as an authentic Mount Meru, dwelling of the gods and pillar of the unshakeable world, in the center of the capital and the kingdom.

Every sanctuary on Phnom Bakheng houses a *lingam*. Since all is Siva, the *lingam* which is his principal manifestation can represent all the other deities. The central shrine is dedicated quite specially to Siva, worshiped under the name of Yasodharesvara, "Lord of Yasodhara," the manifestation of Siva which was the favorite divinity of Yasovarman. This king was a fervent Sivaite, "whose intelligence reposed in the light of the feet of Rudra [Siva.]"[57]

In a ceremony of extreme solemnity the spiritual advisor of the king, the Brahman Vāmasiva, raised up the *lingam* on Phnom Bakheng, thus consecrating

fig. 57

57 Temple of Phnom Bakheng (last years of the ninth century). Becoming king at Hariharālaya, Yaśovarman soon left what had been his father's residence to found a new capital, Yaśodharapura on the site of Angkor. The city was built round the hill of Phnom Bakheng which the king crowned with a great sanctuary dedicated to Śiva. On a five-story pyramid rise the five principal shrines which, arranged in a quincunx, recall the five peaks of Mount Meru, the axis of the world and the dwelling place of the gods.

the surroundings of the hill which, as well as being a Mount Meru, was also a *śivakshetra*, a sacred precinct that surrounds a *lingam* for 1000 cubits round about it. Its dimensions of 650 meters by 440 make the enceinte of the temple of Phnom Bakheng demarcate approximately the extent of a *śivakshetra*. The slopes of the hill formed the park of this holy place which was given over to ascetics for their meditations.

It is only by flying over Phnom Bakheng that one can fully appreciate the imposing harmony of its layout. The five sanctuaries on the summit have unfortunately been mutilated. In the post-Angkorian period the Buddhists tried to build a colossal seated Buddha in dressed stone on the place where the central shrine stands. It is not without esthetic quality, but it was left unfinished. When Phnom Bakheng was restored, this image was removed so that what remained of the original shrine could be seen. The superstructures have disappeared entirely, but the wall decorations are splendid: small figures of orants with their hands joined among foliage scrolls, dancing figures on the stairways, noble *devatā* on the walls. Majestic rather than elegant, as was the taste of the time, these female figures are the guardians of the shrine that opens to the four points of the compass.

From the heights of Phnom Bakheng it is possible to see the moats of the city and over to the northeast the Eastern Baray, called Yaśodharatatāka after the name of its founder. This artificial pool, surrounded by a retaining bank 7 kilometers long by 1,800 meters wide, had essentially religious value, as is proved by the four stelae placed at the corners of the bank. The whole water system of the region was sacred, for the waters of the Stung Siem Reap had flowed over the divine images carved in its rocky bed on Phnom Kulen; the water was as holy as the ablution water that has been poured over an idol in a sanctuary.

How did Yaśovarman populate his new capital? Was the area within the enceinte settled all over? And was the king's residence already on the site of the Royal Palace of Angkor? Nothing has been found to date to give an answer to these questions. We only have documentation for the three monasteries that Yaśovarman founded for Śivaite, Vishnuite and Buddhist monks. The Śivaite and Vishnuite monasteries, the Brahmāśrama and Vaiśanvāśrama, were probably built near the southern bank of the Yaśodharatatāka where their foundation stelae were discovered. The site of the Buddhist monastery is not known since its stele, found at Tep Pranam, had evidently been moved. It is likely however that it was built a little away from the city as were the other two, according to the recommendations of monastic rule. The internal organization of these three institutions is clearly defined in the epigraphic texts. They were centers of teaching and asylum as well as of meditation, and might accomodate lay people. The marks of honor reserved for the various classes of society, and the prohibitions against those considered unworthy, reflect the hierarchy into which Khmer society was divided.

In the early thirteenth century the ramparts of the original Yaśodharapura were no doubt abandoned, the Yaśodharatatāka was certainly at least partially dried out, but Phnom Bakheng, now outside the new city, remained a sanctuary dedicated to the cult of Śiva. On feast days the faithful were still to be seen climbing those steep stairways, guarded by stone lions, to pay their homage to the "Lord of Yaśovarman."

The reigns of the two sons of Yaśovarman did little to change the aspect of Angkor, though Harṣavarman I "to increase the dharma of his parents" founded, at the foot of Phnom Bakheng, the little temple of Baksei Chamkrong, a simple brick sanctuary built *fig. 58* on a stepped laterite pyramid. Enshrined in the forest this little building is full of charm, with the serenity of its lines and the harmonious coloring of

58 Baksei Chamkrong (first half of the tenth century). The son of Yaśovarman founded this little temple to the north of Phnom Bakheng and dedicated it to Śiva and his consort Umā. This shrine was restored in the reign of Rājendravarman who aspired to give it a brilliance comparable to that of Mount Kailāsa, the residence of Śiva. Under the paving of the shrine a central well sinks to a cell on ground level. The shape of Baksei Chamkrong recalls the stepped pyramids which are raised in India over the tombs of certain initiates devoted to Śiva.

59 Pre Rup (mid-tenth century). After being abandoned for nearly twenty years, Angkor was reestablished as the capital city at the accession of Rājendravarman (944), the nephew of Yaśovarman I. After first constructing the temple of the Eastern Mebon to the memory of his ancestors, the new king founded the Śivaite temple of Pre Rup. These two temples are built in pink brick on pyramids of reddish laterite, and each crowned with five shrines arranged in quincunx, reproducing the five peaks of Mount Meru.

pink brick and golden laterite. Here Harśavarman set up golden statues of Śiva and of Umā.

At the time when the last son of Yaśovarman disappeared, there does not seem to have been any other building of durable materials in Angkor, but in the immediate neighborhood of the city there are several little sanctuaries of the early tenth century that must mark the sites of villages long since deserted. One of them is Prāsāt Kravan, a group of five sanctuaries to the east of Yaśodharapura. Its foundation is the work of several dignitaries. An inscription informs us that in A.D. 921 a high official named Mahīdharavarman had an image of Vishnu set up in the central shrine. In Khmer monuments it is usual for the walls of the *cella* to be bare, but in two of the shrines at Prāsāt Kravan the inner walls have reliefs carved in the brick.

Such was Yaśodharapura when in 928 Jayavarman IV became legitimate king by the death of his two nephews, and moved the royal residence. Yaśovarman's

dream of making Angkor the ideal capital seemed to have been abandoned for ever. If Jayavarman IV had managed to establish a long line of succession, Koh Ker might perhaps have remained the dwelling of the gods. In his desire to surpass the work of Yaśovarman had not Jayavarman IV raised, on a sandstone pyramid 35 meters high, a *lingam* of Śiva, Tribhuvaneś- *fig. 51* vara, "Lord of the Three Worlds"? But this enterprise was doomed to failure, for in 944 a nephew of Yaśovarman, Rājendravarman, gave its pre-eminence back to Angkor.

Angkor in the Second Half of the Tenth Century

Rājendravarman "of whom the world praised the budding virtues" brought back the capital to "the holy city of Yaśodharapura that had for long remained empty."[58] In his reign and that of his son the site of Angkor saw the construction of monuments of high architectural and decorative quality. Apart from the buildings executed in the Royal Palace the new foundations are all located to the east of the city. Rājendravarman was anxious to establish his legitimacy as heir to Yaśovarman and his sons. Soon after his accession he restored the Baksei Chamkrong of Harśavarman and gave it a coating of stucco, so that it should shine with the brilliance of Mount Kailāsa, the residence of Śiva and his wife Umā to whom the temple was dedicated. His first great foundation is the eastern Prāsāt Mebon, raised to the memory of his ancestors, on an island in the center of the Yaśodharatatāka. Not until 961 did he build the great temple of his reign, Pre Rup, in the central shrine of *fig. 59* which he had the *lingam* Rājendrabhadreśvara set up, whose name contains the name of the deity of Wat

60 Pre Rup, the northeast corner (mid-tenth century). Pre Rup was the great temple of Rājendravarman's reign, and here in the central shrine he set up the *lingam* Rājendrabhadreśvara, his favorite deity, whose name includes that under which Śiva was honored at Wat Phu, the shrine worshiped by his paternal ancestors who were the founders of the Chenla dynasty. The pink brick of the buildings still preserves a few traces of its original decoration modeled in white stucco.

Phu, Bhadreśvara. Though it was the chief sanctuary of the dynasty, Wat Phu did not belong to the Angkor kingdom until the accession of Rājendravarman, who inherited it from his father.[59] Angkor and the rest of Cambodia he had received from his mother, a daughter of Yaśovarman.

Prāsāt Mebon, its shrines reflected in the waters of the eastern Baray, could only be reached by boat. The approach to Pre Rup was more monumental; before climbing the steps of the first entrance pavilion the faithful had to follow a long avenue, between two rows of boundary stones. The temples of Pre Rup and Prāsāt Mebon are both built on tall laterite pyramids. Their arrangement introduces some novelties. Approximately half way up this base, a broad terrace supports long halls on either side of the passage pavilions and on the axes. They mark a rest in the climb to the central shrines. The base of Pre Rup is much higher than that of Prāsāt Mebon; from its highest terrace the view extends far away to Phnom Bok and even, on the horizon, to the escarpment of the Kulen plateau.

The summits of both temples are crowned with five towers arranged, as at Phnom Bakheng, in a quincunx; but here the material used is brick coated with stucco, not sandstone. The retun to brick construction is significant of Rājendravarman's desire to return to the ancient formulae. He linked himself back in this way, beyond Yaśovarman, to his ancestor Indravarman, whose work of unification and assemblage of lands he was completing by joining to the Khmer monarchy the land of Wat Phu which had been separate from the rest of Cambodia since the eighth century. The return to the art of Indravarman is equally apparent in the decorative sculpture. The corners of the pyramid of Prāsāt Mebon are guarded by stone elephants, recalling those that had been placed in the temple of Bakong, at Roluos. In the composition on the lintels, the plant scrolls are animated by little figures in designs evoking the art of Roluos, though they have perhaps less spontaneity.

The stucco facing has weathered over the years, but it still partly covers the pink brick and is modeled on the sanctuary walls into *devatā* more graceful than the majestic guardians of Phnom Bakheng. The warm colors of the brick and laterite contrast with the grey-green of the lintels and false doorways, so delicately carved in the fine sandstone that it is difficult to imagine that their chiseling has retained such sensitive relief after so many centuries.

After founding these two great temples, Rājendravarman undertook the construction of the Royal Palace. He entrusted the direction of the works to one of his high dignitaries, Kavīndrārimathana, who had also been in charge of supervising the building of Prāsāt Mebon. Inside the enceinte of the Palace the laterite pyramidal base of the Phimeanakas, the "Celestial Palace" was erected. This monument was probably not finished until the early eleventh century. Its high pedestal recalls that of Prāsāt Mebon; and it too is guarded by elephants at each corner. The works on the Royal Palace continued during the reign of Jayavarman V. The surrounding walls and entrance pavilions were probably built at the end of this period.

The second half of the tenth century saw the building of important temples by high officials all round the Angkor region: the two brick towers of Preah Enkosei on the left bank of the Stung Siem Reap, downstream from Angkor, the temple of Bat Chhum, also in brick, dedicated to the Buddha by Kavīndrārimathana, the same who, though a Buddhist, was in charge of the building of Prāsāt Mebon and the Royal Palace, and lastly the temple of Banteay Srei, one of the most famous of the monuments of the Angkor group.

It would be impossible to evoke Angkor at this period at the end of the tenth century without stopping at Banteay Srei, although this monument is situated some thirty kilometers from Angkor and was built in another city, Iśvarapura, the "City of the Lord (Śiva)." Its foundation in 967 was the work of the Brahman Yajñavarāha, a descendant of Yaśovarman and one of the leading men of the kingdom, who exercised a virtual regency during the minority of Jayavarman V. Banteay Srei is built of pink sandstone, and its masonry and carving are carried out with extraordinary care and perfection. The entrance porch of the outer enceinte is massive and monu-

fig. 60

fig. 116

fig. 61

fig. 64

61 Banteay Srei (third quarter of the tenth century). At a distance of some thirty kilometers from Angkor in the now vanished city of Iśvarapura, the temple of Banteay Srei was founded in 967 by the Brahman Yajñavarāha, who was one of the mightiest men in the kingdom and a descendant, on his mother's side, of Yaśovarman. After following a long avenue flanked by boundary stones, and passing through three enclosing walls, the visitor reaches the central shrines. A wide moat surrounds the second enclosing wall; it is crossed by a causeway running along a bank.

62 Banteay Srei, southern shrine and *mandapa* of the central shrine (third quarter of the tenth century). The north and south shrines are simply square *cella*, guarded by *devatā*; the central shrine comprises a long hall, a *mandapa*, in front of the *cella*. All three shrines are built on the same base; staircases give access to the entrances to the shrines and to the *mandapa*. On the string-walls of the staircases, animal-headed figures stand guardian. In front of the southern shrine these "string-wall spirits" are lion-headed men; in front of the southern staircase of the *mandapa* they are two simian figures.

63 "String-wall spirit," Banteay Srei (third quarter of the tenth century). In front of the entrance of the northern shrine the "string-wall spirits" have taken on the aspect of two *garuda*. The face is that of a bird, but the ears are human. The

torso and arms are human, but the lower body is covered with feathers and the legs end in the claws of a bird of prey. On the head is the diadem and top-knot case of the gods.

64 Banteay Srei, the central shrines seen from the west (third quarter of the tenth century). Inside the first enceinte rise the three central shrines and, on the east side, the two libraries. All these buildings are small in scale; proceeding from the eastern entrance to the shrines, in fact, the size of the buildings grows increasingly smaller, so that the ministrants of the temple could only enter the shrines by bending low. The decoration of this little temple of pink sandstone is extremely rich, but harmonizes well with the architectural lines.

65 Rāvana shaking the Kailāsa, Banteay Srei (third quarter of the tenth century). Rāvana, wishing to attract Śiva's attention, shakes, with all the strength of his ten arms, Mount Kailāsa, seat of Śiva and Umā. The sculptor has shown the Kailāsa as a stepped pyramid. The hybrid creatures and hermits who populate the mountain are expressing their terror. On the first step, Nandikeśvara, the monkey-faced guardian of the mountain who was mocked by Rāvana, raises his hand, no doubt to prophecy to Rāvana that one day he will be destroyed by the monkeys. At the summit, Śiva undismayed is preparing to bring the whole weight of the mountain to bear upon Rāvana, while Umā clings terrified to his shoulder.

mental, but as one approaches the center of the temple the passages and surrounding walls become smaller and smaller; the central shrines are so small that the priests had to bend down to enter them. Each of the elements of this temple has an exquisite harmony of line. The rich decoration is executed with the delicacy of a goldsmith or jeweler, yet it gives no feeling of being overloaded. The guardian figures on the walls, male and female alike, have a grace which is unique to the art of this temple. On some of the tympana there are figures illustrating divine legends, rendered in strong relief against a plain background.

fig. 62

Angkor in the Eleventh Century

At the death of Jayavarman V the monuments of Angkor formed two groups within the enceinte of

66 Ta-Keo (early eleventh century). The temple of Ta-Keo has very little carved decoration because it was never completed. The five central shrines are built on the highest terrace of the five-stepped pyramid. The second story has a long gallery forming an enceinte, cut through by passage halls at the axes. Although undecorated the temple of Ta-Keo is one of the loveliest of Khmer monuments, because of the beauty of its lines and the harmony of its proportions.

Yaśodharapura, one centered on Phnom Bakheng, the other to the north, round the Royal Palace. Between the Royal Palace and the two long halls of the Khleang stretched a broad space, the Great Square of Angkor. Outside the city, the royal temples rose in the sector of the eastern Baray, while the foundations of the mandarins were more widely scattered throughout the eastern parts of the region.

In spite of the war of succession between Jayavīravarman and Sūryavarman I it may be, as suggested

67 Baphuon (second half of the eleventh century). Founded by Udayādityavarman, the temple of the Baphuon is one of the Khmer monuments which has suffered the most delapidation. It opens to the east onto the Great Square of Angkor Thom, through monumental entrances (which were in course of reconstruction when this photograph was taken). A long paved avenue resting on columns leads to a cruciform building, then to the eastern staircase of the pyramidal terrace now partially ruined; The shrine built on the top of this pyramid is completely destroyed.

plinth is completely surrounded with a gallery punctuated by passage pavilions on the axes and tower-shrines in the corners. The bare look of the unfinished building brings out the beauty of its proportions and the harmonious lines of this architecture.

by J. Boisselier, that the construction of the temple *fig. 66* of Ta-Keo to the east of the city was undertaken by the former of these two claimants. The elimination of this prince by Sūryavarman I between 1006 and 1010 would explain why the monument was never finished and left without decoration. The volumes of the five crowning towers are well balanced with the mass of the tall base. A first tier of this pyramidal

Becoming king after a civil war, Sūryavarman I was fired with ambition to raise the country from its ruin. He set works going in the Royal Palace at Angkor; but the more ambitious enterprises were those of his son, Udayādityavarman II. He raised the temple-mountain of the Baphuon right up against the south *fig. 67* wall of the Royal Palace; its high base carries two tiers of galleries. At the side of the Great Square a monumental entrance gives access to a raised avenue running to the foot of the pyramid. Nothing remains of the central shrine of the Baphuon. It is however evoked in an inscription: "on the crest of this golden

68 Rāma consoling Sugrīva, Baphuon (second half of the tenth century). The walls of the passage pavilions, *gopura*, are carved with little bas-reliefs illustrating mythological or epic scenes. Here Rāma, accompanied by his brother Lakshmana, approaches Sugrīva, the prince of monkeys, who is weeping bitterly because he has been driven out by his brother Valin. Rāma lays his hand on Sugrīva's shoulder to comfort him and suggest they join forces against Valin and then against Rāvana who has carried off Rāma's wife Sītā.

69 Vishnu recumbent, bronze, Western Mebon (second half of the eleventh century). Only the bust of this colossal image has been found, the most extraordinary bronze statue of southeast Asia. Between two cosmic periods Vishnu, lying on the snake Ananta ("He who has no end"), is resting on the surface of the primordial waters. This statue was cast in several pieces: the arms were separate and the adornments also. The headdress has disappeared, leaving the head bare. Eyes, eyebrows, moustache and beard were probably inlaid.

mountain, in a temple of gold, shining with celestial brilliance."[60] Chou Ta-kuan describes the Baphuon more prosaically as a copper tower. The walls of the *gopura*—the passage pavilions—of the Baphuon are carved with small reliefs, one above the other, illustrating Indian epics, principally the Rāmāyana and Mahābhārata. The artists have portrayed princes in their palaces or in the thick of battle, ascetics in their hermitages lost in the forests, peasants in their villages, and better still, scenes of family life. With the Baphuon reliefs Khmer society is admitted into the art.

fig. 68

The Yaśodharatatāka, installed nearly two centuries before, was perhaps showing signs of drying out. Udayādityavarman decided to build a new reservoir. To hold in the water he built a dike eight kilometers by 2,200 meters, surrounding an artificial pool, the western Baray. In this way he compensated for the inadequacy of the eastern Baray and furthermore gained merit by creating a new *tīrtha*, a holy tank. In the midst of the waters he erected the western Prāsāt Mebon, on an island. It was near this temple forty years or so ago that the bust from a colossal bronze statue of the reclining Vishnu was discovered; it is amazing both in its size and the quality of its workmanship. Bronze working indeed reached its peak in Cambodia in the second half of the eleventh century.

fig. 69

Angkor in the Reign of Sūryavarman II

Angkor Wat is the only monument that can be certainly attributed to Sūryavarman II, though there are other temples in the Angkor group that belong to the same style. Two small shrines in a very pure style, Chau Say Tevoda and Thommanon, were set up on either side of the roadway that runs eastward on the axis of the Royal Palace. At Roluos the central shrine of Bakong had been ruined; it was rebuilt in the twelfth century. This new *prāsāt* with its elegant decoration and sober lines fits perfectly with the sandstone pyramid raised nearly a hundred years earlier by Indravarman.

fig. 70

fig. 71

The temple of Banteay Samre on the east of the eastern Baray is more elaborate; its shrine is enclosed in a double enceinte. Entering from the east a majestic avenue runs up to a terrace guarded by lions and *nāga*. The temple is built of sandstone, but the galleries of the second enceinte are of laterite. The weathered stone and blocks of tawny laterite make an attractive mixture of tones. The carvings in strong relief give versions of Indian epics that seem typically Khmer in character.[61] On the pediments the artists have portrayed the ardor of battle and the nobility of a dancing god no less successfully than the grotesque antics of monkeys.

In the city's center a number of sanctuaries complete the perspective of the Great Square. Just north of the Royal Palace, set back a little, the temple of Preah Palilay was sacred to the Buddha. Its iconography is not derived from the Mahāyāna, however. No *Bodhisattva* are represented, and scenes are recognizable on the tympana that belong quite definitely to Theravāda imagery, such as the Buddha taming the raging elephant or receiving the offerings of the forest animals.

The outstanding foundation of the mid-twelfth century is, of course, Angkor Wat. No other Khmer temple has enjoyed such prestige. Its fame has never suffered eclipse; while Angkor Thom became overgrown by forest it remained a cult center. For centuries Angkor Wat was all that survived of the ancient capital, so much so that at the beginning of the seventeenth century when the king of Siam Prāsāt Thong wished to build in Ayudhyā, his capital, a replica of the city of Angkor, he raised a monument which is a "copy" of Angkor Wat, though a very free "copy."[62]

fig. 73

70 Thommanon, southwest corner of central shrine (mid-twelfth century). Framing the avenue leading to the Gate of Victory stand two small temples, Chau Say Tevoda and Thommanon. They each comprise a single shrine and a library built inside the first enceinte. The decoration of Thommanon is especially carefully done. On the walls are beautiful sculptures of *devatā* in the style of Angkor Wat.

71 Banteay Samre, central shrine (first half of the twelfth century). The temple of Banteay Samre is one of the finest monuments in the style of Angkor Wat. It is built at the east end of the Eastern Baray. On the east it is approached by an avenue of boundary stones, then a cruciform terrace. Two enceintes surround the shrines and the two libraries; a *mandapa* stands in front of the central shrine. The lines of this building are of great nobility. The walls are decorated with great sobriety and have no *devatā* figures; but the pediments are carved in vigorous relief with remarkable compositions.

72 Angkor Wat, Western Entrances (first half of the twelfth century). Whereas nearly all the great Angkorian temples have their main entrances on the east, Angkor Wat is orientated to the west. A flight of steps flanked by lions, then a causeway along a dyke flanked by *nāga*, give access to the Western Entrances. This monumental porch comprises a triple central passage framed by two long galleries forming porticoes which end in carriage gateways. The other entries are smaller and do not open onto roadways.

Taking the oriental view, he was not so much concerned with an exact material representation of Angkor Wat; what was essential for him was to reproduce on the "copy" everything that constituted the religious value of the original.

fig. 75 A wall lined by broad moats describes an area of more than 500 acres given over to the temple. On the axes of this quadrilateral there are monumental passages giving access through the walls. The most honorable entrance opens on the west. On either side of the *fig. 72* central passages of these Western Gateways stretch terraces ending in two great porches, the Elephant Gates by which vehicles and mounts could pass. From *fig. 76* these Western Gateways a paved road, flanked by *nāga*, leads to the cruciform terrace preceding the temple.

A three-tiered pyramidal base more than twenty *fig. 73* meters high carries the five upper sanctuaries. They are linked by galleries that form the first enceinte. A second and third gallery surrounds this central massif at lower levels. The lowest gallery has on its walls the famous Angkor Wat reliefs. The longest are on the north and south, about a hundred meters in length. The composition of these immense tableaux is simple but extremely skilled. The battle scenes, the *fig. 120* battle of Kurukshetra[63] or the battle of Lanka,[64] show two armies advancing from the ends of the gallery to join in the fight which grows more intense to reach its paroxysm in the center of the scene. On the representation of the Churning of the Sea of Milk the long line of gods and *asura* pulling on the body of the *nāga* would create an impression of monotony were it not for the presence of large figures, divine or terrible, who are there to encourage the efforts of the pro- *fig. 148* tagonists. The two galleries at the northwest corner were not carved until the sixteenth century at the time of the ephemeral renaissance of Angkor.

73 Angkor Wat, the upper terrace (first half of the twelfth century). Inside the second enceinte rises the tall base, a three-storied pyramid, that supports the five shrines which are the images of Mount Meru; tracts of gallery link the corner shrines and form the first enceinte whose axial pavilions are joined to the central shrine by passages supported on columns.

74 Second enceinte gallery of Angkor Wat (first half of the twelfth century). While the third enceinte with its bas-reliefs is wide open towards the park, the second enceinte is almost completely closed to the outside. The long galleries are lit by balustered windows which filter the light coming in from the inner courtyard. The rather austere horizontal lines of these galleries contrast with the almost vertical rise of the central pyramid.

Angkor Wat was raised to the glory of Vishnu by Sūryavarman II, whose posthumous name Parama-vishnuloka shows him to have been a sectary of the god. Some of the layout is surprising. The most honorable entrance, as we have said, is on the west, which is the direction of the dead. Then, to follow the sequence of the reliefs the visitor has to go round the third enceinte with the monument on his left, in the inauspicious counter-clockwise direction of the *prasavya*. Was this therefore a funerary monument? Chou Ta-kuan himself is probably referring to Ang-kor Wat in this phrase: "the tomb of Lu Pan is about one *li* from the south gate and measures about ten *li* in girth." P. Pelliot, who translated and commented the text, thinks that Lu Pan, a marvelous Chinese craftsman-builder, is here assimilated to Viśvakarman, the divine architect. The Cambodian legend of Preah Khet Mealea attributes the construction of Angkor Wat to Viśvakarman, though it does not assign it a funerary role. There is no inscription or find to cor-roborate any such association. A similar problem in fact arises with all the temples built on a stepped pyramid; it can only be discussed in the context of the religion of the Khmer monarchy.

Vishnu reigns throughout Angkor Wat, in the gal-leries, on the walls of the corner pavilions, on the

75 Angkor Wat: air view from the southeast (first half of the twelfth century). Air views of Angkor Wat make plain the three first enceintes round the central shrine, with their angle towers and passage halls in the axes. To the west the second and third enceintes are connected by the Cruciform Courtyard. It is the gallery of the third enceinte, starting from the central shrine, that has the famous reliefs of Angkor Wat on the inner side of its wall.

pediments and even on the pilaster bases, in his aspect as Rāma, as Krishna or in one of his other avatārs. As Sūryavarman's favorite deity Angkor Wat *fig. 147* was his dwelling, but under what aspect was he manifest in the central shrine? Was the principal idol of the temple a statue of Vishnu? No Brahman image has been found in the central shrine, neither on a pedestal nor even in the well that is sunk down the center of the pyramid to the level of the ground, and where the two gold foundation disks were discovered, hardly tarnished by the years and so deeply buried that the sacred deposit was safe from pillaging.

For centuries the *devatā* carved on the walls have guarded images of the Buddha. In the central shrine, hieratic and richly adorned, each separate in her niche, they maintain the noble bearing appropriate to divine beings who serve a Supreme Lord. On the walls of the galleries and libraries, sometimes single but *fig. 103* often in groups, they toy with flowers, come forward smiling, link arms, hold up mirrors or even sheets of manuscript. Some are in serious converse, others are merry; here a little *devatā* seems to seek the advice of a companion; there two friends exchange confidences. In all the other temples the *devatā* are always separate; here they join in groups. Their costumes and ornaments show different ethnic types: noble princesses wearing diadems and flowers, hermit women wearing no more than a simple loin-cloth; village girls, some even perhaps from national minorities, are wrapped in plain cloth and leave their locks of hair hanging.

J. Filliozat has extracted the description of the sanctuary of Vāsudeva (Vishnu) from the *Kūrmapurāna* that was said to have stood in Harivarsha, the "Holding of Hari (Vishnu)."[65] The description irresistibly recalls Angkor Wat:

"XVVII, S... in the continent of Hari, they live like gold (as to color) for ten thousand years, fed on sugar-cane juice.

9. There men, mentally creating Vishnu, perpetually adore Vishnu, the god Nārāyana, universal matrix, permanent.

10. There, brilliant like the Moon, clear like a pure crystal, is the sanctuary of Vāsudeva, protected by a wood of pārijāta.

11. Four gates, incomparable, provided with four porticos, provided with ten enceintes, difficult to climb, very difficult of access.

12. Provided with crystal halls, like the dwelling of the king of gods, decorated everywhere with a thousand golden pillars.

13. Provided with stairs of gold, enriched with every kind of jewel, provided with divine thrones, endowed with every beauty.

14–15. Embellished with pools and rivers of delicious water, and filled with *yogin* totally dedicated to Nārāyana, pure, entirely occupied in reciting the Veda, meditating on the Purusha, on Hari, praising perpetually and greeting Mādhava with mantra.

16. There the kings forever express the greatness of the supreme god of gods, of Vishnu of infinite radiance.

17. And, graceful, enchanting, women sing and dance, resplendant with youth, perpetually devoted to making beautiful."

Might not this text, a late addition to the *Kūrmapurāna*, have been inspired by a traveler recounting what he had seen in Cambodia? The towers are reflected in the pools, the moats form remarkable stretches of water, *yogin* carved in stone meditate at the bases of the pillars; and lastly *devatā* animate the *fig. 77* house of the god, pressing round him, like the sixteen thousand wives of Krishna.

Wherever one stands to look at Angkor Wat the architectural masses are admirably organized, and the lines are everywhere balanced into perfect harmony. Every hour of the day alters the colors of the sandstone. It is cloudy grey in the mornings, but the light

76 Angkor Wat, Elephant Gate (first half of the twelfth century). At each end of the long galleries of the Western Entrances, carriage gates allowed elephants and vehicles to enter through the fourth enceinte of the temple, bringing all things necessary for the cult and the ministrants. It is likely that the immense park stretching between the fourth and third enceintes was the scene of full and varied life. Two Buddhist monasteries have since been installed there. A few villagers bring their cows to graze among the trees. In spring there is brilliant blossom to light up the quiet approaches to the Elephant Gate.

126

of midday consumes the colors of the reliefs and models every carved hollow with shadow. In the evening as the sun goes down it casts a golden glow, so that the whole monument can burn like copper against a stormy sky. At night Angkor Wat is a mass of darkness beneath the high silhouettes of its shrines; faint glimmers of light spread over the inner courtyards, cling to the rows of pillars, mold the *nāga* forms on a terrace while on the cruciform forecourt and in the central shrine a little lamp may have been lit by some worshiper, reminding us how once lights shone in every gallery and porch right up to the feet of the gods.

fig. 132

The Rebuilding of Angkor by Jayavarman VII

Yaśodharapura on the eve of the Cham invasion was a city of fine monuments. For three centuries the kings had been concerned to organize a complete politico-religious system, to make it no less invulnerable than the world of the gods. The most serious consequence of the defeat of 1177 was the collapse of this system of religious protection, now shown to be ineffective. With the kingdom defeated and occupied by the enemy, Angkor lost confidence in its destiny.

The town was despoiled of its riches and perhaps too of the palladia that had protected it. It may be that certain traces of fire brought to light by excavations in the Royal Palace correspond to the destruction of royal dwellings. There is however no trace of vandalism on the monuments themselves, either at the Royal Palace or in the temples of the capital. At the most the conquerors carried off some images "into captivity" in order to secure their protection for the new masters.

A few years later Jayavarman VII reversed the situation, drove out the Cham and decided to reinstate Yaśodharapura. To restore the monuments raised by his predecessors to their former glory was but one of his aims. He was determined to organize a system of religious protection superior to the old one which had shown itself bankrupt by the Cham invasion. The establishment of this new organization involved creating holy places both within the capital and in its immediate outskirts.

The ramparts of the new city enclose an almost perfect square some three kilometers a side. "The wall of the city is about 20 *li* all round. It has five gates, each flanked by two side doors. Two gates open on the east, the other sides have only one each. Outside the wall is a large ditch; outside the ditch, approach roads with large bridges. On either side of the bridge there are fifty-four stone guardians like stone generals, gigantic and terrible.

The five gates are identical. The parapets of the bridges are of stone, carved in the form of nine-headed snakes. The fifty-four guardian spirits hold on to the snake with their hands and seem to be preventing it from fleeing. Over the gateways of the walls there are five Buddha heads in stone, their faces turned to the west; the middle one is adorned with gold. On either side of the gates are elephants carved in stone. The wall is entirely built of superposed blocks of stone, about 2 *chang* high. The stones are very carefully and solidly jointed, and no weeds grow in them. There are no battlements....The inside of the rampart is like a ramp of more than ten *chang*, at the top of which there are two large gates which are closed at night and opened in the morning. There are guards at the gates; only dogs are not allowed to enter. The wall is a regular square, at the four corners of which rise four stone towers."

This thirteenth century description might almost have been written today. Now there are no longer guards on duty in the ledges set at each side of the passages under the gateways. There are very few inaccuracies in Chou Ta-kuan's account, but here and there his memory or his notes must have played him false. For instance there were never more than four

77 *Devatā*, Angkor Wat, Western Entrances (first half of the twelfth century). Some *devatā* of Angkor Wat seem to be portraits of young Khmer girls with typically Cambodian features: shapely bodies with high breasts, square faces with large straight eyes and thick lips. A diadem and metalwork flowers crown this young deity whose face is framed in garlands of jasmin buds.

fig. 54 heads over the gateways of Angkor Thom, and they do not all look to the west but to the four points of the compass. It is quite unthinkable that there should ever have been a fifth gilded head. One observation by the Chinese traveler has to be corrected: he mentions four heads and not the four faces that are to be seen on the towers of the Bayon. We should not be surprised at his identification of these carvings over the gates as heads of the Buddha; Cambodian iconography was totally unknown to the Chinese.

The moats are crossed by causeways, not bridges, thus dividing the moats into four independent quadrants. The gateways, too, have only a single passage; this mistake may be due to a confusion with the three-passage entrances of Preah Khan, which are also approached by a roadway bordered by giants. The gateways of Angkor certainly number five, as he says, with two on the east, the Gateway of the Dead and the Gateway of Victory opening onto two avenues, one leading to the Bayon temple, the other to the Royal Palace.

Phnom Bakheng no longer rises at the middle of the new capital, for the center was moved towards the fig. 142 Great Square of Angkor. The enceinte of Jayavarman VII's city even leaves Phnom Bakheng outside the ramparts, 400 meters from the south gateway. The monuments bordering the Great Square, now in the heart of the city, were reinstated in honor. Jayavarman VII completed the monumental aspect of this vast esplanade by having the long Royal Terraces laid out in front of the Palace and the ten Prāsāt Suor Prat along the Khleang. On the south of the square, in the geographical center of the city, he fig. 78 founded the temple of the Bayon.

Khmer temples had always been built with a surrounding wall, an enceinte to mark off the holy ground, but no wall surrounds the Bayon. Its enceinte is that of the city itself, which belongs in its entirety to the sacred precinct of the temple, the strangest creation of Khmer art. Its central sanctuary, ringed by radiating chapels, housed a statue of the Buddha seated in meditation on the *nāga;* this image was broken by vandals and tipped into the central well of the temple. After its discovery it was set up on a terrace near the Great Square. Two enclosing galleries are built on the terraces of the high base of the Bayon; the inner sides of their walls are completely covered with reliefs illustrating mythological and historical scenes. On the outer southern gallery, below a naval battle which is probably the victory of Jayavarman VII over the Cham, runs a series of scenes of everyday life which we have already had occasion to mention more than once.

The indented outline of the plan of the terrace and the higher gallery that follows its recesses gives an impression of confusion to the visitor. Seen from an airplane the arrangement is clear: it follows the magical symbolic figure of a *mandala*. At the center of this design the plan of the central shrine with its radiating chapels creates a lotus flower, the seat of the Buddha.

This layout, unusual to say the least, is not the only originality of the Bayon. Each of the shrines, and they are fifty-one in number, has a superstructure in fig. 80 the form of a tower with four human faces. Over the central sanctuary rose a series of tiers on which faces can still be distinguished, though the whole structure crowning the shrine is much ruined and nothing of its decoration remains. It is surprising that Chou-Ta-kuan never took note of these superstructures with their faces and that he noted simply: "Marking the center of the kingdom there is a golden tower flanked by more than twenty stone towers and hundreds of stone cells. On the east side are a golden bridge, two golden lions placed at either side of the bridge, and eight golden Buddhas placed at the foot of the stone chambers." Was the Bayon then given a facing of gold, at least in part? There remains no trace of it, of course. Stone lions guard the approach terraces. It is not certain that the eight golden statues were of the Buddha. It is hardly thinkable that Buddhist believers should have set up such venerable statues in the inferior positions implied by the words "at the foot of" or "below the stone chambers"; these statues might have represented *dvārapāla*.

No one could look at these towers of the Bayon without feeling moved. On the upper terrace the visitor feels the presence of those faces round and above him; some—crowning the *prāsāt* of a lower story—appear at the height of a man to some one standing

78 The Bayon (late twelfth-early thirteenth century). The temple of the Bayon stands in the center of Angkor Thom at the crossing of the two axial streets of the city. Its plan evokes the design of a *yantra*, a geometric pattern of symbolic import. The central shrine surrounded by radiating chapels figures a lotus flower of which the torus, ringed with petals, is the throne of the Buddha.

on the higher level, others dominate the monument from the top of a shrine raised on the terrace itself. These unique configurations made a strong impression on the nineteenth century travelers who discovered the temple in the middle of forest. L. Delaporte describes the ruins of the Bayon as he saw them a hundred years ago: "In the middle of the great courtyard enclosed within the second enceinte rises a terrace... in the form of a cross.... Now take the trouble to climb one of the steep staircases that are built at the ends of the arms of this block: you come out in the open air on a platform ringed by little *nāga* at elbow height... in the angles of the turrets little aedicules and large heads rear up above the ramp. Each tower, as I have said, is decorated with a quadruple head.

Let us stroll for a minute among these immense figures. They are round, their eyes are wide open and slightly oblique; the mouth is wide, the lips thick; behind their ears festooned with jewels hang splendid diadems....These are strange faces, but regular and of characteristic design, which gives them an air of strength and serenity, half-smiling, which has its own very original nobility. From both near and afar they have a perfect setting in the pilasters that join them in pairs; they adopt naturally the curve of the building, and combine effortlessly with an architectural ensemble that remains, in spite of the superabundance of decorative accessories, correct in design, harmonious in its proportions and grandiose in its general effect."[66]

Jayavarman VII's foundations in the Angkor region spread over a considerable distance. Some are temples of relatively modest dimensions, comprising a tall shrine inside two or three enclosing walls; such are Krol Ko, Ta Nei, Ta Som, to quote only the most

79 The Bayon, *devatā* of the central shrine (late twelfth-early thirteenth century). The *devatā* who stand holding flowers and guarding the central shrine, are richly adorned; each has a diadem and metalwork sprays of flowers on her brow, a broad pectoral over her bosom and a skirt draped with a triangular flap, held on her hips by a belt from which hang pendants. From her shoulders hangs a garland of jasmine buds, sinuous as a snake.

80 Towers with four faces, the Bayon (late twelfth-early thirteenth century). Fifty-one face-towers crown shrines in the Bayon in which it seems the deities of all the different holy places of Cambodia were worshiped. There has been much speculation on the significance of these faces that surround and dominate the upper terrace of the temple. The deep meaning of the Bayon can only be understood in the context of Jayavarman VII's conception of religious protection for the kingdom.

81 Banteay Kdei, cruciform terrace (late twelfth-early thirteenth century). The eastern *gopura* of the third enceinte is preceded by a cruciform terrace guarded by lions on the stringwalls of the steps, and bounded by *nāga* forming a balustrade. On the *nāga* ride *garuda*, enemies of snakes; here the *garuda* keep the *nāga* under the spell of a magic formula. Inside the *gopura* pious worshipers have collected together images of the Buddha.

interesting. Ta Prohm and Banteay Kdei are enormous monasteries; Preah Khan is a real town. The plans of these three large temples are extremely elaborate. They are laid out on ground level. The outer enclosure of these monuments surrounds a park in the center of which rises the temple itself. These surrounding walls stretch for 600 by 500 meters at Banteay Kdei, one kilometer by 600 meters at Ta Prohm and 800 by 700 at Preah Khan. After the outer *gopura* of these temples is passed, the park is crossed by an avenue leading to a terrace that precedes the group of sanctuaries. Monumental passages are pierced in the axes of the enclosures. As one moves towards the central shrine, galleries can be seen extending on either side of the *gopura;* passing along terraces bordered with *nāga*, one can pause in cruciform halls to glance at the friezes of *apsarā* that adorn the lintels and have caused these buildings to be called "halls of the dancing girls." Minor shrines stand in the courtyards, little *prāsāt* with pediments carved with

fig. 81

82 Banteay Kdei, east gate (late twelfth-early thirteenth century). Whereas the entrances to Angkor Thom are each surmounted by four quite distinct heads, the gates of certain temples founded by Jayavarman VII are crowned by four faces belonging to a single head. In the absence of any epigraphical reference it is difficult to identify these guardian figures who watch over the gates of the enceinte of the temple of Banteay Kdei. The east gate opens onto the terrace with the magnificent landing stage, built beside the basin of Srah Srang.

At Banteay Kdei, the east gate crowned by a four-faced tower opens on the outside to a broad piece of water, Srah Srang. A splendid terrace fenced by *nāga* ridden by *garuda*, provides a landing-place. Boats could navigate on this artificial lake which still shows traces of a central island on which a temple, now destroyed, once stood. Whatever the time of day or the light, the charm of the waters of Srah Srang is always irresistible to those who linger by its side.

Ta Prohm, founded in memory of Jayavarman VII's mother and of his *guru*, is one of the most elaborate monuments. Three temples were in fact built within its enceinte. Some galleries give the feeling of labyrinths, shrines seem to overcrowd the inner courts; yet it is quite certain that not one of these buildings was put up without consideration of the whole. Unfortunately the motifs behind the devising of the plan are to a large extent obscure. At Ta Prohm, Jayavarman VII wished to honor his mother in the guise of Prajñāpāramitā, the Perfection of Wisdom. "Doing these good works, this king, by extreme devotion to his mother has made this wish: 'By the good deeds that I have performed, may my mother, once delivered from the Ocean of existences, enjoy the state of Jina.' This king, anxious to maintain the established order, having seen that the practice of the Law was corrupted... has said to the future kings of Cambodia desirous of protecting this foundation: 'Having piously considered the inconceivable bene-

fig. 81
fig. 84
fig. 83

83 Ta Prohm (late twelfth-early thirteenth century). The monastery of Ta Prohm consists of several temples. It has not been completely cleared of forest. The shrines and galleries are arranged in a very complex plan, and at evening the atmosphere of mystery becomes almost eerie. This monument was founded by Jayavarman VII in memory of his mother and of his spiritual advisor. It was from his mother, who was descended from the very oldest Cambodian dynasties, that Jayavarman VII held his most convincing right to the throne of Angkor.

84 Banteay Kdei, the landing-stage of Srah Srang (late twelfth-early thirteenth century). A great basin is laid out facing the east entrance of Banteay Kdei. This is the Srah Srang, the "Royal Bath." Access to this pool is by a splendid landing stage with steps going down from a cruciform terrace guarded by lions and protected by *nāga* ridden by *garuda*. Formerly there was a little cult-building in the center of the pool.

Buddhist images, epic scenes or even episodes of the great Brahmanic myths. Complexity of plan, richness of decoration, albeit sometimes of rather hasty workmanship, and iconography are features common to the three great temples built by Jayavarman VII to the east of his capital, but they in no way detract from the originality of each.

factions received from their mothers, grateful sons should sacrifice all, even their own lives, in the interests of their mothers; it is thus, oh kings, that I who know it well... I beseech you, you who are anxious to protect my foundation'".[67] It is worth remembering that it was from his mother's side that Jayavarman VII held his strongest claim to the throne of Angkor.

The Preah Khan of Angkor was a town built on the very spot where Jayavarman VII was said to have won a victory over the Cham: "At the place receptacle of the enemy's blood, where in the battle he had won the victory (Jayaśrī); he founded a town bearing this name (Jayaśrī); its stones and golden lotus change the color of the ground, and today it still shines as if it were overlaid with blood."[68]

The four entrances of Preah Khan are strongly reminiscent of the approaches to Angkor Thom. Continuing an avenue flanked by boundary posts, causeways cross the moats dug at the foot of the ramparts. On either side, in the guise of parapets, two rows of stone giants, benevolent on one side, terrible on the other, support *naga*. The causeways lead to the monumental gateways, each with three passages for carriage ways. Neither the gateways nor the sanctuaries of Preah Kahn are crowned with towers with faces. The ramparts are splendid. Along the top of the laterite walls, instead of cresting, there are long blocks of sandstone carved into niches that each shelter an image of a meditating Buddha. At regular intervals the architect has set up large sandstone figures the whole height of the wall, of *garuda* holding up *naga* held prisoner in their claws. Carved in high relief these great mythical birds, proudly erect, keep guard over the enclosure. We are certainly here in presence of the town Jayaśrī, a religious city, distant from Angkor by about a kilometer as the crow flies.

G. Coedès observed that Preah Khan is the name given by the Cambodians to the Sacred Sword, the palladium of the kingdom.[69] At Bangkok, the Sacred Sword has kept the name Jayaśrī: "Nagara Jayaśrī, which signified in reality the town of Royal Fortune Victorious, has become in popular usage the town of the Sacred Sword, in Cambodian Preah Khan."

The galleries, passage halls and inner courtyards of Preah Khan have well-balanced proportions; the *figs. 86, 87* decoration is elegant. Some pediments and lintels are animated with well-composed scenes. The central sanctuary is very bare and must originally have been *fig. 85* faced with bronze or copper. In the courtyards surrounding this shrine are a number of little chapels built to the memory of deceased high dignitaries.

Preah Khan is the foundation dedicated by Jayavarman VII to his father, Dharanīndravarman, who probably never was king at Angkor. The victorious sovereign desired it to be remembered that he owed his Buddhist faith to his father who "Finding his satisfaction in this nectar: – religion –, of this moon: – the Śākya –; placing the best of his riches at the disposition of the *bhikshu*, the Brahmans and all his subjects who implored him, desiring to extract the marrow from the body, an impure and marrowless dwelling, he honored without ceasing the feet of the Jina."[70] Dharanīndravarman was worshiped

85 Preah Khan, central shrine (late twelfth-early thirteenth century). The inner walls of the central shrine have only been roughed out, and were perhaps covered with metal sheeting, probably gilded bronze. In the galleries there were ceilings above the friezes; they have fallen to reveal the blocks of the corbeled vault. A *stūpa* in the style of the Thai art of Sukhodaya has been set up in the sanctuary which is open to the four points of the compass.

86 Preah Khan, two-story building on round columns (late twelfth-early thirteenth century). The northeast quadrant of Preah Khan contains a storied building of which the intention is unknown. The Chinese texts and the relief carvings on Khmer monuments give evidence of the existence of two-story buildings of light material. Here, the pillars of the ground floor are circular in section. The upper hall, rectangular in plan, is lit by windows, and a balcony at either end. Access to the upper story must have been by a wooden staircase. A building of the same type, but roughly built, existed at Ta Prohm.

87 Preah Khan, east axial passages (late twelfth-early thirteenth century). A series of passage halls runs along each axis to converge on the central shrine. The vaults have fallen in, but the halls with their intended plan still show the beauty of their lines. Preah Khan was a Buddhist temple dedicated to the memory of the father of Jayavarman VII, Dharanīndravarman. He was probably never king of Cambodia but simply a feudal prince.

at Preah Khan under the name of Jayavarmeśvara, the Lord of Jayavarman, the king's favorite deity. A statue of Avalokiteśvara represented him: "This king Śrī Jayavarman has consecrated here in the year marked by the form, the moon, the moon and the Vedas (1113 Śaka = 1191 A.D.), a Lokeśvara named Jayavarmeśvara which is the image of his father."

Thirty years ago a splendid statue of a radiant Lokeśvara was discovered in the bush not far from *fig. 88* Preah Khan. It is tempting to think of this image as the "Lokeśvara named Jayavarmeśvara," but there is nothing to allow such an identification. This is perhaps the most beautiful of all the Lokeśvara images found until now in Cambodia. The bearing is very noble, the face naturalistic like a portrait, with a wide forehead, slightly hollowed delicate chin, and is lit by a smile that is barely sketched but of great gentleness.

In front of the east entrance to Preah Khan a terrace served as a landing stage, on the bank of a large lake 900 meters by three and a half kilometers, the Jayatatāka. This pool was the *baray* of the town of Preah Khan. "In Jayaśrī which is like the carefully curled lock of hair adorning his queen, the earth; this king has placed the Jayatatāka like a well endowed mirror, colored by stones, gold and garlands. This pool whose water is lit by the light of the *prāsāda* of gold and colored by the red of the lotus, shines as it evokes the image of the sea of blood shed by the Bhārgava [the king of Champa]. Inside [this pool] there is an island standing up, drawing its charm from the basins [that surround it], cleaning the mud of sin from those who come in contact with it, serving as a boat for crossing the ocean of existences."[71] This island was *fig. 89* Rājyaśrī, "Royal Fortune." It is now known as Neak Pean, the "curled up *nāga*," for two many-headed snakes surround the circular base of its central shrine.

The layout of Neak Pean is quite exceptional. In the center of the islet the shrine rises up in the middle of a square of water 70 meters on each side, with steps running down into it. The water of this basin is poured by gargoyles into little kiosks built on the axes from which it runs into four reservoirs, also square, 25 meters on each side. The gargoyles each

have a different head: a man's on the east, a lion's on the south, a horse's on the west and an elephant's on the north.

The central shrine is a *prāsāt* in the Bayon style, very pure in line, enriched with very fine carved decoration. Originally it opened on all four sides; later, except for the east entrance, the bays were filled with carved panels figuring large images of Lokeśvara. In the central basin statues in full relief were placed on pedestals round the shrine: a Vishnu recumbant on the west, and a representation of "a thousand *lingam*" on the north. It has only been possible to reconstitute one group, built up of sandstone blocks: that on the east. It represents the episode of the Horse Balāha, *fig. 90* a manifestation of Lokeśvara, coming to free the merchants who had landed on an island of ogresses, because at the moment when they were to be devoured, they prayed to the compassionate *Bodhisattva*. This group in the round, one of the most famous pieces of Khmer art, shows the great horse swimming across the lake to the central shrine, bearing to salvation the merchants who cling to his sides since Neak Pean washes away "the mud of sins."

The studies of G. Coedès, of L. Finot and of V. Goloubew have made it possible to identify Neak Pean with Lake Anavatapta, a mythical lake in the Himalayas, whose waters pour into four rivers through the mouths of heads carved in stone; representing a lion, a horse, an elephant and a bull; symbolic of the four continents. At Neak Pean the bull is replaced by a man. J. Boisselier has demonstrated how the presence of Lake Anavatapta on the soil of Cambodia was supposed to assure that the kingdom lasts until the end of the present *kalpa*;[72] for this lake is supposed to be the last of all to dry up at the end of the cosmic

88 Statue of a smiling Lokeśvara from Preah Khan, National Museum of Phnom Penh (late twelfth-early thirteenth century). The statues of Lokeśvara can be identified because of the image of Amitābha Buddha worn in his headdress by the *Bodhisattva*. Jayavarman VII is known to have set up a statue of his father in the aspect of a Lokeśvara, at Preah Khan; there is however nothing to allow the identification of this magnificent image, with its delicately carved face and almost dolorous smile, with the effigy of Dharanīndravarman.

89 Neak Pean (late twelfth-early thirteenth century). Neak Pean was a representation of Lake Anavatapta, the mythical Himalayan lake from which rose four rivers. Here the waters of the central basin flow into four axial basins and then into canals figuring the four rivers. Of all the water on earth, Lake Anavatapta will be the last to dry up at the end of our cosmic period. Its possession must therefore render Cambodia indestructible until the end of the *kalpa*.

period. The Horse Balāha and the Brahmanic images gave additional symbolism to Neak Pean; Rājyaśrī was one of the essential elements in the system of religious protection established by Jayavarman at Angkor.

The god of the shrine has disappeared. It was no doubt an image of the Buddha, as is confirmed by Chou Ta-kuan's description: "The *North Lake* is

90 Group with the horse Balāha, Neak Pean (late twelfth-early thirteenth century). In the central basin there is a sculptural group representing people clinging to the sides of an enormous horse that is swimming towards the central shrine. The horse Balāha is a manifestation of Avalokiteśvara who saved some merchants who were shipwrecked in a storm on an island populated by ogresses. Terrified by the fate in store for them, they invoked the compassionate *Bodhisattva*. He bore them to material salvation, just as he leads his worhipers to spiritual salvation.

five *li* north of the city. It contains a square golden tower, dozens of little stone houses; a golden lion, a golden Buddha, a bronze elephant, bronze bull, bronze horse, nothing is lacking." The arrangement of the basins and the elegance of the shrine make Neak Pean one of the most enchanting of Angkor's monuments, while at the same time, being a replica of Lake Anavatapta, it was one of the surest guarantees of the indestructibility of the Kingdom.

Layout of the Approaches to the Capital

For half a millennium the Khmer monarchy attempted to build the ideal capital at Angkor, assured against all dangers by a system of religious symbolism. The holy places that were to make the city indestructible were the great temples, often related to holy basins. The provision and maintenance of water for these basins called for large-scale works. The city had also to be provided with the material conditions for its existence. Hydraulic works were necessary for providing the town itself with water, for irrigating the region and also for communications, since during the rainy season overland transport became very difficult. Canals held a very important place in the economy of the city.

Hydraulic works, undertaken as soon as the reign of Yaśovarman I began, continued for as long as the Khmer monarchy lasted. There were two quite separate programs: one of religious inspiration concerned the creation of *tīrtha*, holy basins; the other was purely economic and was directed to setting up reservoirs and canals for water supply, irrigation and transport. The *tīrtha* were essentially the two Baray, Eastern and Western, and the great pool laid out to the east of Preah Khan, surrounding the islet of Neak Pean which Chou Ta-kuan calls the "Northern Lake."

The waters feeding these *tīrtha* came largely from Phnom Kulen. They were made sacred by running over the bed of the Stung Siem Reap, carved with divine images: *lingam*, the recumbant Vishnu, Brahma. The epigraphy makes it quite clear that the Baray were not for bathing, for nothing could be allowed to soil its water. These great sacred reservoirs are not excavated reservoirs; the water is held by a dike built on four sides. The Yaśodharatatāka owes most of its nourishment to the Stung Siem Reap, but this river was also responsible for its drying out. The works of the reign of Yaśovarman had deflected it from its course; its contours became unbalanced, it began to dig its bed once more, and in consequence it gradually drained the Eastern Baray. The Western Baray, the work of Udayādityavarman II, has remained partially full of water until the present day. The Baray of Preah Khan was dried when breaches were made in its dikes during the Siamese invasion of 1431.

The soil of the plain of Angkor is favorable to crops, but it needs water. During the dry season only the banks of the Stung Siem Reap are green. If the fields are to be cultivated during most of the year, even without trying to get four crops, the land must be irrigated. To do this the peasants have ponds to hold rain water. These *trapeang*, or reservoirs, are innumerable. Many are dry at the present time, but in their time they kept the villages supplied with water and were used as watering places for the cattle. Some of these basins are simply ponds, others are faced with laterite and lined with steps. As B. P. Groslier has observed: "Khmer hydraulics are works of economy and redistribution."[73] Barrages built across the rivers created reservoirs of water that could then be used for irrigating the fields. For distributing the water the Khmers might use locks; their most usual method was simply to cut channels through the barrages that they filled in again in the rainy season. The network of irrigation channels is very close and complex, the result of several centuries of development. The little banks surrounding the ancient rice fields follow extremely regular patterns; the evidence of Angkorian agriculture their vestiges provide show that the population was dense all round the capital.

In Angkor Thom a canal system was laid out in connection with the moats. The moats surrounding the city are a hundred meters wide and five or six deep. The approach causeways divide them into four independent quadrants. Those on the northeast and southeast were fed by the river of Siem Reap and the

Eastern Baray, the northwest quadrant took water from a reservoir established to the west of Preah Khan. The excess water from the northeast quadrant was led inside Angkor Thom by a vaulted conduit under the town wall. A canal thirty to forty meters wide ran right round the town thus supplying it with its needs, and the ground has a gentle slope sufficient to make it drain towards the southwest corner where the waste water collected in a pond, the Beng Thom. Passing under the ramparts by conduits the surplus water flowed into the southwest quadrant of the moats. Connecting with this interior peripheric canal, trenches were dug on either side of the avenues that ran from the Bayon and the Royal Palace to the five town gates. This urban water system still existed in the time of Diego do Couto: "And on either side of this roadway stretched other very fine canals, full to the brim with water coming from the great moat surrounding the city, and which enters by the two gates of the north and east sides, then returns to flow into this same moat by [the gates] of the south and west, so that the water of the moat never diminishes, for however much water enters by two gates, it returns again by two others. As for the great moat, it is always full, for large and abundant rivers flow into it and because of the excess of water it is even necessary to run some off at certain places to prevent flooding. And in this way each of the streets that runs from each of the gates is flanked by two others of water plied many boats which come in from the interior of the country on the river outside: full of provisions, of wood for burning and other necessities that they unload at the very doors of the inhabitants who all have one access onto the canal and another onto the river. And thus the city is washed of all its rubbish...."[74]

The description by Diego do Couto gives us to understand that boats laden with merchandise could come right into the city. In fact, communication between the moats and canals was only possible by conduits passing under the ramparts and no more than a meter high. Nor did the interior canals form a continuous system. If goods were transported on the interior canals they must have been transshiped at the entrance to the city. Then again the houses could not have had two landing places, one on the canal and one on the river, for the two waterways were too far apart. B. P. Groslier believes that Diego do Couto was confused because he never saw Angkor and was relying on the recollections of another missionary for his description. On the other hand it is not certain that the Cambodians of the sixteenth century built their houses where their Angkorian predecessors had built theirs.

The interior canals of Angkor Thom were certainly not the only ones used by boats. Apart from the city moats, a multitude of waterways threaded the region, connecting together the reservoirs and the trenches of the great temples.

The description by Diego do Couto is strongly reminiscent of the floating market in Bangkok as it was only twenty years ago. Plied generally by a woman, the long craft full of fruit, vegetables and different wares would glide along the canals, stopping at the steps of some little landing-place. The owner of the barge would sell, here a few mangoes, there a watermelon or cardoons. On other boats fishwives recommended their wares to the housewives who hailed them from their windows over the water. We may imagine such scenes taking place every day in some of the quarters round Angkor Thom.

ACTIVITIES OF THE PEOPLE

The ramparts of Angkor Thom were, as we have said, the real enceinte of the Bayon; they marked off a consecrated area. It is very likely that most activities of ordinary people went on outside these walls; indeed, much of the ancient Yaśodharapura lay outside the city of Jayavarman VII.

The popular quarters were certainly wide-spread and picturesque. The houses of the humble folk cannot have been very different from those of the villagers. It has always been like this. There are photographs of Phnom Penh less than a hundred years old that show the town looking exactly like an enormous village. Yet the activities of these quarters were those of a city. If we follow the relief of the south gallery of the Bayon we find ourselves transported into the middle of a popular quarter. The center of animation is the market place; all round it are craftmen busy in their workshops and booths.

One street resounds to the regular blows of a hammer or an axe splitting wood, the clatter of planks being stacked, the creaking of a beam as two journeymen join their efforts with a shout to lift it on end. We *fig. 91* are in a carpenter's workshop. One man is using a longhandled axe to square off a tree trunk; kneeling beside him a fellow joiner is preparing a plank with hammer and chisel. "Carpenters have no saws and only work with axes. Thus a plank needs much wood and much time. Anyone who has to make something of wood also only works with a chisel." In another corner of the workshop a carpenter is tapping with a mallet on a long handle to adjust it in a piece of wood. Other workmen are carrying away prepared planks while an apprentice is brandishing in both hands a

long kind of brush to clean shavings and sawdust off them.

Next door to the carpenter's shop we can watch the preparations for a feast. A host of cooks and scullions *figs. 92, 93* are milling round clay stoves under a kind of awning stretched between trees. With precise movements a master cook is about to plunge a little pig into a great cauldron which is placed over a fire fanned by an assistant. Another cook is crouching down to set the lid carefully on a pot that is to be cooked over a

91 Carpenters, the Bayon, outer south gallery (late twelfth-early thirteenth century). The bottom of a Bayon relief shows the activities of a village. Here carpenters are preparing planks with chisels and hammers, according to a technique described by Chinese chroniclers. Other workmen are carrying planks while a journeyman is brandishing a leaf broom to dust off the sawdust.

92 The kitchen, the Bayon, outer south gallery (late twelfth-early thirteenth century). On the left a cooking pot has been placed on the tripod of a clay oven, similar to those made to-day in the region of Kompong Chhnang. A man is pouring grains into the pot; though they are so large they may perhaps be rice. On the right a cook is about to plunge a pig into an enormous cauldron under which an assistant is blowing up the fire. Behind them a waiter is carrying a tray of cakes, or dishes cooked in little jars.

93 Cooking kebabs, the Bayon, outer south gallery (late twelfth-early thirteenth century). A meal is being prepared in the open. Here two men are grilling skewers over the flames of a wood fire. The pieces, probably of meat, are not spiked on the skewers, as is usual today, but slipped between the two blades of a stick split lengthways. On other reliefs fish are cooked in the same way. In every Cambodian market place there were little vendors cooking meat, fish and even bananas over embers in this way.

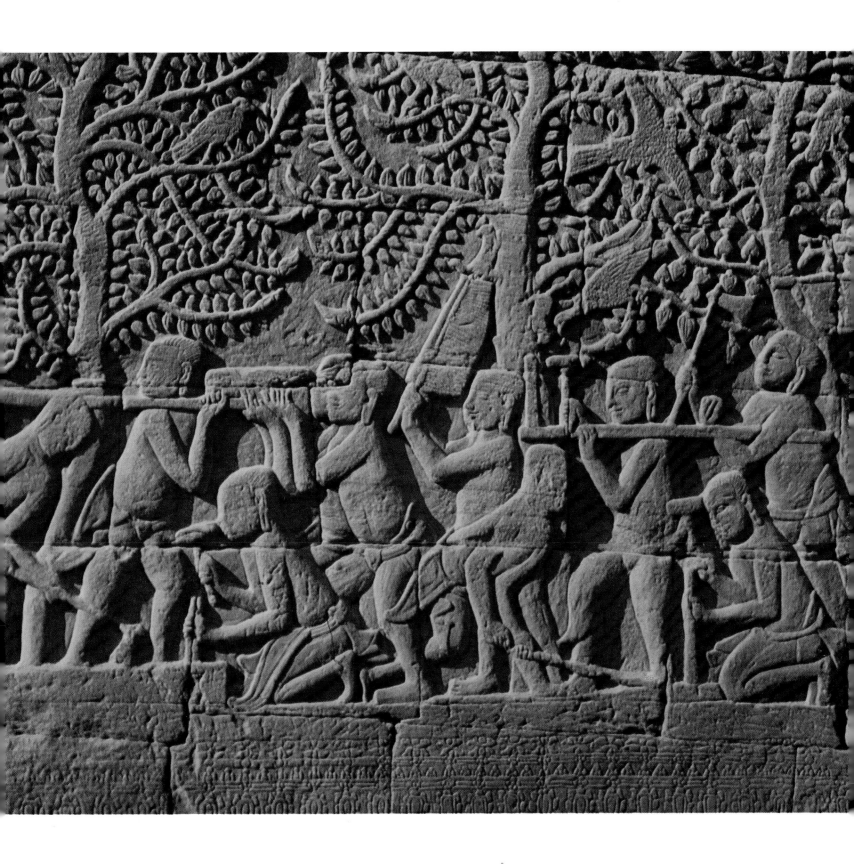

water-bath. A baker is preparing dough for rolls or biscuits that are to be fried or steamed. Nearby, rice is being poured into a pan. Two men are grilling skewers over a brasier. All round the cooks bending over their work are servants coming and going, arranging what is already cooked on dishes, carrying these off on their heads to a street stall or feasting hall. It is hot round these stoves and one has to hurry. Amid the boiling of saucepans, the sizzling of frying and the crackling of flames round the skewers, the waiters and cooks exchange jokes, laugh at the clumsiness or the clowning of one of the scullions, complain of the fussiness and bad temper of their clients.

Another street is where the goldsmiths work, fully aware of the nobility of their craft. One has set out his tools before him on a little bench. Near him burns an oil lamp; he will make a blow pipe from a simple tube that will do to make the metal soft. Taking a burin he engraves a delicate stylized foliage motif; then with a little chisel he chases the precious metal or carves out a relief. He also has to set the carefully polished gems: rubies from India, stones of varying value from the west of the country. All the parts of the jewel are ready; one after the other he places them on the two-horned anvil and taking up a riveting hammer he places the minute rivets with skillful movements, puts the motifs together, hangs on the pendants.

Goldsmiths are never out of work. Even though humbler folk could afford no more than a ring or two, the rich and all who revolve round the court are enamoured of sumptuous jewels. All the diadems carved with serrations and flowers, necklaces incrusted with stones and hanging with pendants, the multiple bracelets for arms and wrists, the belts with their rich clasps and the heavy ankle-rings that adorn *fig. 94* the gods and *devatā* on the reliefs, are copied from the Khmer jewelery worn by the princes and princesses of the Angkorian court. The few pieces of jewelery that have been found show how skillful were the Khmer artists. They worked also for the gods. Rich donors felt it an obligation to adorn the statues of their favorite deities; inscriptions proclaim the munificence of such gifts. We see that the "holy image of the queen mother" of Rājendravarman, represented as a goddess, received among other gifts a crown, two ear pendants, a necklace, two rings, two armlets, a ring with a gem, five pearl necklaces and a garment gold in front and silver behind.

The goldsmith has fixed the last pendant to the edge of a necklet; the piece is finished, brilliant with gold and glistening jewels. The artist pauses a minute to examine it, but there is more work waiting. A great dignitary has been accorded by the king, as a mark of honor, the right to be shaded by a gold parasol and carried on a golden palanquin, or more exactly gold-covered. The artist has to fashion the precious metal, working repoussé motifs of volutes, flowers, and leaf scrolls to cover the supports of the palanquin and the handle of the parasol. After this he also has an order for a ewer, cups and dishes of gold or silver.

Manufacturing the attachments for palanquin was usually the work of bronze smiths who plied their *fig. 95* craft away from the commercial streets. They needed room for preparing their molds and installing their braziers. They only used the *cire perdue* technique which has been handed from generation to generation until our own day. The bronze smiths of Phsar Dek near Udong have preserved the methods of their Angkorian ancestors in their open-air workshops. The composition of the bronze varies from piece to piece. According to Cambodian tradition it includes copper, gold, and silver; but the alloy often contains tin, zinc and lead as well. Some Siamese texts add mercury and bismuth to this list. The artist models the object to be cast in wax over a clay core; he carves all the detail, then covers the wax with clay and encloses it all in a mold of clay mixed with rice chaff. Within the mold he reserves a cell containing the metal which when melted will take the place of the wax.

94 *Devatā* ornaments, Angkor Wat, *gopura* II west (first half of the twelfth century). The ornaments of the *devatā* are certainly representations of real jewelery. The rare fragments of jewelery that have been found bear witness to the skill of the Cambodian goldsmiths. It was perhaps in the period of Angkor Wat that the tiaras worn by the *devatā* were the most beautiful. Above the diadem, the hair-bun is adorned with three flowering sprays, doubtless chiseled in precious metal. Zigzag motifs, beading and rows of flower petals decorate the bracelets and the broad pectorals hanging with pendants.

Bronze smiths have very diverse commissions to execute and each one has his speciality. Journeymen prepare the casting while the craftsmen finish the molds for fine utensils, such as bowls and cups. Seated at a distance, an artist is carving a litter hook in wax with a *nāga* head; absorbed in his work, he is indifferent to all going on around him. In another workshop the master and his assistants are all concentrating on the preparations for a ceremony before proceeding to the casting of a statue of a deity, which will be consecrated as an image for processions.

fig. 96

In a poor quarter weavers are making rough cloth. "They only know how to make cotton cloth, and even then they have no spinning wheels and make their hanks by hand. They have no looms for weaving; they merely attach one end [of the weaving] to their belts and continue working at the other end. For shuttles they just use bits of bamboo." Yet if we return to the market place we shall perhaps be lucky enough to see women bent over looms between the piles under a house, weaving some of those fine cloths worn by rich citizens.

fig. 99

To go round the market we have only to follow the scenes along the south gallery of the Bayon. The first stall belongs to a fishwife. Her hair is dragged into a bun on top of her head, a coarse cloth is wound round her hips, and she is squatting on a kind of wide bench, with her heap of fish piled in front of her. Beside her an elegant young lady has come to make her purchases and discuss the price. Behind the fishwife two gossips are jeering at the young customer, who is perhaps too pretty for their liking. Next we come to a market gardener who is weighing vegetables chosen by a customer. Forgetting the load hanging at each end of his yoke, a passer-by is gaping at two men in a violent quarrel who are shouting abuse at each other. Here our eyes are drawn to an enormous fish offered

fig. 3

95 Palanquin hook, National Museum, Phnom Penh (late twelfth-early thirteenth century). Solid bronze hooks attached the hammock of the palanquin to the shafts. The upper part of the hook forms a wide ring to slip over the shaft. Here the richly chiseled hook has female orants on the ring, which is held by a *garuda* with spread wings; in his claws the bird holds the body of a *nāga* which forms the spike of the hook.

154

by a young woman sitting in a little kiosk. Shouts
are rising from a group surrounding two fighting
cocks. With many exclamations the betting is going
well, and the owners are holding back the two champions who are trying to get at each other, flapping
their wings, clawing at the ground, squawking madly
and ready to tear each other apart with beak and claws
in a whirlwind of flying feathers. All this flurry
causes no concern, a cock fight is no novelty, and
there are always plenty of backers. And the lady beside all these worked-up men is paying them no attention, for she is entirely engaged in listening to the
client who is whispering sweet nothings in her ear.
This couple is no more interested either in the animated conversation going on between three friends who
are recounting some event with great gestures. They
speak loud, and laugh out, but without awakening
a peasant woman who has dropped off to sleep near
her basket full of fruit. She sleeps with her fists clenched, unaware that a little girl is stealing the contents
of her basket; but a neighbor is about to wake the
sleeper and is threatening the little girl who will very
soon make off with her booty. Behind the kiosk
sheltering this scene two men are taking a meal with
their backs turned to the market; in countries with
an Indian civilization people do not like eating out of
doors, and perhaps for this reason they are hidden in
a corner. If we are to believe Chou Ta-kuan there
were goings-on round the market place that shocked
our Chinese friend: "In this country there are dozens
of pretty young things who go around in groups of
ten and more on the market place. They are always
trying to seduce the Chinese, in return for rich presents. It is hideous, it is shameful."
On the street running alongside the market place are
peasants leading their ox-carts. Some are heaped with
large bundles wrapped in mats and tied round with
rattan. Others are carrying pots buried in straw: jars

fig. 97

fig. 98

fig. 16

96   Statuette of a deity in bronze, National Museum, Phnom
Penh (late twelfth century). This male four-armed deity is not
easy to identify. The hands are broken off. The sign decorating
his brow does not seem to be Śiva's frontal eye. Small bronze
images were often worshiped on family altars. Larger bronzes
might be images for carrying in processions.

of every kind, very large and with wide open mouths for collecting rain water, smaller and taller ones for keeping rice or oil; oval ones with narrow necks to contain alcohol. The best pieces are large vases with a molded foot and ovoid belly, and a wide flaring lip, as pure in line as an amphora. Fragments of such vases are often found in Angkorian temples. Khmer ceramics have a dark brown glaze that gives them a rather severe aspect, though it brings out their beauty of line. Of less value, the rough unglazed pottery is more summarily wrapped, some are even hung from the roof of the cart. Cooking pots of all sorts, stoves, and pans are of pretty pink earthenware, with darker

97 Cock fight, the Bayon, outer south gallery (late twelfth-early thirteenth century). In the middle of the market place men gather round two fighting cocks which their owners are holding back with difficulty. Passers-by weigh up the form and make their bets on the two champions. The poses of the figures are observed and rendered with a sense of humour bordering on caricature.

98 The little fruit thief, the Bayon, outer south gallery (late twelfth-early thirteenth century). It is hot, a woman has dropped off to sleep by the fruit she has brought from the village to sell at market. A little girl takes the chance to dip her hand in the basket and seize a fruit. A third person however is wagging a finger at the little thief and on the point of waking the careless sleeper. The sculptor has noted the supple movement of the child and the abandon of the sleeper, with legs bent and arms folded.

patches caused by the firing. They are fragile, it is true, but cost very little.

Meanwhile the cock fight is over. Pleased to have won, or annoyed at losing, the backers turn away from the two twitching animals, the victor being himself in such a bad state that he may well not survive his adversary. Those who were watching return home or stop at a house to do business.

Commercial exchanges are important at Angkor. Business is not only a man's job, however. "In this country it is the women who understand trade. Thus a Chinese who takes a wife on arriving there profits in addition from her business acumen. They have no permanent shops, but use a kind of mat that they spread on the ground. Each person has his place. I have heard it said that they pay a rent to the mandarin for it. For little transactions they pay in rice, cereals, Chinese objects; then comes cloth; they only use gold and silver for the biggest affairs."

Foreigners coming to do business in Cambodia were well received, to the great satisfaction of Chinese pride. "In general the people of this country are very simple. When they see a Chinese they show respectful awe and call him Fo (Buddha). As soon as they see him they throw themselves on the ground and prostrate themselves. Just recently some of them have begun cheating the Chinese and doing them wrong. This is because so many have come there."

Many kinds of merchandise were traded. "What is most prized is Chinese gold and silver, and then mottled silks, light with double thread. After these products come Chen-chou tin, lacquer trays from Wen-chou, Zaitun blue porcelain, mercury, vermilion, paper, sulphur, saltpetre, sandalwood, lotus root, musk, hemp, cloth, *huang-ts'ao* cloth, umbrellas, iron

99 *Devatā* costume, Angkor Wat, Western Entrances (first half of the twelfth century). The female costume is a long piece of cloth draped with two flaps; one, very long, passes over the left wrist, and the other is folded back to hang over the right thigh. All the central part of this length of cloth is decorated with a scatter of flowers; the broad border of the folded flap is decorated with stripes, lozenges of flowers, zigzags. The brocaded motifs of modern ceremonial *sampot* are very close to the decoration on the skirts of the *devatā*.

saucepans, copper, trays... sieves, wooden combs, needles. Ming-chou mats are less valuable. What they want to get above all is beans and wheat, but export is prohibited." It is true that the Chinese forbade the export of starch foods.

Cloth figures among the products imported by the Khmers. As we have seen, textiles were made in Cambodia, but foreign cloths were the fashion among well-to-do people. "There are many qualities of cloth. The prince wears some, valued at two or three ounces of gold; they are the finest in color and weave. Although cloth is woven in the country, much is brought from Siam and Champa, and the most prized is that coming from the western seas because of its skillful manufacture and fineness." Silk textiles were luxury items and especially appreciated. "The Cambodians do not raise silk worms and their women do not make clothes....Recently some Siamese started cultivating silk worms; mulberry trees and silk worms come from Siam....The Siamese weave clothes of dark tussor from their silk." Were silk worms cultivated at the beginning of the century in the Menam basin that was then under Khmer dominion? Cambodia has never been a great silk producing country. As for the reproach that the Chinese levelled at Cambodian women, that they did not know how to sew, it is not surprising since at that period all clothing was draped.

The Cambodians had long known iron working. The ore of Phnom Dek, the "Iron Mountain," is specially pure. But the smiths of Phnom Dek devoted themselves mainly to making arms: arrow tips and spears, daggers and knives of every kind, and the machete with a curved blade fixed into a wooden handle by thongs. The form of the machete has been preserved into modern times and is used by the peasants in the region of Siem Reap for cutting wood, splitting coconuts or cutting a path through the bush and creepers of the forest. In the Angkorian period this machete is the noble and redoubtable weapon held by Sūryavarman II and his high officers at the parade in the Historical Gallery of Angkor Wat. Tradition has it that the blade of the Sacred Sword preserved in the Royal Palace of Phnom Penh came from Angkor. Sword and knife blades have been found on Angkorian sites, but they are badly corroded, and it is very difficult to date them. More than any other manufactured objects, weapons were for the court and aristocracy, who had the task of arming the soldiers who fought under then.

fig. 99

ARISTOCRATIC DWELLINGS

Nothing remains of the aristocratic dwellings; they have disappeared as completely as the huts of the poor. Were there aristocratic quarters? Or did modest houses huddle round the residence of a great family?

"The palace, the official dwellings and noble houses are all orientated to the east....The dwellings of princes and great officers are arranged differently and are different in size from the houses of the people. All the outbuildings and outlying dwellings are covered with thatch; only the family temple and private apartments may be covered with tiles. The official rank of each person decides the size of the dwelling."

The large residences of the Angkorian period consisted of a number of buildings. On the Bayon reliefs the composition in registers results in buildings being shown one above the other which were really one behind the other. On the lower registers are the annexes, servants quarters and offices. The family residence is always carved on the upper part of the relief; the master of the house could not be shown below his subordinates and servants. These buildings are shown with roofs, so the registers do not represent the stories of one building but different buildings. Exceptionally we see a few houses of more than one

story. On a pediment of Banteay Srei it is on the upper level of his palace that Kamsa is put to death *fig. 125* by Krishna, while scenes of lamentation are going on in the neighboring rooms and on the ground floor. At the Bayon there is a relief called "The Chinese man's house" because of the physical type of the master; a reception is going on in the upper story while on the ground floor, probably between the piles, the servants are getting the feast ready. Sometimes the staircase is shown that gives access to the *fig. 100* upper floor. It can be accepted that when the registers show buildings with roofs they are to be read as standing one behind the other, but when just a floor separates two registers we are often being shown a house with more than one story. In several of the scenes in a great house, the offices are all on one floor while the master's house has an upper story.

Since the reliefs invite us, let us go into one of the aristocratic residences. There is no getting in without showing one's credentials, for the entrance is watched by guards armed with stakes to persuade the undesirables to change their minds about going further. Servants are coming and going in a low building, setting down heavy baskets, carrying victuals to the kitchens, pausing for a minute's chat. Now we are in the tree-planted courtyard that surrounds the master's lodging. This building is of wood, like the gateway and offices, but it has been raised with extreme care. Dominating all the other buildings, it rests on heavy pillars carved from tree trunks. On the upper floor is a verandah, with slender columns supporting a roof decorated with pediments. In the center of the gables a monster's head protects the

100 Scene in a noble house, the Bayon, outer east gallery (late twelfth-early thirteenth century). A festivity is taking place in a great house. Under the house priests are apparently about to participate in the ceremony; behind them a woman brings a cup of offerings. Fan bearers climb a stairway to join ladies already seated on the verandah. The scene inside the house is unfortunately not depicted.

house from all evil influences. Above the tiled roof rises a tiered superstructure tapering to the top, rather like those of the sanctuaries.

This architecture is reminiscent of the temples; and if we are to believe Chou Ta-kuan every dwelling did in fact include a chapel. No doubt images of the deities who protected the family were worshiped on a private altar. Whereas temples are all built in stone, here everything is of wood, carved, lacquered and gilded. The delicacy of the woodwork and the rich colors are the products of a very refined art which has been perpetuated in southeast Asia into modern times. The dwellings of men are built of perishable materials, but they are no less richly furbished than the temples of the gods.

At this moment there is no one on the verandah. Mats hang between the columns; they keep this part of the house shady and cool. They will be raised after the heat, when the master comes to sit in this secluded spot.

A relief in the south gallery of the Bayon shows men coming together for a feast. This scene is depicted on a register above the open-air kitchen that we passed when going to the market. Perhaps it was for this great repast that the scullions were preparing in such agitation. At the far left of the register the guests are arriving. With two of his household—perhaps his sons—at his side and a little behind him, the master, seated on his heels, is receiving his guests; they kneel before him and all greet each other with joined hands. They exchange words of welcome and thanks. They all are dressed simply, but the *sampot* is elegantly draped, and each one has adorned his neck with a necklet with pendants. Only men join in these feasts; the women remain in the private apartments.

When all the guests are assembled the master requests them to adjourn to the banquet. In the garden under the trees the servants spread a great awning and in its shade they have covered the ground with mats. The custom of serving meals in a tent on festive occasions had persisted in modern Cambodia. For a wedding or other family celebration the master of the house invited all his relatives, his friends and even his neighbors. A Cambodian house, be it ever so spacious, would not be able to accomodate such large numbers.

Humble people built a shelter on the pavement in front of their house and sometimes in front of their neighbor's too; in the wealthy houses the feast took place under an awning in the garden, as it is shown on the Bayon reliefs.

Now the guests have taken their places on the mats. Squatting on their heels they are grouped in twos, fours or fives. The waiters place the dishes in front of them, and they help themselves, choosing a piece of meat or a little rice with their fingers. It is not easy to eat elegantly with the fingers. The Bayon sculptor has skillfully rendered the delicacy and elegance of the gesture which remains that of Indians taking their meals today, or of the Lao preparing mouthfuls of sticky rice. The guests at this feast are clearly well bred. They serve themselves with an elegance which contrasts with the rather rough behavior of the two fellows lunching in a corner of the market place and even more with the greed of the boor who is plunging his arm into a cooking pot at the other end of the relief. Once the meal is finished there is no staying behind to make speeches; each guest takes leave of his host, who retires to his private apartments to take some rest.

When the sun goes down the master of the house will perhaps enjoy the cooler hours on his verandah, where the servants have put aside the blinds; there, with a relative or a friend, he will start a long game of chess. Now they are both kneeling before a little low table *fig. 101* on which the board is spread. Deep in his calculations, one of them is preparing to play and raising a hesitating hand to take an ivory piece while his opponent patiently awaits his turn. While chess provides an agreable way of spending the evening in the well-to-do houses, it is also a past-time during long journeys by water. At Angkor Wat on a relief in the southwest pavilion, chess players have settled down on the deck of a boat in the shade of a little carved wooden pavilion.

The chess game has gone on until nightfall. Servants are coming to light candles fixed in bronze candlesticks, or lamps with wicks soaking in coconut oil. In the main rooms there are tall cressets standing like those on the Banteay Chhmar reliefs, to shed a brighter light all round. The host has pushed aside the

101 Chess players, the Bayon, outer south gallery (late twelfth-early thirteenth century). In the shelter of a pavilion two men squat on their heels to play chess. One has his hand raised and leans over the board as he plans his next move. Here the chessmen are larger and fewer than in the representations of chess games at Angkor Wat, but the shapes are the same and resemble those of modern chessmen.

chess board and is pausing to chat with his friends. There is no lack of subjects to talk about. Family problems, the crops he intends to rear, perhaps a law suit in process, his official duties that he takes up again tomorrow morning at the Palace, and then all the little court intrigues, all provide an inexhaustible fund of topics for discussion.

While the head of the family is detained at the Palace by his functions as a high dignitary, or devotes himself to entertaining his friends, the great house is the scene of many varied doings as each occupant goes about his daily tasks. The servants are cutting wood, bringing in jars full of oil or palm sugar, or cleaning the cooking utensils. Women prepare mortars for husking rice, as "for rice, they do not use millstones but husk the rice in mortars." The servants come and go, exchanging jokes, or a friendly word, sometimes a not-so-pleasing remark. One servant who is ill has gone to lie down in the servant's quarters. He has companions round him trying to comfort him and listening to the doctor's advice.

In the private apartments the master's wives and daughters pass the time at their toilet, receive their friends, wander in the gardens, and, perhaps, get bored. The first wife has supreme control over the whole household. She may not appear beside her husband at banquets, but it is she who gives orders to the servants and supervises everyone's conduct. She controls all expenses and the receipt of money. A younger wife perhaps enjoys the favors of the master, but she must willy nilly bow to the authority of the first lady of the household. And indeed who would dare to stand up to this august person with her commanding presence and cutting remarks? The young wives, the daughters and serving maids can do no more than exchange knowing glances or whis-

102 *Devatā*, Angkor Wat, southwest corner pavilion (first half of the twelfth century). Bands of metalwork keep the hair of this *devatā* in place, in the manner of a net. Strings of little rings hang from her ear lobes. Her costume is reduced to the narrow loin cloth draped with long flaps which is worn by dancers. She wears rich ornaments and both necklet and belt are hung with finely worked pendants.

per in another's ear some impertinent answer they dare not speak out.

For the noble ladies of heavy stature no less than for the elegant young girls, dressing was the great event of the day. They all spent hours sitting mirror in hand while their maids arranged their hair and painted their faces. A detailed examination of the *devatā* carved on the temple walls is the only means of gaining an adequate idea of the amazing variety of hairdos worn by the young women of high Angkorian society. Obviously the princesses could not have worn the heavy diadems of finely wrought metal except on special feast days. *fig. 102*

Every morning each lady's maid would carefully comb her mistress' hair after treating it with coconut oil; then she arranged it in a halo round her face or *fig. 103* piled it all on top of her head, knotting it in several buns and leaving a few tresses hanging, or else she would patiently plait it in a series of fine plaits and join them all together in one large bun. An inconspicuous frame might be needed to prevent a large bun from collapsing. A gold ring holding the base *fig. 104* of a bun, a delicately worked gold pin stuck through a coil of hair, or gold thread plaited in with the hair might be used to enrich these coiffures, though often the young women preferred to decorate their heads with a wreath of jasmin buds and stick a spray of *fig. 105* brightly colored flowers into their hair.

One young person, mirror in hand, is watching the patient work of her maid. She is pleased, her hair is dressed to suit her fancy; now she has to choose the garment to wrap round her thighs. She picks out a watered silk, unfolds it... throws it to one side. She hesitates, and then at last decides on a cloth decorated with a scatter of flowers and edged with broad zigzags. Now she stands up very straight for two dressers to fix the garment, wind it round her hips and drape it so that a large triangular section hangs down in front to show off the beauty of the border. In the early thirteenth century, fashion is no longer for the complicated draperies affected by the contemporaries of the Angkor Wat *devatā*. A necklace and a few rings for arms and ankles complete the young lady's turnout. She gives a final glance at herself in the mirror and smiles with pleasure.

103 *Devatā*, Angkor Wat, library of the second enceinte (first half of the twelfth century). On the walls of the small libraries built at the foot of the great west staircase of Angkor Wat, the artists carved their *devatā* in an atmosphere of gaiety and fantasy which is found nowhere else. These two *devatā* have lifted up their hair to make a halo round the face, while the long plaits are knotted and held by some device or armature; then they have stuck flower sprays in the knots. Arm in arm they seem bent on some joyous escapade, just like young Angkorians.

It has taken several hours for these ladies to prepare themselves; now it is hot, and they go to find somewhere out of the sun to sit, in one of the rooms of the private apartments. The children of the household play round them or come to be fondled. Soon other young women come to join them, and they all nibble the little biscuits and choice fruits brought to them by serving maids on dishes or in goblets. Sometimes bowls and cups were of precious metal, but excavations have shown that Chinese ceramics were much prized during the Angkorian period in rich households. Khmer houses were on the whole rather sparsely furnished. "They spread Ming-chou mats on the floors, or tiger, panther, deer skins, or rattan mats. Recently they have begun to use low tables, about a foot high. For sleeping they use only mats, and sleep on the floor. A few people have recently started to use low beds, generally made by Chinese. They cover their table utensils with a piece of cloth." In southeast Asia, however rich they may be, town dwellers sleep like country people, on mats placed on racks. When it is as hot as that, it is pleasanter to lie on a hard surface, and a mat is cooler than cloth. Perhaps the Cambodians of this period were already weaving the lovely supple mats that are now made precisely in the region of Siem Reap. The reliefs show seats decorated with balusters and elbow rests in the form of *nāga* and carved wooden chests. Though the quantity of furniture is small, there are many precious objects: ewers, trays, bowls, vases of all kinds. The furniture and utensils are all extremely elegant and

104 Female deity from Prāsāt Trapeang Totung Thngay, National Museum, Phnom Penh (second half of the eleventh century). The bust of this young deity is free of jewels. Her hair is plaited and lifted on the top of her head with a simple decoration of pearl garlands and a metalwork ring to hold her top-knot. The fine pleats of her costume mold her contours. This image was perhaps the effigy of a young princess, represented in the aspect of a deity.

105 *Devatā*, Banteay Srei (third quarter of the tenth century). In costume and ornament the *devatā* of Banteay Srei are different from all those carved on the other great Khmer temples. Heavy earrings drag down their ear lobes and garlands of pearls hang from their belts. Their costume is of fine cloth, loosely draped.

bear witness to the artistic feeling of the cabinet makers and gold smiths of Angkor.

On certain days towards evening the mistresses and maids all leave the great house to go and bathe in the river. "Every three, or four, five or six days, the women of the city, in groups of three, or five, go to bathe outside the town in the river. When they reach the river bank they take off the lengths of cloth wrapped around their bodies and go into the water. There are thousands of them like this in the river at a time. Even noble women like to go and feel no shame about it. Anyone can see them, from head to foot. In the great river just outside the city, not a day passes without this happening. The Chinese, on their days off, often go along there to watch, as an amusement. I have heard it said that there are also people who take advantage of the situation, in the water. The water is always warm and feels as though it had been heated over a fire; it is only at the fifth watch that it cools off a little; but as soon as the sun rises it warms up again." Cooled and refreshed by the waters of the river, and taking no notice of the indiscreet eyes of the Chinese, the women return to the city, gossiping over the news they have heard while bathing. Since they hardly get a chance to leave the private apartments all day long, this walk to the river once or twice a week is the one occasion when they can see the animation of the city before returning once more within the walls of the great house.

Indoors everyone is at his tasks again. Waiters are spreading mats on the verandah floor, preparing a drink for the master, arranging fruit in a bowl. In the kitchens fires are flickering under cooking pots. The sounds of the city penetrate as far as the inner courtyard, where the air is laden with the scent of champa flowers.

THE SIGHTS OF THE CITY STREETS

fig. 107 Porters with yokes over their shoulders, peddlars, idlers, and peasants driving ox carts keep up a picturesque and noisy bustle in the streets. Everyone draws aside to give passage to a noble personage borne in a palanquin. Sometimes a whole cortege will proceed down the street. Magistrates have been judging a number of offences and now those convicted are led through the town to the place where the sentences are carried out. "Formerly they did not have punishment by flogging, but only, I was told, the imposition of money fines. In very serious cases they do not behead or strangle; outside the western gate they dig a ditch and set the criminal in it, filling it in round him with firmly compacted earth and stones. As a lesser punishment they cut off toes and fingers, or amputate an arm." However, it was apparently not forbidden to exact justice oneself: "Debauchery and gambling are not illegal; but if a husband discovers his wife in adultery he squeezes the feet of the lover between two boards and he, being unable to bear the pain, hands over all his possessions and then is set free.... If a dead body is found at the door of a house, it is dragged with ropes outside the city onto some waste land; but there is nothing approaching a serious inquest. If anyone catches a thief he can confine him and torture him." Note that Chou Ta-kuan describes here the "squeezed foot" torture mentioned in the inscriptions.

It is sometimes very difficult to prove the guilt of an accused or to judge who has right on his side in a private quarrel. There is then no other recourse for the Khmers of the Angkorian period than to trials by ordeal. "They have another excellent procedure. If someone loses something and suspects someone else of being the thief, and he denies it, they boil up oil in a cauldron. The suspect has to plunge in his arm. If the man is guilty his hand is burnt; if not, the flesh and skin are unaffected. This is how the foreigners do it. It may happen that two families have a dispute and it is not known who is right or wrong. In front of the palace are twelve little stone towers. *fig. 142* Each contestant sits on one of these towers. At the foot of the two towers are the two families facing each other. After a day, or two, three or four, the one in the wrong ends up by showing it in some way: either he gets ulcers, or boils or starts up some catarrh or malignant fever. The man in the right gets no disease. In this way they decide between the just and the unjust. It is what they call 'the judgment of Heaven.' Supernatural intervention works in this way in this country." We find it more difficult nowadays to appreciate the "excellence" of such proceedings. Chou Ta-kuan does not seem to have been really convinced himself. We may be sure, however, that in the thirteenth century there was no lack of onlookers thronging to watch the outcome of "divine judgment" day by day.

There are other processions filling the city streets. An important personage has died, and his funeral is about to take place. It is possible that corpses were sometimes exposed to the birds and wild animals, but the reliefs do not seem to depict this type of funeral, though they show at least one cremation. According to Chou Ta-kuan only those of Chinese origin cremated their dead. One relief in the inner north gallery of the Bayon, unfortunately badly eroded, shows a cremation ceremony. The dead man was obviously a very distinguished person, probably a prince, perhaps even a king, for all the mourners are in princely garb and, even more telling, the body is enclosed in an urn. In modern Cambodia it was only kings, princes and religious and lay dignitaries of princely rank who had the prerogative of cremation in an urn. Did this custom already exist, then, in the time of the Angkorian monarchy? It seems likely that the rich classes had adopted cremation for their dead. The hearse, preceded by the bearers of offerings, had to cross the whole city to reach the place of cremation.

The funeral procession has gone past, but the ordinary folk hurrying along on foot do not have the street to themselves for very long, for here is a cavalry detachment riding into the center. It is followed by elephants on whose backs the mahouts have loaded huge packages which are to be delivered to the Royal Palace. These are gifts sent by a vassal prince as tribute.

fig. 106

Now and again at nightfall the street is filled with music and singing and shouts of joy. A young girl is being carried in a sedan chair to the house of her betrothed. Every year at the same season, in the fourth month of the Chinese year, according to Chou Ta-kuan who is the sole source for this report, occurred the ritual defloration of the girls who had reached puberty. "Between the ages of seven and nine for the daughters of the rich, for the poor sometimes not before eleven, they have a Buddhist or Taoist priest appointed to deflower them. This is called the *ch'en-t'an*. Each year the mandarin chooses a day in the month corresponding to the Chinese fourth month and makes it known throughout the country. Every family in which there is a girl who should undergo the *ch'en-t'an* informs the mandarin. The mandarin gives her a candle on which he has made a mark. On the given day, as night falls, the candle is lit and when it has burnt as far as the mark the moment of the *ch'en-t'an* has arrived. A month, a fortnight or ten days before this date the parents choose a Buddhist or Taoist priest, according to whether they live near a Buddhist or Taoist temple. Some have a regular clientele. Bonzes of some distinc-

tion and fame are preferred by officials and rich people; the poor have no choice. Officials, and rich people give presents of wine, rice, cloth, silk, betel nut, silver objects weighing up to a hundred piculs, and worth from two to three hundred tael of Chinese money. The presents of the less well-to-do vary between thirty and forty or ten and twenty piculs; it depends on the people's generosity. Thus the reason why poor girls reach eleven years old without having gone through the ceremony is that they do not have enough to meet these expenses. There are also some priests who refuse the silver and perform the *ch'en-t'an* free for the poor; this is regarded as a charity. A bonze is only allowed to deflower one girl each year; if he has accepted for one he cannot promise for any others. On the evening a great banquet is organized with music, and relatives and friends are invited. They set up a raised platform outside the door and put clay figurines of men and animals on them, sometimes more than ten, sometimes three or four. Poor people do not put any. This is an ancient custom. They leave it all there for a week. In the evening they set off to fetch the bonze with a palanquin, parasols and music, and bring him back. Two tents are erected with silks of different colors; the girl sits in one and the bonze in the other. No one knows what they say to each other. The music is deafening. That night there is no prohibition on noise and disturbance. I have heard it said that when the moment comes the bonze goes into the house with the girl; he deflowers her with his hand and then dips his hand in wine. They say the father and mother, relatives and friends then all mark themselves on the forehead with it; some say they also taste it. And some say too that the bonze has full intercourse with the girl, though others say not.…At dawn the bonze is taken home

106 Procession of elephants, south end of the Royal Terrace (late twelfth-early thirteenth century). Elephants advance in line, each driven by a mahout sitting on his neck. The saddle, which may be shaded by a parasol, is fixed by ropes to the chest, belly and tail of the animal. Hanging from the saddle are bells that jingle in time to the heavy tread of the beasts. People walk alongside the elephants; one of them has two loads hanging from a yoke on his shoulder.

107 Street scene, the Bayon, outer south gallery (late twelfth-early thirteenth century). People walk in a street in front of a portico, perhaps the entrance to a great house. A porter bears a yoke on his shoulder, balancing on one end a basket, on the other a tall jar. A man and woman are pointing out some unusual object. Other people go about their affairs. The women wear the long scarf round the bust that Cambodian women still wear when visiting the pagoda.

with palanquins, parasols and music. The girl must then be bought back from the priest with presents of cloth and silk, otherwise she would always belong to him and could not marry anyone else....On the night of the *ch'en-t'an*, there are sometimes more than ten families in one street carrying out the ceremony. In the city the people accompanying the bonzes or Taoists are all passing each other in the streets; there is nowhere without the sound of music."

Was this rite really practiced? Has not Chou Ta-kuan merely reported some more or less garbled hearsay that was current among the Chinese colony at Ang-kor? He himself adds: "The Chinese of course do not get much chance of witnessing these things, so the exact truth cannot be known."

There were feast days all the year round. The greatest, which is to say the only ones of which we have any knowledge now, were on the whole royal ceremonies. When the marriage or *ch'en-t'an* processions are over life resumes its normal course in the city. The activities of craftsmen and tradespeople enliven the streets during the day; at night all is calm. Only occasionally will some private family celebration prolong the lights, music and pleasant talk far into the night.

THE WALLED CITY

Did the urban life portrayed for us by the reliefs and the stories of the Chinese chronicler enliven the walled city as well as its outskirts? In medieval towns in the West all activity was concentrated within the shelter of the city walls. Was it the same in Angkorian Cambodia? This would seem unlikely. The ramparts of Angkor are not really defensive fortifications, they are the enclosure of a temple, the Bayon. The walled city thus had a sacred character. In every country, the capital is always a privileged place in the center of the kingdom; thus criminals could not be executed within the city walls. But Angkor Thom has an even greater religious importance; it is an authentic holy place, a dwelling of the gods. Even when it was no longer a capital, it remained in the eyes of all the people of southeast Asia Indraprastha, the dwelling of Indra on the summit of the mountain, with the same name as that of the Pandava capital.

This does not mean that Angkor Thom was a town without inhabitants. There was a population living inside the ramparts, but its activities were primarily ordered by the temples and the Royal Palace. Chou Ta-kuan reports that between one and two thousand women, at least, were employed at the Royal Palace, but that they were married and lived outside the palace. We may assume that these families lived inside the city. Yet it is unthinkable that activities can have gone on within the precincts of Angkor that were not in keeping with the sacred character of the city of the gods. It was because of this sacred character that entry to the capital was formally forbidden to dogs and "criminals whose toes have been cut off."

In the time of Yaśovarman I the town was centered on Phnom Bakheng. Unlike the Bayon, the temple on the Phnom Bakheng had its own enclosure. The world of the gods was thus enclosed within these walls which probably also created the periphery of a *Śivakshetra*. In Indian towns the main temple rises in the center of the city, and this is how the temple on Phnom Bakheng had been built. Houses, market, craftsmen's workshops could be set up all round. It is quite likely that after Jayavarman VII's city was built these quarters of old Yaśodharapura continued to exist. And the port where the travelers and merchandise from afar were disembarked, was installed on the river's edge and so outside the ramparts of the walled city.

The five entrances to Angkor Thom are well guarded by the two rows of fifty-four giants who hold a *nāga* on either side of the avenue. As one enters the city,

108 Angkor Thom, South Gate (late twelfth-early thirteenth century). The gates of Angkor are surmounted by four clearly separate heads, corresponding to four different people, probably the Four Kings of the four points of the compass (J. Boisselier). On either side of the gate, Indra is shown mounted on the three-headed elephant. The pediments and lintels above the entrances have fallen, making the passages much higher.

109 Causeway giant, Angkor Thom (late twelfth-early thirteenth century). Of giants bordering the access avenue to Angkor Thom, some are of godlike benevolent aspect, the others are grotesque rather than ferocious. The giants who support the heads and tails of the *nāga* are taller than the rest; they have many heads and multiple arms and legs. The sculptors have endowed these strange figures with extraordinary power.

the giants on the left have the benevolent aspect of *deva* while those on the right are terrifying with bulging eyes, bared teeth and heads bristling with leaves. The gates are framed by two figures of Indra riding the three-headed elephant Airavata. The four heads that crown the gateways are said by J. Boisselier to represent the four Mahārājikka, guardian kings of the four directions.[75] The enceinte of the city and its moats have the cosmic force of the mountain chain and ocean that limit the world itself.

It is sometimes suggested that the two rows of giants holding the *nāga*, appearing on one side as *deva* and on the other as *asura*, are intended to represent the myth of the Churning of the Ocean of Milk. We do not agree.[76] Only one serpent is involved in the Churning of the Ocean of Milk. Furthermore the giants are turning their backs on the gate that would constitute the pivot of the churn, and they are not pulling on the snake. On the contrary, as Chou Ta-kuan observed, they "are holding back the snake, and look as if they are preventing him from fleeing."

These monumental gateways are extraordinarily beautiful. It is impossible to approach the city without falling under their powerful spell. The composition is charged with symbolism. The *nāga*, water deities and guardians of treasure, are to be identified with the arch of Indra, the rainbow that unites the world of men with the world of the gods, watched over by the kings of the four directions. Passing through this gateway and following the long avenue with its canals on either side, the visitor reached the temple of the Bayon and the Royal Palace at the center of Angkor Thom.

This city that he aspired to make indestructible was not only a residence for Jayavarman VII but the very center of the whole religious system that he had set up to assure the duration of his kingdom: more than that, "The city of Yaśodharapurī the well-matched (spouse), adorned with powder and jewels, burning with desire, nobly born... was wedded by this king during a feast at which nothing was wanting, with the dais of his glory unfolded and spread out, with a view to the procreation of the happiness of the Universe."[77]

fig. 56

fig. 108

fig. 109

176

Part three:

LIFE IN THE PALACE

110 Angkor Thom, central stairway of the Royal Terrace
(late twelfth-early thirteenth century). A monumental stairway
rises in three flights to the upper level of the Royal Terrace
which appears to have been occupied originally by the audience hall. The wall of the lower level is carved with atlantes:
lions alternating with *garuda*. At the higher level are ferocious
guardians. *Nāga* and more lions complete the protection of this
terrace.

The Royal Terraces majestically raised in front of the Palace of Angkor Thom create a harmonious façade for the west end of the Great Square. The three monumental staircases of the central Grand Terrace (Terrace of Honor, as the French call it) project in a series of separate flights in front of the two long wings of the Elephant terraces. Delicate reddish lichens give a warm flush to the sandstone retaining walls with their relief carvings; supporting figures, alternately rampant lions and *garuda* guard the Grand Terrace; all along the walling of the side terraces are elephants hunting wild beasts in the forest.

Crossing the Grand Terrace the visitor comes to the eastern *gopura* of the Royal Palace, and passing through this monumental entrance, finds himself in a park. Before him rises a temple, the Phimeanakas. To the north are two walled pools. Walking in the park he will find several low terraces adorned with molding or *hamsa* friezes, but not a trace of dwelling houses. Together with the humble abodes of the poor and the great houses of the aristocracy, the apartments of the Royal Palace, built like them of perishable materials, have entirely disappeared.

The building of the Palace was undertaken in the mid-tenth century by Rājendravarman when he brought back the capital to Angkor. J. Boisselier has explained how this king aspired to make his palace a replica of the dwelling place of Indra. Of the works of this period the largest is the first state of the Phimeanakas. This temple was built in the Royal Palace on a high pyramidal foundation-base of laterite,

and reached by staircases on the axes. There was at this stage no enclosing gallery on the top level, this was not built until the early eleventh century, and the *gopura* date from this time as well. Thus the main structures of the Royal Palace complex were put up between the accession of Rājendravarman II and the death of Sūryavarman I. Much later, Jayavarman VII started up new works inside the enceinte. The ground was completely resurfaced. B. P. Groslier, excavating in 1952–53, recognized four successive occupation levels north of the Phimeanakas. These higher floors had in fact buried the whole base of the temple, which only regained its original aspect when the whole footing was cleared by the Angkor Conservation Authority. A variety of works was completed in the reign of Jayavarman VII. The supporting walls

111 Five-headed horse, Angkor Thom, Royal Terrace (late twelfth-early thirteenth century). Four reliefs have been uncovered in the interior of the north wing projection of the Royal Terrace. The center of each of these compositions is held by an enormous horse with five heads: a royal animal since each head is crowned with a tiara. Round it a series of frightened little men are cowering against large warriors. At the corner of one relief an elephant is lifting up soldiers, who are shouting out in terror, in its trunk.

112 Elephant relief, Angkor Thom, Royal Terrace (late twelfth-early thirteenth century). The walls of the long wings of the Royal Terrace are carved with elephants involved in game hunts in the forest. Some are in combat with large felines, others have overthrown deer or wild ox with their trunks.

179

of several terraces were carved with reliefs at this time, and so were the south and east walls of the great pool on the north of the Phimeanakas. This period too saw the construction of the splendid Royal Terraces in front of the east *gopura* which lend the Palace its culminating majesty.

The Royal Palace is surrounded by a double enceinte, making an enclosure of 600 × 250 meters. The two

fig. 103

laterite walls are separated by a 25 meter wide moat. There are five gateways into the enclosure: two each on the north and south and one on the east; the back wall is blind. The east *gopura* is one of the most beautiful examples of building in the Khleang style, with its unassuming lines and well-balanced masses. The sober plant decoration is however enlivened by a few very charming *devatā* appearing on the super-structures. The east *gopura* of the Palace contains one of the most interesting specimens of Cambodian epigraphy: carved on the jambs is the text of the oath of loyalty sworn by a certain class of officials to king Sūryavarman I.

The traces of walls uncovered behind the Phimeanakas are evidence that the western part of the enclosure was divided into several courts and comprised several terraces and two water basins. We have now no means of telling what these courts were used for. The largest of the five pools of the Royal Palace was sited north of the Phimeanakas; it measures 125 meters from east to west and 45 from north to south. The wall surrounding it is stepped into 13 levels and carved on the south and west faces in three registers corresponding to the three top steps. One category of mythical beings dominates each register: male and female *garuda*, *nāga* and *nāgī*, and, on the lowest register, sea monsters among fish. Below the sea creatures the steps disappear into the water.

What kind of buildings were there between this pool and the Phimeanakas? Excavations carried out by M. Marchal and later by B. P. Groslier have shown traces of walls. Interesting small finds also have come to light, but nothing to indicate the type of buildings that were put up inside the Royal Palace. We must turn to the accounts of Chou Ta-kuan and a study of the reliefs to learn what we can about the life of the monarch and his court.

Some Pictures of the Royal Palace

"The Palace lies north of the Golden Tower and the Golden Bridge. Counting from the outer gateway, it is five or six *li* in circumference. The tiles of the private apartments are of lead; those of the other buildings are of clay, and yellow. The piles of the bridge are enormous; there are carved and painted Buddhas on them. The mass of buildings is magnificent. The long verandahs and covered passages are bold and irregular, without much symmetry....I have heard it said that there are all kinds of marvelous places inside the Palace, but the guards are very strict, and it is impossible to get in to see them." It is known that Chou Ta-kuan's Golden Tower is the *fig. 78* Bayon, and the Golden Bridge must be the terrace on the east of this temple. The Royal Palace does in fact lie north of the Bayon. Excavations confirm the asymmetrical arrangement of the buildings of the royal residence.

113 Angkor Thom, Royal Palace, north *gopura* (eleventh century). Monumental passage-ways, *gopura*, give access to the interior of the enceinte of the Royal Palace. They were built by King Sūryavarman I. On the jambs of the eastern *gopura* this king had engraved the text of the oath to be sworn to him each year by a certain category of officials. These *gopura* have very sober decoration, primarily of plant motifs. A few gracious *devatā* figures appear, however, in the superstructures.

114 Angkor Thom, Terrace of the Leper King (late twelfth-early thirteenth century). To the north of the Royal Terrace rises a Terrace that owes its name to the statue called "The Leper King" which is in fact a representation of a ferocious figure. The outer walls of the terrace, consisting of a number of returns to follow the many projections of the plan, are covered with figures arranged in registers: *nāga* and *nāgī*, female figures and an occasional male figure holding a weapon. Excavations have revealed a second wall two meters behind it, similar to the outer wall in every particular, and corresponding to a first state of the Terrace.

115 Basins of the Royal Palace (late twelfth-early thirteenth century). Several sandstone-walled basins were laid out inside the enceinte, whose walls can be seen on the right. Plain steps surround the pool in the foreground. In the background a much larger basin has walls carved with fish, fantastic marine creatures and *garuda*.

On the reliefs of the eleventh and twelfth centuries the "long verandahs" and "covered passages" are the usual background for the palace scenes. These are long galleries with tiled roofs resting on columns. Clearance and excavation inside Angkor Thom has produced large numbers of fragments of pink and yellow pottery tiles; eave tiles are raised into a triangular motif which often has a molded decoration: a broad lotus petal, a small arcade framing a flower, or a mythical animal. As far as we know, no lead tiles have been found, but that is not surprising, since these ruins have been systematically robbed for every kind of metal.

In the shelter of these galleries officials take counsel together, and guards stand at arms; on the verandahs of the private apartments princesses converse or watch the progress of a dance, while servants are busy about their tasks. The king's residence is an imposingly monumental pavilion. No effort has been spared to make this building sumptuous. The light shines on the lacquered columns that hold up the carved and gilded pediments; it catches on all the relief of the superstructures, the stages of the towers and the slender domes. The sun's rays glisten off the gildings of the molded cornices, the notched slopes of the pediments and the raised *nāga* heads in which they end. The private apartments are not always wide open. Balusters adorn the windows and form a screen against prying eyes. They filter the sunlight and help to keep the rooms cooler.

"In the palace there is a golden tower, and at its top the king sleeps. All the natives say that there is the soul of a nine-headed snake in this tower who is master of the earth of the whole kingdom. It appears every night in the form of a woman, and the king has first to sleep and couple with it. Even the king's first wives would not dare to go in. He comes out at the second watch and can then sleep with his wives and concubines. If one night the soul of this snake does not appear, then it means that the king's death is at hand. If the king fails to come on one single night some misfortune occurs." The golden tower is the Phimeanakas which was a Śivaite temple. It is hard to discover the legendary source of the coupling of the king and the *nāgī*; it is possibly connected with a memory of the mythical foundation of the Chenla dynasty by the marriage of a Brahman and a *nāgī*. Chou Ta-kuan's account becomes more precise when he describes the council chamber. He probably knew it at first hand, for he says that he has been in the palace. "The council chamber has windows framed in gold; to the right and left are square columns carrying forty or fifty mirrors to face the windows. Below are representations of elephants." This last observation *fig. 112* allows us to suppose that the council chamber was on the Royal Terrace. The royal residences of modern times still provided for a hall at the end of the palace where the king could appear before his subjects. At Phnom Penh the Chanchaya hall was thus built against the palace enclosure, in the axis of the Throne Room. It is worth noting that this building has no walls: the roof is supported on columns so the king could appear on the balcony of this hall. It is in this manner that kings are often shown on the Angkor reliefs, and that Chou Ta-kuan describes the king appearing: "As for me, each time I have been to the palace I have seen the prince come out with his first wife and sit at a golden window of the private apartments. The people of the palace lined up beneath the window on either side of the verandah, and saw him in turn."

The king, the princes and high court dignitaries spent almost all their lives inside the enceinte of the Royal Palace. The king, in fact, should never be totally absent from his palace. If he is obliged to go into some province or has a duty to accompany his army on some military operation, his presence has to be maintained symbolically. While he departs on his elephant his throne has certain regalia placed upon it: generally his bow and quiver, fans, cups and cases. On the reliefs showing such scenes, the nature of the

116 Temple of Phimeanakas (second half of the tenth-early eleventh century). The tall, stepped base was built in the tenth century in laterite, in the heart of the Royal Palace; the surrounding gallery, forming an enceinte on the third level, in the reign of Sūryavarman I. According to a Chinese chronicler the king had to climb the Phimeanakas every night to couple with a *nāgī*, otherwise the kingdom would have been overcome by catastrophe.

regalia is liable to vary. We only very rarely know the names of the kings who were the lords of these palaces. Probably the insignia differed mainly according to whether the king was a simple feudatory or a *chakravartin* monarch. It is possible that the royal presence was symbolized by different objects according to whether the king had absented himself on a peaceful mission, a pilgrimage or a military expedition.

Allowing free rein to his imagination, E. Aymonier has given the following description of the Royal Palace when the splendor of Angkor was at its height: "the prince's dwelling must have comprised... waiting rooms, vast audience halls, halls of justice, reception rooms, with painted and gilded colonnades, rich hangings, paneling loaded with carving and ornaments; then the open belvedere, the astrologers' observatory, the pleasure pavilions covered with colored bricks and steeples inlaid with mosaics of gold, glass and colored stones. Behind were the gardens and secret apartments of the harem. There were spread out precious cloths, embroideries and fringes tastefully composed to create a form of decoration so highly prized that the sculptors reproduce their graceful designs on the pillars and walls of the stone buildings. Outside the women's quarters were the guard rooms, the royal store houses, the workshops of skilled craftsmen, endlessly employed in the service of the court."[78] We are unable to identify the different buildings described by E. Aymonier in the Royal Palace. Were there really halls of justice and a belvedere for astronomers? Obviously, no trace of them can be found. Yet this description of an Angkorian palace by an author who was well acquainted with the Cambodian court of King Norodom is not pure invention. In the Royal Palace of Angkor, the area behind the Phimeanakas certainly seems to form a private enclave. It is not inadmissible to draw a parallel with the Royal Palace of Phnom Penh; there, behind the Throne Room which, it should be noted, contained a little dynastic shrine, an enclosing wall shut off private gardens dotted with palaces and pavilions, the dwellings of the kings and members of the court. The Royal Palace of Angkor doubtless had rather similar arrangements, as was thought by the first scholars who cleared the area. While the temple of the Phimeanakas and official buildings stood in the eastern part of the enclosure, the whole of the western part would have been reserved for the private apartments.

117 Śiva and Umā, Banteay Srei, National Museum, Phnom Penh (second quarter of the tenth century). This attractive group represents Śiva seated with his wife on his left knee. The two deities are wearing the ascetic's top-knot together with the royal diadem. Their pleated garments, draped with one edge overhanging, is characteristic of tenth century art. They have no necklace or armlets, and were probably adorned with real jewelery. In his right hand Śiva holds a blue lotus, its flower hanging over his wrist.

118 Military parade, the Bayon, outer gallery (late twelfth-early thirteenth century). In the foreground march foot soldiers, holding a sort of javelin in the right hand while the left arm is passed through the strap of a long shield. They wear the little loincloth of ordinary folk and a short jacket as well.

In the second plane of the composition march the elephants. The mahouts, seated on their animals' necks, hold a hook in the right hand and a small round shield in the left. Behind the mahout is no doubt the officer, seated on a saddle of carved wood.

THE FUNCTION OF ROYALTY

All-powerful master and proprietor of the whole surface of his kingdom, the king is the protector of his subjects and the conserver of the *dharma*, of the Law founded on religious and moral rule. Thus we see that "King Śrī Rājendravarman, enlightened, liberal, ceaselessly implores the future kings of the Cambuja with this thought: protect this great work which he has done....Oh you who are wise, may you in all your good works *(dharma)* be possessed increasingly of your own duty *(svadharma)*....You have conquered the earth... you must protect all that is found on its surface. Your care must not slacken for one instant...."[79] Rupture of the established order would bring the worst of catastrophes. By his vigilance, by the choice of his delegates, the sovereign must ensure the well-being of the kingdom. He is master of armies and diplomacy in order to ensure the reign of peace. Even more important than his function as ruler of the political and social order, is his role as guardian of religious order. All religious foundations are under his safeguard. In the inscription of Pre Rup, Rājendravarman II addresses his successors to come with anguished insistence: "Oh you who are plunged by fortune in that dream which is the enjoyment of royal power, if this work should crumble, awaken in its favor, like Nārāyana [asleep] on the Ocean of Milk....Oh you who come to royalty, be always attached to the *Dharma*, be excellent by the virtues of generosity, eminent by majesty, rich in treasures and armies, like the ancient kings....It is truly said that supplication is the death of kings, when it has as its aim the realization of their desires. But when by passion for the *Dharma* I offer supplication with the sole aim of the prosperity of the *Dharma*, [this supplication] is the immortality towards which all must aspire."[80] This text deriving from Rājendravarman, in the first century of the Angkorian monarchy, leaves no doubt about the duties of the king in the exercise of his power.

The texts of the inscriptions show a respect and admiration for the king that place him on an equality with the gods. Among the titles attributed to him there are some, such as *Śrī,* "His Fortune," which are borne not only by the gods, but by princes and high dignitaries; but the Khmer titles of *Vrah pād,* "Holy Feet" is applicable only to the gods and the king. It is the same with *Vrah Kamraten jagat,* "Holy master of the world."

Succession to the Throne

A glance at the king-lists of Angkor shows clearly that the royal succession belonged to the eldest son of the deceased monarch. To quote only the earliest examples, the crown passed from Indravarman to Yaśovarman, then to Harśavarman I. In the absence of a direct heir this male succession by primogeniture brings in the accession of a brother or a nephew of the last king. On the other hand the importance of matrilineal filiations is also undeniable. G. Coedès points out how much Yaśovarman insists on the links that united him, through women, with the ancient pre-Angkorian dynasties. Jayavarman VII himself held his right to the throne through his mother, daughter of the most ancient Khmer dynasties, whereas his father, as J. Boisselier has shown, was certainly no more than a feudatory king. In fact it seems that transmission of male right prevailed in royal succession; but that in the absence of a direct heir, a member of the royal family might be accepted as legitimate sovereign by right of the female line.

The care devoted by the kings to the education of their eldest sons confirms the rule of male succession by primogeniture. The upbringing of the heir apparent was entrusted to the Brahmans. The stele of Prāsāt Komnap speaks of the education received by the future founder of Angkor during his "childhood without constraint." "The wisdom from the mouth of his guru which entered his mouth solely by the organ of the voice, was as ambrosia leaving the disk of the moon and entering the image of Indra by the organ of the carotyd. He devoted himself zealously to the practice of every kind of art, which he performed gently, as though they had been mastered and learnt by affection and kindness."[81]

The question of succession to the throne raises that of regency, in the eventuality of the new king being a minor. Throughout our period there was no true regency seen to function, although in the tenth century there was at least one minority, that of Jayavarman V who became king in 968 but did not finish his education until 974. In this case the king's spiritual advisor, the Brahman Yajñavarāha, himself grandson of Harṣavarman I through his mother, exercised a veritable guardianship. Udayādityavarman I was a very small child when he became king, but it is not known who wielded the power during his very short and troubled reign.

Several successions were the occasion of civil war or usurpation. When the usurper himself had insufficient title to aspire to the throne he tended to legitimize his accession by force, by producing a somewhat "touched up" genealogy and marrying the daughter or widow of his predecessor. Having eliminated Jayavīravarman, Sūryavarman I cited the relationship of his wife Vīralakshmī with the sons of Yaśovarman; in fact Vīralakshmī may well have been the widow of Jayavīravarman. There were however some usurpers who had very real rights to the throne, such as Sūryavarman II, the nephew and probably

the heir of Dharaṇīndravarman, who revolted against his uncle whose reign went on too long to please him. Jayavarman VII was probably not related in any way to his two predecessors, Yaśovarman II and the usurper Tribhuvanādityavarman. He took over the vacant throne, re-established the lost strength of the Khmer, and then had himself anointed king. The crown he had won by hard fighting was certainly his own: his mother, a daughter of Harṣavarman III, had passed on to him the rights of the most ancient dynasties. "As from Brahmarshi the goddess Aditi had [as son] the king of the Gods [Indra], from this king [Dharaṇīndravarman] the daughter of Śrī Harṣavarman had a son of radiant power, the king Śrī Jayavarman, who, founding himself on the law, killed in combat the leader of the enemy with a hundred million arrows to protect the land..."[82] The legitimacy of Jayavarman VII is here proclaimed at the same time as the superiority of his mother, raised to the rank of a goddess, while his father is only compared to a Brahmarshi, an ascetic Brahman sage.

Whether he succeeded by right to the throne, or legitimized the power dubiously acquired, the king was the protector of the land and thereby the uncontested chief of the army and the administration.

The King as Army Chief

A stanza of the stele of Pre Rup recounts how king Rājendravarman assembled his troops in his capital at the beginning of the rainy season, the period when military operations are suspended: "Coming in haste from every direction at the sound of his voice, deep like the murmur of the ocean, the armies assembled as do the rivers in haste [at the voice of] the rains whose beginning is announced by the experts."[83] In time of war, a royal order must send off the armies in like haste to the threatened frontiers. The Khmer empire was often engaged in fighting its neighbors, and must have very soon possessed a highly organized army. Even in the seventh century the *History of the Sui* mentions that "more than a thousand guards in armor and armed with lances stand in ranks at the foot of the steps to the throne, in the halls of the

119 Parade of the army of Sūryavarman II, Angkor Wat, Historical Gallery (first half of the twelfth century). The Siamese contingent, identifiable from a short inscription, leads the march. The aspect of these warriors is strange. Their garment, a pleated skirt with a flowered pattern, is held on the hips by a belt with very long pendants; a braided jacket covers the trunk. The headdress is no less curious. Their hair is plaited into numerous little pigtails; a kind of bun-case, decorated with plumes, is perched on the top of the head. The sculptor has noted certain racial characteristics: small slit eyes, a short moustache on the upper lip. The warriors following them are each armed with a stiff cuirass and a helmet crested with an animal's head.

palace, at the doors and in the colonnades....It is the custom of the inhabitants always to go about in armor and with weapons... so that the slightest quarrel is liable to end in bloodshed." Scenes of fighting appear among the earliest Khmer reliefs. The walls of Angkor Wat and the Bayon display a series of great battles and imposing military parades. Thanks to these reliefs and the information gleaned from the inscriptions we can work out some of the features of the military organization of Angkorian Cambodia.

At the beginning of the dry season, before going on campaign, the king orders the hosting. In peace time this army must have been no more than the royal guard and a few troops. Before embarking on hostilities it was necessary to enlarge the forces. Perhaps each feudatory brought a contingent. It is quite likely that the king employed merceneries. It is not known whether the Siamese detachment that leads the military review in the Historical Gallery of Angkor Wat is to be seen as a troop of mercenaries or the battalion of a feudatory prince from the Menam Basin. When danger threatened, the king might have recourse to a levy of troops among the people. At the end of the thirteenth century "in the war against the Siamese, the whole people was obliged to fight." Exceptionally the king could even call on the slaves attached to the service of a deity in a temple, for we find an inscription stating: "the king, supreme over the earth, is not to employ in his own service any of the slaves of Śrī Indreśvara, nor of the other gods. In the event of an army invading the kingdom, and only in such an event, he may call upon them to destroy this army."

We do not know how the recruiting entrusted to certain officers was carried out. The text of an inscription reports how the younger son of an old Brahman family of officials "fulfills the extremely honorable functions of the recruiter of soldiers for the royal guard who wear helmets... and hold a weapon."[84] Were the men capable of bearing arms enrolled freely or constrained? Their departure was a dramatic moment in peasant life. On the outer east gallery of the Bayon, soldiers are leaving their families. The farewells are painful. Some of the recruits only reluc-

tantly tear themselves away from their wives and children.

The Khmer artists more than once embellished temple walls with armies marching to the rhythm of the band, but there is nowhere any such scene to compare with the departure, apparently to the wars, of the army of Sūryavarman II, carved in the Historical Gallery of Angkor Wat. After sitting enthroned at the center of his assembled court, the king comes down from his palace and sets off among his officers and troops. In each battalion, horsemen, archers and lancers are grouped round the leader who is mounted on a elephant. It is notable that on the wall of the Historical Gallery of Angkor Wat, and therefore in a contemporary military parade, the artists have not depicted any chariot, whereas on the reliefs of the other galleries in the same temple, devoted to epic battles, the war chiefs fight from horse-drawn carts. Quaritch Wales is probably right in thinking that the Khmers, like the Indians, had by this time abandoned this method of fighting, since the sculptors only used it with archaizing intent in mythical and legendary scenes.

The parade in the Historical Gallery is like a splendid triumphal procession. First comes the Siamese contingent. With plumes on their heads and their costume decorated with long pendants hanging over their skirts from belt to knees; warriors from the Menam plains must have looked a strange sight to the Khmers who stood to watch them pass. The other soldiers wear the *sampot*, and some a short jacket as well. With a view to startling their enemies some have given a monstrous look to their shields and put on extraordinary headdresses, diadems bristling with leaves, helmets horned or crested with animal heads: deer, horse or bird. Many wear a cylindrical leather or metal breastplate, without shoulder straps, simply cut out under the arms; an arrangement of straps allows the soldier to fix the plate over his chest and slip one or two daggers in behind his left shoulder. Some warriors have little curved knives hanging over their throats from a necklace. Round the war leaders on their elephants prance the horsemen with raised spears, the foot soldiers move forward in serried ranks, lancers alternating with archers. Standing bolt

fig. 118

fig. 119

upright, dominating their battalions, the leaders look down from their elephants whose heads are painted in bright colors round the eyes and ears. At their sides on the benches servants hold parasols and banners, wave fans and fly-whisks, their numbers depending on the importance of the lord. The ensigns hold poles crowned with images: Vishnu standing on the shoulders of *Garuda*, Nandin, or Hanuman dancing. Bands give the army their marching rhythm: the musicians bang gongs, blow trumpets, beat drums, clash cymbals. Clowns gesticulate and tumblers, with ludicrous contorsions, balance the long poles of standards on their foreheads, on one thigh or on the palm of one hand.

In this bright and noisy procession come Brahmans surrounded by parasols and insignia, bearing on their shoulders the long shafts of a litter supporting the Sacred Fire, identified by a short inscription in Old Khmer, "Vrah bhloeng." Behind the ark a Brahman superior is carried on a palanquin ; he is very old and very thin and his head lolls on his chest. Other Brahmans are gathered respectfully round him.

About half way along the procession comes the royal guard, preceding the king. As G. Groslier noted, "a characteristic detail is the way the royal guard preceding the prince carry their lances, held obliquely across the shoulder with the point turned down... this is the way the few lancers who precede the present king hold their arms when they accompany him on a solemn occasion."[85] The king comes forward in his turn, standing on his elephant. He wears a diadem and an ornament over his knotted hair, the top-knot case, and holds the handle of a sword with its blade across his shoulder. Round him servants raise fifteen parasols. In majestic pose and with supreme elegance, the king turns back to the battalions that follow him and bring the long procession to an end.

Sūryavarman II's army has no war machines. Chou Ta-kuan claimed that the Cambodians had "neither bows, nor arrows, nor ballistas, nor shot, nor armor, nor helmets." They certainly had no knowledge of firearms even though they used powder for fireworks; but they had the other personal weapons, both defensive and offensive. As for ballistas, we can *fig. 121* see on the Bayon reliefs that there were little catapults

carried on elephant back or pulled on wheels. According to G. Groslier: "two bows held face to face were simultaneously braced by sliding the cord fixed to the hinder bow, and let fly together."[86] P. Mus thinks that this weapon of Chinese origin might have been introduced into Cambodia through Champa.

Chou Ta-kuan, who indeed has only the feeblest notion of the military organization of the Cambodians, says again: "They have neither tactics nor strategy." In fact, we have no knowledge of how the Khmers of Angkor conducted warfare. The operations probably consisted of incursions into the enemy's territory, followed by a few battles and sieges. At Angkor Wat the scenes of the battles of Lanka and Kuruk- *fig. 120* shetra give the impression of a confused melee. The two armies, having marched one against the other, are engaged in man to man fighting in which each man chooses his adversary. The main objective is the occupation of the enemy capital, whose fall will bring about the collapse of the kingdom. This is what happened to Cambodia in 1177, and the fate that the Khmers in their turn inflicted on Champa. We have a few accounts of battles in inscriptions. There is the fight to the death engaged in by the future Sūryavarman II in revolt against his uncle, Dharanīdravarman I, told in the inscription of Prāsāt Chrung: "after fighting for a whole day king Śrī Dharanīndravarman was despoiled by Śrī Sūryavarman of the royalty which was defenseless,"[87] and the Ban That inscription adds: "launching onto the field of war the ocean of his armies, he [Sūryavarman II] made terrible war; leaping onto the head of the elephant of the enemy king, he killed him, as *Garuda* descending on the summit of a mountain kills a snake."[88]

Often the texts of the inscriptions insist on the military prowess of the king, but they only report military operations in terms of how the enemy submitted at the sheer sight of the king. "His Majesty, having the brilliance of the weapon of Nārāyana, was a veritable fire... for the mass of raw flesh of the enemy army, a bush fire for the forest of weapons, a moon for those lotus that were the bowed-down enemy kings. Seeing the terrible aspect of this king in battle with his weapons, the enemies shut their eyes and their arms, like snakes, dropped their arrows, while the missiles they had for so long been sending seemed to stop short."[89] For the enemy are powerless before a *chakravartin* king, and submit of their own accord. Jayavarman VII, who is the king celebrated in the Ta Prohm inscription just cited, appeared as an authentic *chakravartin* king.

The King as Chief of the Administrative and Judiciary Organization

All administrative, civil and judiciary power resides in the person of the king who seems frequently to have exercised it without delegation. "Twice every day, the king holds audience for affairs of government. No list is drawn up. Whoever of the officials or the people wishes to see the prince sits on the ground and awaits him." The settlement of all disputes is in his hands. "Peoples' disagreements, even if they are quite insignificant, always come before the sovereign." It is obvious, nonetheless, that the king could not assume such authority unaided, and that he had to rely on counselors and delegates.

The king's counselors all belong to the noblest families in the kingdom and they are even sometimes members of the royal family. "Most of the time princes are chosen for office; if not, those who are chosen offer their daughters as royal concubines." These great Mandarins played an important part in the state. In the tenth century, one of them is known who bears the title of *rājakulamahāmantrin* and occupied a considerable position under Rājendravarman II. Even more important was the *vrah guru*, the king's spiritual advisor. The fame of two of these high dignitaries has survived: Yajñavarāha in the tenth century, and Divākarapandita who really seems to have directed policy from the reign of Harśavarman III to that of Sūryavarman II. Dignitaries were chosen on the whole for their knowledge and ability; the texts of the inscriptions insist on their knowledge of the Indian texts, the *Dharmaśāstra* and *Arthaśāstra*. Their activity was extremely varied. The king not only entrusted them with administrative duties, but with diplomatic missions and military commands; sometimes he even ordered them to preside over important building works: thus on the instructions of Rājendravarman II, Kavīndrārimathana supervised the works at the Royal Palace and the temple of the Eastern Mebon.

These important people lived on a grand scale. In the palace of one of them, Sadāśiva Jayendrapandita,[90] the king, Sūryavarman I, "took pleasure in enthusiastically lavishing in the prescribed form the most acceptable marks of honor, such as marvelous banquets etc. ...This [palace] was embellished with statues of carved stone, made very seductive, covered with a series of decorations, adorned with women: how could one think of speaking of other beauty? Cups of gold, a fly whisk, a shining seat, a palanquin in the form of a three-headed serpent, a dazzling parasol; heaps of splendid gems by the thousand: rubies etc.; a hand basin [complete with] a golden ewer, a vase and a shell; a hand basin [complete with] a cup, another cup, a vase and a shell; a jug with a spitoon and any number of wonderful things."[91] The list of the riches of this noble gentleman continues for fifteen stanzas.

Some religious dignities and some court offices were hereditary, and it is possible it was the same for high administrative office. In the genealogies of the great families whose title to nobility generally goes back to Jayavarman II, important administrative functions were entrusted, through the centuries, to the members of successive generations. In one line the title of "inspector of magistrates" is borne by the head of the family for three generations; this would imply that the office was hereditary. A long text engraved on a stele ends with a short history of the career of one of these families: "the said Vāgīśa, head of the town of Chok Trakvān, was a mandarin of king

120 The Battle of Kurukshetra, Angkor Wat, west gallery III (first half of the twelfth century). The armies of the rival cousins, the Pāndava and the Kaurava, have come to grips. The ground is already littered with the dead. This last battle of the Mahābhārata is a fatal combat from which few heroes will emerge alive. A warrior is preparing to fling his javelin. His headdress, a diadem decorated with leaves, is that of ferocious characters.

Udayāditya[varman]....Having entered the respectable family devoted to the noble office of fan bearer in the service of the thirteen kings who have reigned successively since the king of kings named Śrī Jaya-[varman], sole possessor of the white parasol, until the king named Sūrya[varman] favorite family of the king....In the reign of Udayāditya[varman], the plant of this family, having this (Vāgīśa) as its root, well watered by the regular rain of good works... having as its sap its fidelity to the king, as its main stem observance of the rule, as flower the protection of virtuous people who had turned to it in times of trouble, and for fruit its effort with the glory of heaven in mind, obtained a Lakshmī of gold as badge of its office."[92]

The inscribed texts reveal the existence of an official hierarchy which is in fact quite impossible to reconstruct. "In this country there are counselors, generals, astronomers etc., and below them every kind of small official: only their names differ from ours." The recruitment of all these officials was decided by the king; "it is in consideration of their ages, their connections, their manner of serving, and their qualities that he distinguished his servants." The names of two categories of elite officials have been transmitted down to us: the *sanjak* and the *tamrvāch*. G. Coedès thought the title of *sanjak* might be that of "dignitaries seeming to enjoy the special confidence of the kings, and giving proof of a devotion which even reached sacrificing their lives for him." The title of *tamrvāch* was given to less illustrious persons. Again according to G. Coedès "these people formed a sort of elite guard rather than a body of administrators, and from them the sovereign chose the men he most relied on." The *tamrvāch* were numerous; the inscription with the oath of loyalty of the officials lists about four hundred of them.

It was essential to the king that all these officials be loyal. To make sure of their faith, he required an oath from them when he came to the throne, and it was renewed every year. In the reign of Sūryavarman I the text of the oath of the *tamrvāch* was engraved on jambs of the east *gopura* of the Royal Palace. "Here is [our] oath: we all belong to the division of the *tamrvāch* of the first class, at the moment of swearing,

we cut off our hands and offer our lives and our grateful devotion, without fail, to His Majesty Śrī Sūryavarmadevadar who completely enjoys legitimate royalty from 924 *shaka*, in the presence of the sacred Fire, the sacred Jewel, of the Brahmans and the *āchārya*. We will revere no other sovereign but he; we shall not oppose him; and we shall not be abettors of his enemies....All the deeds which are the fruit of our grateful devotion to His Majesty Śrī Sūryavarmadeva, we will endeavour to accomplish. In case of war, we shall endeavour to fight with all our hearts, not to cling to life....If there is a service for which His Majesty the king orders us to travel far away, because there is an event of which he has heard, we shall try to find out the affair in detail, and each to keep to his oath....If there are traitors among us who do not keep exactly to this oath, may they be reborn in the thirty-two infernos, as long as the sun and the moon endure. If we keep this oath without fail, may the sovereign give his orders for the maintenance of our families, because we are devoted to our master His Majesty Śrī Sūryavarmadeva. ...The reward of those who are devoted to their masters, may we obtain it from this world into the next."[93]

The sovereign owed it to himself to be generous to those who served him well. The *tamrvāch* begged him not to abandon their families if they suffered misfortune. To those who had been successful in their missions the king accorded titles, honorific distinctions and even gifts of land. These gifts of property were the foundation of the fortunes of more than one great family. Sanskrit titles or even inscription into a caste were sure to have been much appreciated favors. Besides titles, officials might obtain marks of honor from the king, generally palanquins and parasols. "The insignia and the following also depend on rank. The highest dignitaries use a palanquin with

121 Balista, the Bayon, outer gallery (late twelfth-early thirteenth century). A soldier is pushing a balista mounted on wheels. This very simple war machine consists of two bows flexed with a single string. The release of the two bows gave great propulsive force to the machine. On the same relief are balistae carried on elephant back.

golden shafts and four parasols with golden handles; the followers have a palanquin with golden shafts and one parasol with a golden handle, or simply a gold handled parasol; below that they have simply a parasol with a silver handle; there are some also who use a palanquin with silver shafts. The officials who are entitled to the gold parasol are called *pa-ting* or *an-ting;* those with silver parasol are called *ssŭ-la-ti.* These parasols are made of red Chinese taffeta; they have fringes reaching the ground. Oiled umbrellas are in green taffeta and have short fringes."

The parasol handles and palanquin shafts were certainly not solid gold or silver but of wood plated with repoussé gold or silver. Palanquins were decorated with *nāga*, and it seems that the number of *nāga* heads might be three, five or perhaps even seven, according to the grade of the owner of the palanquin. On the reliefs of Angkor Wat and the Bayon we see a great variety of shapes and decoration of parasols, with festoons, streamers and fringes, with plain, embroidered or embossed cloth; we do not know of any with fringes falling to the ground. Some are open, others shut, some have several layers one above the other. The numbers vary. Chou Ta-kuan speaks of four round the highest dignitaries, but in the Historical Gallery at Angkor Wat there are twelve accompanying a war lord and fifteen carried behind the king.

Inscriptions abound in texts mentioning distinctions granted by the king. There is a young man called Śrī Sūryapandita, for instance, rewarded by Sūryavarman II: "at the age of nineteen, having acquired the knowledge of his father, wise, ceaselessly attached to duty, affable; he was, in recognition of his good qualities, gratified by the master of the earth with a golden vehicle, with a Brahmanical cord [of gold], with a tablet and a fan of gold."[94]

Throughout these texts, the king always appears not only as the supreme head of all administration, but also as the dispenser of favors. Though he may ask much of his servants, he rewards them; while he may at times pronounce very hard sentences on those who violate the *dharma*, he is also capable of clemency. He is not unapproachable in his palace, for the people as well as the mandarins are able to come to him when he gives audience.

KING AND COURT

fig. 122 The Khmer king rules over his kingdom like Indra on Mount Meru. The identification of the sovereign with Indra is quite clear, even before the foundation of Angkor. It was said of King Indravarman: "he possessed the venerable lion throne, the Śrī Indrāyana, the Śrī Indravimānaka and the Śrī Indraprāsādaka, made of gold according to his own design."[95] The Śrī Indrāyana is Indra's vehicle; the Śrī Indravimānaka, his palace and the Śrī Indraprāsādaka, his pavilion. Does this mean that the assimilation to Indra makes the king a deity? One interpretation of an eleventh century inscription that records the sacring of Jayavarman II on Phnom Kulen made it appear likely. It records the initiation of a rite for the cult of the *devarāja*. It appoints the Brahman Śivakaivalya, and his descendants after him, in charge of this cult. It was thought that the cult of the *devarāja*, translated "god-king," was addressed to the spiritual "ego" of the deified king. But then J. Filliozat translated *devarāja* as "king of the gods," which is the exact translation of the composite Sanskrit word. "King of the Gods" is generally used of Indra, but J. Filliozat points out that the Tamils refer to Śiva in this way. So the *devarāja* must be Śiva, of whom the Śivaite kings in fact considered themselves to be the incarnation.

In the Historical Gallery of Angkor Wat, Sūryavarman II is seated on a throne in truly royal majesty, surrounded by his sedulous attendants. His vassals wait in a long line to pay homage and offer their gifts. Seeing this relief we can understand what the Chinese chronicler meant when he said: "they may be just a kingdom of *Man* and *Mo*, but they certainly know what a prince is." The representations presumed to be of Jayavarman VII show the king in much simpler array. On the Bayon relief he is watching the progress of a naval battle, and is dressed no differently from the warriors fighting under him. State costume such as is worn for the triumphal procession would be unsuitable for a king involved in fighting. Again, the famous statues that are thought to be portraits of Jayavarman VII show the king as an *upāsaka*, a zealous Buddhist; he could not keep on his royal garb in the presence of the Blessed One. However the sovereigns carved on the Bayon reliefs, which certainly portray the reigning monarch, appear in full royal panoply.

In the thirteenth century, despite the misfortunes of war and dubious successions, the Khmer king maintained the royal pomp of his predecessors. He was distinguished from his subjects, even from the noblest, by his more sumptuous apparel. "Only the prince can wear cloth with a close floral pattern. He wears a golden diadem....When he is not wearing the diadem he twines garlands of scented flowers like jasmin round his topknot. He has about three pounds of large pearls round his neck. On his wrists, ankles and fingers he wears bracelets and rings of gold with catseyes set in them. He goes barefoot, and the palms of his feet and hands are stained red with a red dye. When he goes out, he carries a golden sword in his hand."

The first queen shared her husband's glory; it was after all through their wives that several of the kings were confirmed in their titles to legitimacy. Early in the thirteenth century, when Jayavarman VII was at *fig. 123*

the zenith of his power, the first queen was Indradevī. The king had bestowed on her the title of chief queen, *agramahishī*, the "queen who is at the summit," after the death of his first wife Jayarājadevī, the younger sister of Indradevī. The king had other wives. No confirmation has been found of Chou Ta-kuan's assertion that "the king has five wives, one for the private apartments properly speaking, and four for the four cardinal points." The names of several wives of some of the kings are mentioned in the epigraphy.

fig. 124 The *agramahishī* is the first lady of the kingdom; she is in command inside the palace. If she survives her husband and one of her sons comes to the throne, she retains an important position at court and acquires merit by multiplying her pious works.

The Great Stele of the Phimeanakas, on which the text was composed by Indradevī herself, in memory of her sister, reveals something of what these sisters

fig. 126 were like. Jayarājadevī married Jayavarman when he was still only a prince. She lived through all the troubles and uncertainties of his youth, often separated from him, wondering what fate had in store for him. She passed much of her life enduring heavy penances in the hope of winning success for her husband and his return. Despite these practices, her beauty, "burnt by asceticism" was "neither destroyed nor diminished." In these spiritual exercises she was

122 A sovereign giving audience, the Bayon, inner gallery (late twelfth-early thirteenth century). In a pavilion, accompanied by his wife and female entourage, a king is giving audience to two people humbly kneeling before him. One of them has set down an offering before the king, who is giving him advice, or an order. Behind the pavilion that shelters them can be seen coconut palms.

123 Statue presumed to be of Jayavarman VII, Krol Romeas, National Museum, Phnom Penh (late twelfth-early thirteenth century). Several statues of this slightly corpulent man, seated in meditation, have been found in the territory of the ancient Khmer kingdom. The silhouette is similar to that of the commander presiding over the naval battle in the Bayon relief. The subject has removed all royal apparel; his head is shaved, though on the splendid head found at the Preah Khan of Kompong Svay the hair is gathered into a little bun. The modeling of the torso and legs is specially naturalistic. The face looks older than that of the Preah Khan head, but the reflective expression is of great beauty.

"instructed by her elder sister Śrī Indradevī, and considering the Buddha as the beloved to be reached, she followed the calm path of the Sugata [The Buddha] which passes through the fire of torments and the sea of sorrows." When Jayavarman VII returned victorious to Angkor "having found her husband once more, now king of kings, in gratitude she poured onto the earth a rain of magnificent gifts,

124 Scene in Paradise, Angkor Wat, Gallery of Heaven and Hell (first half of the twelfth century). In a celestial palace supported by *garuda* reclines a young lady who has successfully undergone the judgment of Yāma, god of death, and can be reborn as a divine being. She is seated like a princess, in luxury, surrounded by servants to attend to her every whim. The atmosphere can differ little from that of an Angkorian palace. A woman is holding a baby in front of the young goddess, as the nurses of royal infants must have done.

125 King Kamsa's Palace, Banteay Srei (third quarter of the tenth century). In the palace of Mathura, Krishna puts to death his cruel uncle, king Kamsa, who had so often tried to take his life while he was a child. Terrible confusion reigns. The palace is built of wood and richly carved. The first story rests on columns which serve, no doubt, as piles; garlands hang between these columns. Upstairs the great hall is flanked by smaller rooms; behind Krishna, the sculptor has shown the folds of a hanging.

like a Gangā [come down from heaven] after her asceticism.... She poured out gratitude by dispensing the king's wealth on earth; and the king himself dispensed the riches... belonging to the queen: they were well known for helping each other....Charitable, she placed the essence of her wealth at the

disposition of the gods and the poor... by gifts of food and by lamps for the cult worthy of the royal treasure." Unfortunately her happiness can only have been short-lived. Perhaps exhausted by over-strict asceticism "although she was faithful to the love of her husband unto nirvāna, she entered nirvāna

straight away after her master had been invested with the midday rites." There are several female statues, all almost identical, discovered in different temples in the Bayon style, that may represent Jayarājadevī; it is known that Indradevī had statues of her sister set up, as well as of the king and of herself.[96] These show a frail looking woman, with a slender bust, and thin face, just as we might imagine the first and younger of the two queens.

This death was surely deeply distressing to Jayavarman VII. "When this queen who was the joy of the world came in possession of nirvāna, her elder sister named Indradevī, having received the king's sacring, appeased the fire [of sorrow] which was burning the worlds." It is noteworthy that Indradevī is the only queen to be mentioned as receiving the sacring. The text she composed, in excellent Sanskrit, shows that Indradevī was a highly cultivated woman. She surpassed "with her grace, the grace of those who are endowed with much; with her knowledge, the intelligence of the philosophers; and with the splendor of her happiness, adverse fortune. In the Buddhist temple of Nagendratunga, the foremost in the land in religious science, and in that of Tilakottara, appointed Chief Instructress by the king, she instructed a crowd of women."[97] Furthermore, "placing the king's feet on her bowed head, and thus dominating the Gangā who, in anger, put hers on the head of Śiva, she bestowed the favors of the king upon the women enamoured of knowledge, in delicious nectars, in the form of learning. Intelligent by nature,

126 Statue presumed to be of Jayarājadevī, from Preah Khan, Musée Guimet (late twelfth-early thirteenth century). While the future Jayavarman VII was fighting in Champa his wife, Jayarājadevī, practiced harsh austerities. Once he had thrown back the invader and re-established peace, he was not reunited with his queen for long, because she died. He then married the elder sister of the deceased queen, Indradevī, who set up several statues to Jayarājadevī.

127 *Devatā*, Banon (late twelfth century). The face of this *devatā* is serious, as though conscious of her responsibility as she guards the sanctuary of Banon. She wears a draped skirt with long embroidered flaps, and the edge turned down round her waist to make a corolla. Her tiara and necklace, however, have been left without carving the detail. She holds a lotus stem that twines over her shoulders, between her two hands.

wise, very pure, devoted to Śrī Jayavarmadeva...
and leaving aside all other talent, she shines with
brilliance."

On the reliefs in the temples, queens and princesses
are figured beside the kings. Their garments and
jewels scarcely differ from those worn by the loveliest
devatā, carved on the sanctuary walls. Each has a
diadem on her brow; often the knot of hair is covered
with a cone of worked gold. In the twelfth century
an extremely elegant coiffure was adopted by some
of them; still wearing the diadem they adorn their
hair with three branches of flowers, probably of
precious metal incrusted with gems. At the end of the
century this floral decoration changed into a triangular motif adorned with rosettes and plumes. To the
broad collars carved with rosettes and hanging with
pendants, they add a belt-necklace made of two bands
of worked metal, crossed over the chest between the
breasts; sometimes they wear a row of pearls instead
of this gold or silver band. In the thirteenth century
pearls or beads were very fashionable for jewelery.

At court the princes came immediately below the
king in rank. Though only the king is entitled to wear
cloths with close floral designs, the princes can wear
floral designs, but sparser ones. They have certain
privileges, such as the right to use the passage of
honor to cross the enceinte of certain temples. The
king could grant the title of *yuvarāja* to the crown
prince. However, the title cannot always have been
attributed solely to the heir to the throne, for Jayavarman VII bestowed it on a Cham prince whose
loyalty he felt had survived the test.

A large staff was employed to serve in the palace.
"As for the concubines and daughters of the palace,
I have heard numbers mentioned of between 3,000
and 5,000, divided into several classes....Every family with a pretty daughter tries to get her into the
palace. Below them are the women who do service,
called *ch'en-chia-lan;* there are no less than a thousand
or two. They are married and live anywhere. But
they shave their hair high above the forehead... and
mark this place with vermilion, and both sides of
their temples; this is their distinguishing mark. Only
these women may enter the palace; no one beneath
them may do so. The *ch'en-chia-lan* are always about

in great numbers on the roads in front and behind the
palace." All important functions of this service were
entrusted to women of comparatively high rank. One
inscription at Phnom Prāsāt Preah Nat Preah praises
one of these women who was a florist at the palace:
"In this town was born the [lady] named Madhya-
deśā, in whom, as in Parameśvarī, were united the
good, the agreable and the useful. She was the most
virtuous among women of virtue....Because of her
beauty and her intelligence among women, she was
florist at the royal palace." These women had always to be dressed with elegance and richly adorned.
Diadems and hair-knot coverings of metalwork were
probably reserved for princesses. The women of the
palace, like the lower ranking *devatā*, had to wear
their costumes smartly draped; jewels adorned their
necks, arms and ankles. They put flowers or metal
pins in their plaits, which they lifted to frame the
face, or knotted on the top, leaving a few locks
hanging.

The female staff in the royal entourage also comprised
dancers and musicians. In the palace scenes the
artists have often carved dancers performing ballets
to the music of an orchestra of young women; these
latter sing, play the harp, the little Khmer violin, and
a monocord of one or two gourds, an instrument
related to the Indian *vīnā*. The dancers and musicians
are very elegantly dressed and wear tiaras like princesses; the dancers wear short *sampot* which leave
them free to move.

There were also many men employed in royal service.
Beside the ordinary palace officials who were only
allowed to wear cloth "with two groups of flowers"
the high dignitaries had clothes "with scattered floral
designs." Plenty of inscriptions trace the careers of
officials, informing us of the titles with which they
were honored. But unfortunately it is impossible to

128 Girl dancers and musicians, Banteay Srei (third quarter
of the tenth century). Here a young woman is dancing, accompanied by two girls playing the cymbals. The graceful movement of the arms and the feet tapping the ground to mark the
rhythm are closely observed. The three young women wear a
hair-bun coiled on the side of the head, a characteristic hair
style of the women at Banteay Srei.

work out the hierarchy of these officials, or even to know what duties these appointments carried. Young men recruited from the greatest families in the kingdom saw, as pages, to the immediate service of the king. Some officials were seconded to the royal treasury with such titles as "guardian of the holy registers," "treasury steward," or "treasury inspector." There were others, such as "chief of the storehouses," who were in charge of the palace warehouses.

The king rewarded those who served him well with higher and higher office. Inscriptions describe the successive promotions of certain people. The reasons for these promotions are not always what might be expected. In one inscription, unfortunately mutilated, the members of a family, recalling the high deeds of their ancestors, record this exploit of one of them: "In the reign of His Majesty Paramavīraloka; Lon Vijaya, our maternal ancestor, was chief of the arsenals. His Majesty Paramavīraloka ordered him to smite a fierce bullock; at the first stroke the handle broke..." All the same Lon Vijaya must have slain the beast, for "the king deigned to confer on him the name of Śrī Vīraparākrama, to give him land, with the office of guardian of the bedroom at Vnur, and a rank in the pages' corps as Senāpati [army chief]."[98] The functions of guardian of the bedroom of the king, and guardian of the royal couch must have been entrusted to persons very close to the king, but we have nothing to go on in deciding what their functions were. Another rather surprising title is that of "inspector of qualities and faults." As J. Boisselier has pointed out, respect for the *dharma* needs watching over, both among the living and the gods. In Indian mythology, this was done by the four Mahārājikka, gods of the four cardinal points, who come to report to the thirty-three gods seated in council on Mount Meru under the presidency of Indra.

130   Buddha seated on the *nāga* (late twelfth-early thirteenth century). This Buddha seated on a *nāga* was found lying among other pieces in a cave. The Blessed One sits with legs crossed on the coiled body of the serpent Muchilinda. His hands rest in his lap. The faintly smiling face is of great gentleness.

Some appointments belonged to professional families; we find trace in the epigraphy of the rise of families of doctors, artists and also of archivists, one of which keeps the manuscripts concerning the Kambu family and the various departments of the royal household, manuscripts concerning the high deeds of the sovereigns, "from His Majesty Chrutavarman to those of His Majesty Śrī Sūryavarmadeva. ...The collection of these holy writings is conserved [through its care] on sheets deposited at Śrī Chikhareśvara [Preah Vihear]...."

High sacerdotal functions at court belonged to members of the great Brahman families, famous for their learning, particularly their knowledge of the Indian texts. High Brahman dignitaries exercised their influence on king and court according as they were *purohita, hotar* who were in charge of reciting the

129   Dvārapāla, Banteay Srei (third quarter of the tenth century). The central shrine of Banteay Srei is carved on the walls with figures of young men acting as *dvārapāla*, "door guardians." In Khmer art the *dvārapāla* are generally given a rather repulsive aspect, but at Banteay Srei they are young and elegant, as the pages must have been who are mentioned in the inscriptions.

sacrificial formulae, *āchārya* or *guru*. With their knowledge of the Veda and the magic and mantic texts, the *purohita* were attached to the person of the prince in the capacity of chaplains. This was the title granted by Jayavarman II to the Brahman Śivakaivalya who was put in charge of the cult of the *devarāja*. The *guru*, like the *āchārya*, was a spiritual advisor; the education of the young prince was his most important function. The king sometimes conferred on this personage the title of *Vrah guru*, "Holy master." Generally after being the king's tutor the *vrah guru* presided over the ceremonies of his sacring. He was in charge of certain other ceremonies also; thus the *vrah guru* Vāmaśiva erected the central *lingam* at the foundation of Yaśodharapura. Among the *vrah guru* were two great politicians who virtually governed the Khmer kingdom: Yajñavarāha in the tenth century and Divākarapandita in the early twelfth century.

Yajñavarāha was a Brahman on his father's side, and through his mother the grandson of king Harśavarman I. He seems to have inherited the political gifts of his great grandfather, Yaśovarman. His cousin Rājendravarman bestowed on him the title of *vrah guru*. By the end of this sovereign's reign he was the leading figure in the kingdom. He built the temple of Banteay Srei. At the death of Rājendravarman and the accession of Jayavarman V who was still a child, he took over the reins of government and exercised a veritable regency. Even after the young king attained his majority the *vrah guru* continued to countersign all the edicts of "king Jayavarman, who was always advised by his *guru* and with his heart always disposed to favor him."

The most brilliant of political Brahmans was certainly Divākarapandita. He had a very long career and certainly merits the name of "king-maker." He entered the service of Udayādityavarman II at the time of the consecration of the Baphuon. When the king died he continued his offices for the new sovereign Harśavarman III. When Harśavarman disap-

peared from the political scene, the great Brahman favored the accession of Jayavarman VI to the throne, the founder of the Mahīdharapura dynasty, and legitimized his seizure of power by sacring him king. At the death of Jayavarman VI in 1107, Divākarapandita performed the same ceremony for Dharanīndravarman I, the brother of the king who had died who "without having desired royalty, when his younger brother the king returned to heaven, simply out of compassion and ceding to the prayers of the human multitudes bereft of a protector, governed the land with prudence."[99] Divākarapandita did not remain loyal to this unambitious monarch for long. When the young and brilliant Sūryavarman II revodlte against his uncle, he found the great Brahman at his side. When the unfortunate Dharanīndravarman died on the field of battle, Divākarapandita proceeded once more to the sacring of a sovereign. Heaped with honors by Sūryavarman II, he was then charged to take offerings in the name of the king to several sanctuaries in the kingdom, and first of all to Wat Phu. He went; but he must have been very old. It was more than fifty years since he had taken service with Udayādityavarman II. He died while still enjoying all honors, during the reign of Sūryavarman II.

Although the celebration of Hindu ceremonies was not stopped by the accession of the Buddhist king Jayavarman VII, the dignitaries of the great priestly families no longer played the role allotted to them during the three preceding centuries. Jayavarman VII reorganized the kingdom along very different lines. As a Buddhist he in no way rejected the Brahmanic deities. He regarded them as deities of the terrestial world who should have their place in the protection of his kingdom, but he did not consider any of them as a supreme deity. The Brahman high priests continued to preside over the ceremonies, but they had very little influence on the government of a king whose personality would never brook such an ascendency over his own power.

JAYAVARMAN VII AND THE REORGANIZATION OF THE KINGDOM

At the beginning of the twelfth century Jayavarman VII reigned over Cambodia after reconquering his kingdom from the Cham, now reduced to vassal status. Before the Cham invasion of 1177 he had had no opportunity to play a leading role. At the time of the usurpation by Tribhuvanādityavarman, he was fighting in Champa and was unable to intervene in favor of Yaśovarman II. Only after the Cham had invaded Cambodia, put the usurper to death and occupied the capital could Jayavarman VII press the right to the throne he held from his mother, a descendent of the old pre-Angkorian dynasties. Having driven out the Cham he had himself anointed king in the capital he had undertaken to rebuild.

Jayavarman VII seems to have been haunted by the fear that the catastrophe of 1177 might be repeated. All his work was dominated by a determination to make such a disaster impossible in the future. He saw to the material means of defence, but all material is in its essence impermanent; in consequence such precautions are illusory. Religious protection, to his mind, was the only effective one. That provided for Angkor by his predecessors had shown itself to be impotent; it was therefore necessary to find a superior system, without destroying what had been done previously; for that, though defective, remained the work of his predecessors. To destroy what they had done would have been a slur on the legitimacy of the whole Khmer monarchy. J. Boisselier has demonstrated how Jayavarman VII, taking Buddhist texts as a foundation, superposed a politico-religious organization that he thought indestructible on a system that had crumbled. We will do no more here than quote some of the conclusions drawn by J. Boisselier in the long study he has made of the work of Jayavarman VII.

In founding Phnom Bakheng, Yaśovarman had es- fig. 57 tablished a Mount Meru in the center of Yaśodharapura. Jayavarman VII made the whole of Angkor Thom into the Trāyastrimśa, the dwelling of the thirty-three gods, situated at the top of Mount Meru, over which Indra reigns. In the same way as the *asura* of Buddhist legend gained no more than a transitory victory before being thrown down from Mount Meru by the gods led by Indra,[100] so the Cham invasion of 1177 had only temporary success and was followed by the dazzling victory of Jayavarman VII. From its foundation the Royal Palace of Angkor was regarded as the palace of Indra. Besides the palace the city of Indra comprised, in its center, the Sudharmasabhā, the council chamber where the gods hold well-ordered assembly every month on the eighth day of the moon; the four Mahārājikka, the kings of the four cardinal points, surround them. Brahman Sanatkūmara, the "Ever young" then comes down from a higher heaven and, multiplying his appearances, stands beside each god. The Bayon might fig. 78 be this assembly hall of the gods in Angkor. Against any new offensive by the *asura*, the four Mahārājikka keep watch over each of the five gates of the city; thus Angkor Thom is a replica of the city of Indra in the center of the Trāyastrimśa.

In order to assure the permanence of the kingdom for the duration of the present *kalpa*, the present cosmic period, the king caused the basin of Neak Pean to be built, figuring Lake Anavatapta, a mythical lake in the Himalaya which will be the last place on earth to go dry at the end of the *kalpa*. The kingdom which possessed this marvelous lake should remain unshakeable until the end of the *kalpa*.

It is from Lake Anavatapta that the water must be taken for the ablutions of the *chakravartin* king, the universal monarch.[101] All Khmer kings aspired to be *chakravartin* kings. The model adopted by Jayavarman VII was the Indian emperor Asoka who is regarded as a *chakravartin* king. A universal monarch shows on his body the marks identifying him as an exceptional being; marks which he alone bears, apart from the Buddha. A power emanates from him which forces his enemies to bow of their own accord before his superiority, without fighting. Lastly the *chakravartin* king must multiply pious works, some of which can only be carried out by a universal monarch. The inscriptions mention the existence of such marks on Jayavarman VII's body and the confusion of enemies in his presence. The charitable foundations conform to the image of the *chakravartin* monarch held by this king. It is this conception of royalty which, in a Buddhist spirit, inspired in Jayavarman VII his infinite compassion for all suffering and made him say that he was more affected by the maladies of his subjects than by his own sufferings.

fig. 131 The king had a duty to live sumptuously as well as to be accessible to his people. Doubtless the royal audiences of the late thirteenth century differed little from those in the reign of Jayavarman VII. The scene of these audiences was splendid: "the council chamber has window frames of gold; to right and left are square columns bearing forty or fifty mirrors set on the sides facing the windows. Below are representations of elephants.... Twice every day the king gives audience for government affairs. No list is drawn up. Those among the officials and the people who wish to see the prince sit on the ground and wait for him. After a certain time you hear far-off music in the palace; and outside they blow conches to welcome the king. I have heard it said that he only used a gold palanquin; he does not come from far. A moment after, you see two of the palace girls lifting the curtain with their slender fingers and the king, holding a sword in his hand, appears at the golden window. The ministers and people hold their hands together and touch the ground with their foreheads; when the conches have ceased sounding they may raise their heads. According to the king's pleasure they come up and sit down near him. At the place where one sits down, there is a lion skin which is regarded as a royal object. When business is over the prince turns round; the two palace girls let the curtain fall; everyone rises."

The throne room with its pillars hung with mirrors, its gilded windows and precious hangings, has disappeared. We can no longer admire more than the terraces which probably supported it. Yet this lovely terrace, supported by atlantes, lions and *garuda* and carved with the wonderful elephant frieze, allows some idea of the luxury and splendor of the palace buildings. It may be that the tall pyramid of the Phimeanakas in the center of the royal enclosure did not every night witness the visit of the king coming to unite with the *nāgī*, but in the morning the priests certainly climbed the steep steps of the stairways to carry out the rites of homage to the god. While, in the administrative buildings, the mandarins and officials applied themselves gravely to their duties; in the courtyards of the private apartments the sandstone-bordered pools reflected gilded pavilions and the brightly draped silhouettes of the princesses and their attendants. In these years of the early thirteenth century, Jayavarman VII might well consider the splendor of his palace with some confidence, this center of the capital he had rebuilt as a city of the gods and hoped to make indestructible, "for as long as the sun and the moon endure."

131 Scene in Paradise, Angkor Wat, Gallery of Heaven and Hell (first half of the twelfth century). Having undergone the judgment of Yāma a man is residing in a celestial palace, upheld by *garuda*. He wears the ornaments and garments of a prince. Women press round him, among whom his wife is recognizable by her tiara. This king appears surrounded by a female court, like the king of Cambodia in the audiences described by Chou Ta-kuan.

132 The Great Avenue, Angkor Wat (first half of the twelfth century). Angkor Wat has always been the most important sanctuary of Cambodia. Pilgrims have never ceased to come to worship the holy images there. Two Buddhist monasteries have been established within the very enceinte of the temple. Often at nightfall, the monks go to meditate in the deserted galleries, while some worshiper lights a lamp in the central shrine to shine afar until day breaks.

Part four:

LIFE IN THE TEMPLES AND CEREMONIALS

ASCETICS IN THE FOREST

The texts of inscriptions are all of religious inspiration, and together with the representations in the temples bear witness to the two cults practiced in Cambodia, Hinduism and Buddhism. Their study throws some light on the philosophical systems and sects that were followed in the country. Both religions were introduced into Cambodia at the beginning of the Hinduisation of southeast Asia, in the first centuries of the Christian era. Until the accession of Jayavarman VII all the sovereigns seem to have been Hindu. The posthumous name of Sūryavarman I, Paramanirvānapada, made earlier scholars believe that this king was a Buddhist, but in fact the term *nirvāna*—extinction, final liberation from material life—is not purely Buddhist and, in the sense of absorption into the supreme godhead, may well form part of the posthumous name of a Hindu. For the most part, the kings of Angkorian Cambodia were Śivaites, although Sūryavarman II was a Vishnuite; his posthumous name Paramavishnuloka confirms this, as does the iconography of the temple of Angkor Wat,[102] his great foundation. But while Hindu monarchs succeeded each other on the throne, Buddhism was being practiced by a considerable number of Cambodians, and by people of some quality. We have seen how in the mid-tenth century Rājendravarman II entrusted the conduct of works in the Eastern Mebon and the Royal Palace to a Buddhist dignitary.

With the accession of Jayavarman VII Cambodia came under the rule of a fervent Buddhist. The Buddhism of Cambodia in this period was still Mahāyāna. But the Brahman cults continued and in many temples the artists carved not only images of the Buddha and of *Bodhisattvas* but representations of the Hindu gods and the myths concerning them. There is nothing surprising in this, since the gods of Brahmanism have their place in Buddhist cosmology. On the walls of the Bayon and Preah Khan the sculptors depicted the most famous Brahman myths; the dance of Śiva, the sleep of Vishnu, the exploits of Rāma at the battle of Lanka and of Krishna destroying monsters or raising up Mount Govardhana, together with episodes in the life of the Buddha and representations of *Bodhisattvas*. In the thirteenth century Cambodia turned to Theravāda Buddhism, the doctrine of the Ancients (Monks) deriving from the creed abusively termed Hinayāna, "Lesser Vehicle of progress towards salvation." With the introduction of this doctrine the images of *Bodhisattvas* disappeared, but Brahmanic representations were not abandoned. In most Angkorian Buddhist temples the images of the Buddha have been hacked down, and the *Bodhisattvas* mutilated and sometimes transformed into Brahmanic deities. It has been suggested that after the reign of Jayavarman VII there was a reaction by the Brahmans and a wave of iconoclasm. There is no record of any such movement.

133 Hermit chased by a wild beast, the Bayon, inner gallery (late twelfth-early thirteenth century). Soldiers are marching through a forest where hermits dwell. One of these, chased by a wild beast, is scaling a tree trunk while one of his fellows, clinging to a creeper, seems to be giving him advice. The scene of the hermit chased by a great feline appears more than once in the reliefs of Khmer art. The artists have rendered with humor, and perhaps with some malice, the terror of the holy man, curling up in his efforts to get out of the animal's reach.

The description of the religious situation in Cambodia by Chou Ta-kuan has its picturesque side: "The scholars are called *pan-ch'i;* the bonzes are called *ch'u-ku;* the Taoists are called *pa-ssu-wei*. I do not know whom the *pan-ch'i* worship. They have nothing resembling a school or any place of instruction. It is difficult to know what books they read. They go about dressed like other people except for a rope of white thread that they wear round their necks; it is the distinctive mark of scholars. The *pan-ch'i* who enter public service rise high. The neck cordon is worn throughout life." As E. Aymonier has already observed, the word *pan-ch'i* certainly comes from *pandita*. The white Brahman cord that they have to wear all their life leaves no doubt of this identification of the *pan-ch'i* with the Brahmans. As we know, Brahmans could be appointed to the highest posts. They were certainly scholars. Though they may have transmitted some of their knowledge by word of mouth, they possessed great numbers of texts written in Sanskrit, evidently inaccessible to a Chinese.

"The *ch'u-ku* shave their heads, wear yellow clothes, leave their right shoulder uncovered; they knot a skirt of yellow cloth over the lower part of the body and go barefoot. Their temples may be covered with tiles. The interior only contains one image, entirely similar to the Buddha Śākyamuni and which they call *po-lai*. It is clothed in red. Made of clay, it is decorated with vermilion and blue: that is the only image in the temples. The Buddhas of the towers are different, however, and all cast in bronze. There are no bells, no drums, no cymbals, nor *ex-voto* of hanging silk, nor dais. All the bonzes eat fish and meat, but drink no wine. For their offerings to the Buddha, they also use fish and meat. They have one meal a day, prepared in the household of a host, for there is no kitchen in the temples. The texts they recite are very numerous; they all consist of palm leaves very regularly piled. On these leaves they write black characters, but as they use neither brush nor ink I do no know what they write with. Some bonzes also have the right to the shaft of a palanquin and a parasol handle of gold or silver; the prince consults them in serious cases. There are no Buddhist nuns."

This description of the bonzes and the life they lead is perfectly applicable to Buddhist discipline as it has remained until modern times. The only meal the bonzes take each day must be offered them by the faithful, either at the morning collect, or in the house of a donor, if the priests have been invited on the occasion of a ceremony. The prohibition on wine drinking, and the permission to eat fish and meat are still in force. The distinction between two types of temple is interesting. The first type of building, covered with tiles and so probably built of light materials, and containing only the image of the Buddha Śākyamuni, might well correspond to a Theravādin Buddhist sanctuary. The "towers" presumably are the Mahāyānist temples of stone in which images of the Buddha and *Bodhisattvas* were venerated.

The identification of the third group of religious named by Chou Ta-kuan is more difficult. "The *pa-ssu-wei* wear ordinary clothes, except for a piece of red or white cloth that they wear on their heads like the *ku-ku* of Tartar women, but a bit lower. They have temples also, but smaller than those of the Buddhists: Taoism has not become as prosperous as Buddhism. Their only cult image is a stone which is rather like the stone of the altar of the god of the earth in China. I do not know whom they worship either. There are Taoist nuns. Taoist temples may be covered with tiles. The *pa-ssu-wei* will not share food with other people and do not eat in public. They drink no wine. I have not seen them reciting prayers or accomplishing meritorious exercises for their fellow men."

This description leaves many points obscure. The name *pa-ssu-wei* itself is difficult to explain. We do not know what the headdress of Tartar women was like; some ascetics shown on the reliefs have their topknot wrapped in cloth; perhaps the text refers to something of this kind. P. Pelliot thought that the block of stone as a cult object might be a *lingam*. Perhaps the *pa-ssu-wei* belonged to a Brahmanic sect? L. Finot suggests they were adepts of the Śivaite sect of Pasupata.

Hermits must have existed in Cambodia at this period and long before. Representations of ascetics, *rishi*, are numerous in both pre-Angkorian and Angkorian art. Some, both carved in the round and in relief were placed in the superstructures of *prāsāt;* some can be

134 Preah Khan, chapel near the central shrine (late twelfth-early thirteenth century). This wall of a chapel in Preah Khan is decorated with a forest landscape surrounding five hermits seated in meditation under arches. The arches probably signify shelters into which these religious have retired to meditate, taking up a *yogin* posture with crossed legs and hands held together in front of the chest.

seen at Banteay Srei. On the bases of pilasters *rishi*
frame the entries of sanctuaries; on the walls of the
little chapels of Preah Khan they sit meditating under
a series of arcades arranged in friezes, in the midst of
a decoration of foliage. Some places venerated in
Cambodia, such as Phnom Kulen and the rocky
spikes perforated with caves in the region of Kampot
or Battambang, have sheltered hermits to this day,
and sometimes women hermits as well. The texts of
the inscriptions give very little information about
eremetical life. The reliefs of the Baphuon, of Angkor
Wat and the Bayon however have many scenes showing hermits living in the forest.

Rishi might live in isolated hermitages, alone or with
their families. The Vessantara Jātaka, the last incarnation but one of the Buddha, provided the artists with
the theme of the hermit-prince who, with his wife and
children, adopted this way of life. More numerous
are the representations of hermits grouped round a
master in a hermitage, an *āśrama*. Young people come
to them for instruction, like Rāma and Lakshma to
the sage Viśvamitra. Some *āśrama* form vast forest
dwellings. Pupils crowd round the spiritual master
to receive the word of wisdom, while other disciples
set apart devote themselves to the practice of yoga.
Standing on one leg with the other foot against his
ankle, his left arm raised, with a rosary in his right
hand, an ascetic remains motionless "turned into a
pillar" in a posture of austerity well known in
India.

Rishi must not neglect the duties of the cult. First and
foremost they have to maintain the flame in the fire
hut. Under a little shelter attached to an *āśrama* in the
midst of the forest, a Brahman is cutting small firewood for the fire into which milk will be poured at
the ceremony of the *agnihotra*, the "fire offering";
this sacrifice must be offered twice a day, at sunrise
and in the evening when the first star appears.

Rishi also have to attend to all their material needs;
they feed the cows, churn butter, gather plants and
roots in the forest. Animals gather round them without fear. Rabbits frisk all around, monkeys play in
the trees, deer dash into thickets. It is curious to note
that the artists have sometimes enjoyed showing the
hermits with less than perfect reverence on the reliefs, putting them in uncomfortable and humorous
situations. One scene repeated several times shows a
hermit running away from a tiger and climbing a
little tree while the beast sniffs hungrily at the holy
man. In scenes showing the *bhikṣātanamūrti* of Śiva
there are *rishi*, over-vain of their merits, put in the
rather ridiculous role of jealous husbands whose
wives have fallen madly in love with a naked hermit
who is no other than Śiva himself. On a relief at
Angkor Wat showing this scene, the *rishi* are made
to show their rancor by grotesque gesticulations.
The Khmers respect holy hermits, but the cowardly
ascetic, too sure of himself and hypocritical, can be
cruelly pilloried.

When the reliefs show hermits living in monastic
buildings surrounded by trees it is hard to know if
the scene is taking place in a forest far from other
dwellings or in the park of a great sanctuary, for
some large temples were monasteries. Thus at Ta
Prohm there are rows of monks' cells built of stone
inside the enclosure of the domain.

LIFE IN TEMPLES AND MONASTERIES

To build a temple is the most generous gift that a devotee can make to a deity, since the temple is his dwelling place. Every religious building of any importance has to be built of brick or stone, laterite or sandstone. Such an enterprise required a large labor force and quite elaborate techniques.

Temple Building

When a sovereign or rich founder decided to build a sanctuary the master builder had first to seek out the materials. In the pre-Angkorian period builders used large bricks that might be anything up to 30 cm. long. Later they were always smaller. The bricks were carefully polished by friction all over the surface, then joined by a mastic composed mostly of vegetable matter. Though brick continued to be used until the end of the Angkorian period it had nothing like the status of stone in construction. The foundation bases and surrounding walls were always built of laterite, sometimes called limonite. This is a ferruginous clay which hardens after extraction. It forms a stone which is coarse but has a lovely fawn color. Sandstone is the noble material. Stone cutters went to extract if from the quarries of Phnom Kulen. The blocks were brought to the site by boat, sailing up the broad canals.

The technique used for setting the blocks in place is little known. The equipment was probably very simple, with rollers to slide the stone along, pegs, crampons, hoists and ropes. Cement was never used. Until the twelfth century the methods of assembling stone remained similar to those for wood; for example the angles forming frames for the bays were mitered. But the builders lacked confidence in using stone, so much so that in the eleventh century they adopted the habit of piercing holes in the non-decorative lintels so as to reinforce them, as they thought, by introducing beams into the cavities. The result was often disastrous; in the course of time the beams rotted and the lintels, reduced to hollow stone without their wooden armature collapsed under the weight of the walls they were supposed to support. In the twelfth century they gave up this procedure, but kept the technique of assembling blocks with mortice and tenon, or with recessed tongues, and jointing with double ties of sandstone and iron.

After laying all the courses of a *prāsāt*, the masons had to trim the blocks for decoration. They began at the highest parts, using the scaffolding set up for building. The decorative lintels and colonnettes were roughed out before being set in place. The dressed surfaces might receive a decoration of which the lines were first engraved with a point. For some motifs that were repeated they would probably use a stencil. From this engraved design the sculptors would gradually carve out stylized leaves, hooks, scrolls, chevrons, rows of lotus buds and zigzags. Some friezes, pilasters, arcades, and even guardian figures and relief scenes have been left unfinished and show the different states this work went through. Coatings of plaster covered brick walls and were given carved decoration. Metal sheets must have lined some bare walls in the most venerated sanctuaries. When Chou Ta-kuan mentions gold or copper towers he must means the existence of copper, gilt bronze or even gold sheeting on the roofs.

Shrines and Their Images

Kings and rich founders raised temples to their patron deities who would be worshiped in the central shrine, but the secondary shrines housed other gods. In the central tower of Pre Rup Rājendravarman II established: "this principal *lingam* named Śrī Rājendrabhadreśvara,"[103] surrounded by four deities, one in each of the four shrines at the angles of the upper terrace. The inscription enumerates these images. The first is another representation of Śiva. "For his own prosperity, and as if it had been his own royal substance, he placed this Iśvara Rājendravarmeśvara in the region of Agni [southeast]." Then comes a statue of Vishnu: "And he has also made this Rājendraviśvarūpa, ravishing Hari, with the aspect of the Omnipresent, here in this [temple] which is like the heaping up of all the beauties of the three worlds." In the third shrine "he has set up the daughter of the mountain [Umā], protectress of fortune, so that Jayadevī, mother of Śrī Harśadeva, and younger sister of her mother, may obtain heaven." Lastly another image of Śiva was placed in the fourth shrine: "This king of kings has made this Iśvara Rājendravarmadeveśvara for the fortune of his junior, the king Śrī Harśavarman." Other deities were venerated on the lower levels of the temple. The text of the stele makes it clear that the images of Umā and of Rājendravarmadeveśvara had been erected in favor of the dead: the aunt of the king and his cousin Harśavarman II, who had died at Koh Ker after a reign of two years.

On the stele of Ta Prohm Jayavarman VII refers to the foundation of this temple, then called the Rājavihāra, the "royal monastery," a monument "whose limbs are adorned with gold and resplendent with gems." The text then enumerates the deities placed in the shrines: "He has erected Śrī Jayarājachudāmani whose body is brilliant with jewels, and in this one the image that he put up was that of his mother. ...He has set up the image of his *guru* and an entou-

135 *Devatā*, Prāsāt Sen Keo (second half of the eleventh century). Prāsāt Sen Keo is a monument in Baphuon style in the north of Cambodia. The sculptures decorating it are executed with extreme care. The *devatā* guarding the walls are very refined and their supple sinuous silhouettes betray some slight lassitude. This *devatā* holds her head bent down, her face meditative, with almond eyes elongated towards the temples; a faint, almost melancholy smile plays about her lips.

rage of 260 deities." It is interesting that the text of this latter stele gives a sort of description of the temple of Ta Prohm, listing among the donations made to the foundation: "39 pinnacle towers, 566 groups of stone dwelling houses, 288 groups of brick dwellings; 76 braces wide and 1,150 braces long in total for the long pool and the basin; 2,702 braces of surrounding wall in limonite [laterite]."[104] It is difficult to tell what these buildings correspond to, but it is strange to find them quoted in the inventory.

The Personnel of the Temples

Temple service employed considerable personnel. At Ta Prohm the inscription enumerates: "there are here 400 men, 18 principal officiants, 2,740 officiants, 2,232 assistants, among whom 615 women [who are] dancers; in total 12,640 persons, including those who have a right to lodging; 66,625 men and women perform there the service of the gods. In total 79,335 with the Burmese, the Cham, etc." One wonders how the author of the inscription arrived at such high figures. At Preah Khan the total attached to the temple is even more imposing: 97,840 men and women among whom "444 chefs; 4,606 servants, cooks and others; 2,298 serving girls, of which 1000 dancers; 47,436 individuals offering the oblation." The temple domains were certainly very extensive: 150 acres for Ta Prohm, 140 for Preah Khan. This however is very little for a population of 80,000 and more. Most of these people must in fact have lived in villages attached to the temple, though a considerable personnel probably lived inside or close to the enceinte. The only people attached to the shrines were those who carried out the cult ceremonies.

136 Statue of Śiva, Phum Bavel, Museum of Wat Po Veal, Battambang (late tenth-early eleventh century). Śiva is shown with two arms, according to Khmer iconographic tradition; movable attributes could be slipped into his half open hands. The god has the third eye on his brow and the crescent moon on his top-knot. This statue is of veined grey sandstone, and the carving of high quality; the expression of the face is gentle and benevolent.

The personnel, probably slaves, that saw to material needs was attached either to the service of the god, or to the service of the monks. The inscription of Kuk Roka specifically mentions the cooks of the god and those of the monks. Domestic staff also included women to grind grain, spinners, weavers of garments and rainy season rugs for the monks, and slaves whose functions are not described. Mention must also be made of the plantation keepers, the animal keepers and the slaves for the rice-fields.

fig. 128 The girl musicians, singers and dancers were also slaves but of much superior rank. Was their position that of the *devadasī* of Indian temples? In India these women were dedicated to the god from childhood; they were appointed to sing, to dance, to serve the image of the god, to fan him. As dedicated to the god they were sacred prostitutes; hierogamy was indeed a very ancient fertility rite, and the *devadasī* enjoyed great respect. Was it the same in Angkorian Cambodia? The sources at our disposal are absolutely silent on this subject, as on all that concerns the life of the personnel attached to the temples.

The Gifts Made to the Temples

In some inscriptions donors give long lists of their offerings to a shrine: clothes and food for the priests, cult objects and above all ornaments and clothing for the statues of the gods. When a founder had a temple built, he endowed it with lands and villages to ensure its revenue. Later other donors, often descendants of the founder, added further gifts, mainly rice, oil, butter.

Cult objects such as are listed in the inscriptions were extremely varied in nature. After founding the temple of Banteay Srei the celebrated Yajñavarāha offered, among other things, "cups in the form of skulls,[105] water vases, drinking vases of gold and of silver... jars, mirrors, spittoons; all the venerable utensils for the cult in and out of doors, covered in divers jewels and ornaments of price." Still in the tenth century, the stele of Prāsāt Komphus lists: five palanquins of gold, gold plate, a conch, four disks, a great silver ewer, two spittoons of silver, all

137 Frieze of girl dancers, Preah Khan (late twelfth-early thirteenth century). A frieze of celestial dancers, *apsarā*, is carved above the doors of a cruciform gallery at Preah Khan. Halls of the same type with the same decoration exist in several other great temples built during the reign of Jayavarman VII, particularly at Ta Prohm. These *apsarā* wear tall tiaras, necklaces, and metalwork chains crossed between their breasts; their *sampot* are short and draped with broad flaps. It may be that ritual dances were performed in these cruciform halls.

kinds of silver boxes, four mirror stands of silver, a great Chinese mirror, four gold handled parasols, two peacock feather fans, two silver candelabra, and in addition: a spoon, a ladle, two cruets for clarified butter, a libation cup and many other precious objects; to these gifts are added various utensils: red copper pots, door chains, holders for cow dung, standard lamps and divers musical instruments: gongs, conches, lutes and drums.

As time went on the accumulation of offerings added increasing luster to the ceremonies and increasing wealth to the temple treasuries, in which the gods' adornments were the most prized pieces. The authorities in charge of a monastery were in duty bound to see that it became "abundantly enriched" and to protect "the personnel as it increases."

The Workings of a Monastery

Some idea of how a great temple functioned can be gleaned from the foundation stelae; it is from Yaśo-varman I, however, that emanated the most interesting documents on this subject. Three inscriptions engraved at his behest are really foundation charters for three monasteries, corresponding to the three religious sects of the kingdom: Śivaite, Vishnuite and Buddhist. The three texts are very similar. They define the condition of the monks, their discipline, their cultural and charitable activities and what must be their behavior towards outsiders, guests or unfortunates who ask for asylum.

The stele of Prāsāt Komnap[106] concerns the foundation of the Vishnuite monastery and begins like a royal edict: "The king Śrī Yaśovarman who possesses the majesty of Vishnu has made this Vaishnavāśrama for the maintenance of the Vishnuites. Let this decree of the king Śrī Yaśovarman be observed in this hermitage by the Superior and by all the servants. This is [the king's command]."

The monastery is open to all Vishnuites worthy of being monks "who are solely attached to good conduct and study and have freed themselves from the duties of a householder; who continuously restrain their senses," and to those "who, during the rainy season, have no shelter elsewhere; who are satisfied with one meal a day." Discipline was very strict: "No Vishnuite of this Vaishnavāśrama is to have relations with a woman, even in the vicinity [of the hermitage], even if she is his legitimate wife." Those who live in the monastery and respect its rules are provided with their needs: "Three tooth-picks, a portion of husked rice, forty leaves of betel and six arec nuts... a bundle of firewood, all this will be given without fail to the Vishnuites." These allocations are greater for the masters and students and less for the young boys who no doubt assisted the monks.

All those presenting themselves as guests are to be received at the monastery by the Superior who "will carefully honor the guests and extend the hospitality. ...If the king comes here with his wives, he will take care to honor him as a god, according to the resources

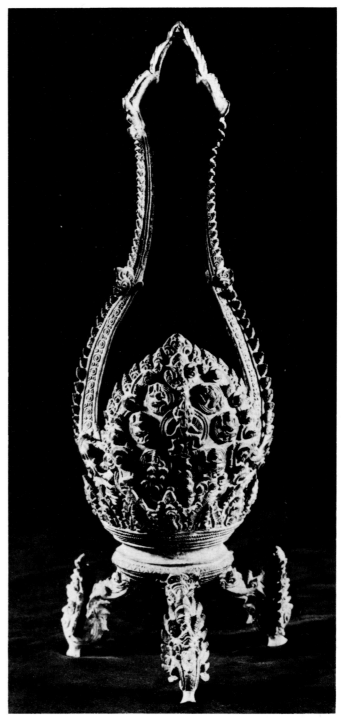

138 Bronze conch, National Museum, Phnom Penh (late twelfth-early thirteenth century). A large number of ritual bronzes has been found, primarily bells and conches. These latter will have been used as musical instruments or to hold water for dousing. This conch, supported on a tripod, is one of the finest pieces of Angkorian bronze art. It is decorated with an image of a dancing Hevajra, a Mahāyānist Buddhist deity, surrounded by *apsarā*.

of the hermitage, for... who ever fails in respect to the king, the guru of the whole world, does not see his gifts, nor his sacrifices, nor his offerings to the spirits bear fruit. After the king, the Brahman shall be honored above all others; if there are several, account will be taken first of their conduct, then of their good qualities, lastly of their learning. The prince, the mandarin, the army chief, the nobleman shall be honored in the order here named.... Immediately after him who possesses the three Vedas shall be honored the master well versed in grammar; among masters of equal learning, preference shall be given to the one who observes celibacy....The daughter of the king, the granddaughter of the king, the old wives of the king, the well-born woman shall be honored here like the other guests, but they shall not go up into the cells." On the other hand, "women whose coquetry is notorious shall not be admitted here, even if they present themselves [to ask for] hospitality."

The Cult

"In the reign of His Majesty Paramavīraloka, I have sought out a stone [to make a] Śiva *lingam;* I have cast a Brahma; I have cast a Nārāyana riding on *Garuda;* I have cast a Gauripatīśvara riding on the bull. I have invited K.A. Vrah Guru to perform the installation ceremony, and I have given him elephants and horses as honorarium."[107] This text, engraved in the eleventh century, commemorates a gift of images and confirms the fact that in a newly constructed shrine the erection of the statue of the god was the occasion of a consecration ceremony of which unfortunately we know very little. It appears that the two most important consecration rites were the baptism (sprinkling with holy water) and the "opening of the eyes" of the image by engraving or placing the pupil on the eyeball. After accomplishing these rites it was declared that the image was inhabited by the god. The daily cult consisted in serving the effigy of the god as the master of the house; consequently it received ablutions and was anointed with oil and perfume. An inscription by Rājendravarman con-

cerns a donation of oils intended for anointing a statue. The attentions lavished on the image consisted further of offering it food, and as we have seen a cook might be delegated to its service. During the heat of the day it was fanned and in the evening the ministrants protected if from mosquitoes; some inscriptions mention among the gifts veils of Chinese silk for protecting the feet of the statues from mosquitoes. Then of course the effigies of the gods were also clothed and adorned.

When the idol is a *lingam,* it may be covered with a casing of gold or silver; a lining of precious metal may also cover the outflow carrying the water from the washing of the *lingam.* If the deity is anthropomorphic, it is decked with royal jewels. Some inscriptions contain long lists of jewels. One such text will suffice, the one engraved on the stele of Prāsāt Komphus. It lists the ornaments given to the "holy image of the queen-mother," no doubt the mother of Rājendravarman, depicted in the aspect of a divinity: 1 crown, 1 club, 2 pikes, 2 ear pendants, 1 necklet, 2 armlets, 1 buckler, 2 rings, "1 garment in gold in front and in silver behind with 26 jewels," 1 cord, 1 ring with a jewel, rosaries, 5 pearl necklaces and a drain sheath in silver. In the midst of his list the donor mentioned a club and a buckler; these are the attributes of the goddess Durgā Mahishāsuramardinī in whose aspect the queen mother must have been depicted.

All these marks of reverence were assigned to statues erected in shrines; but there were also, in Cambodia as in India, images for processions. A stele at Phnom Bayang mentions an "image in gold of Śambhu [Śiva] that is still borne on a shield."[108] The effigies carried in processions were generally gilt bronze statuettes, or even precious metal. The soil of the

139 Silver head of Vishnu, region of Wat Phu (seventh-eighth century). This splendid head of solid silver was discovered about ten years ago by two companions who tried to share it between them by dividing it into two with an axe. It entered the collection of the Princes of Champassak in this mutilated condition. The eyes must have been inlaid; gold leaf still covers the lips. From under his cylindrical mitre Vishnu's curly hair covers the nape of his neck. The very gentle face is lit by an ineffable smile.

fig. 139

ancient Khmer kingdom has not delivered up any images of precious metal except the wonderful silver head discovered near Wat Phu, but that is too large to have belonged to a portable statue. "Holy impressions," little Buddhist images impressed on gold or silver leaf are a much later form of votive offering. A considerable number of bronze statuettes up to some 50 cm. high do seem likely to have been portable images for processions, on the other hand.

Many deities set up in shrines were effigies of the dead, worshiped in the aspect of the deity into whom they had wished to be absorbed after their death. Such illustrious dead would have cults celebrated to their memory of course, but there were also rites performed to revere the other dead, even the humblest. The regulation of the Vishnuite monastery founded by Yaśovarman lays down that "at the moment of the offering to the spirits of the dead, in times of eclipse, and when, at the two equinoxes, there is a presentation of funeral cakes, an offering of a *khari* of husked rice shall be made for him who has sacrificed in the hermitage. Those who by devotion have fallen on the battle-field, the devotees who have rendered up their souls, those who have died without food, unfortunate, abandoned, in infancy or in old age; for all these shall be made at each month's end a funeral offering of cakes for which four *adhaka* of rice shall be used. The cakes shall be made in this hermitage, then they are to be carried all together and the offering shall be made right on the edge of the pool of Yaśodhara." These rites have not vanished, since the Cambodians have continued into modern times to make funeral offerings of cakes on the occasion of the feast of the dead.

The knowledge we now have of the cult ceremonies is very restricted. The authors of the inscriptions did not think of describing rites which every one of the priests and devotees, who performed them daily, knew thoroughly. Thus Yajñavarāha performed "every day, as regularly as eating, the offering of a garland of eight flowers to Śiva, oblations on the fire and yoga exercises. Each month, at the four phases of the moon, he lavished gold, garments and cows with swollen udders on the Brahmans."[109] Cows themselves received a cult. The statues of the Vishnuite monastery recommend the honoring of "a brown cow by presenting it with grass, and by rendering homage to it."

To be valid, these detailed rites, most of them inherited from India, had to be performed to the last letter, without fault. No doubt, just as in India, it was often not a Brahman who performed them, but Brahmans presided over the ceremonies and supervised their correct execution and could set right any errors committed by expiatory rites. They had knowledge of the texts and especially of the ritual books, for the *āśrama* and temples were centers of Indian culture.

THE CULTURAL ROLE OF TEMPLES AND MONASTERIES

From the start of the Hinduisation of southeast Asia, Indian religious texts penetrated Cambodia. In the following centuries the Khmer kingdom remained in constant contact with India and was aware of the doctrines being worked out there.

Philosophic and Literary Knowledge

The epigraphy provides plenty of evidence of the Indian contribution to philosophy and literature in the land of the Khmers. A late ninth century stele recounts how a Brahman savant of Cambodia learnt "the *shāstra* [from the mouth] of him who is called Bhagavat Śankara, and whose lotus feet are licked by those garlands of bees that are the heads of all the sages."[110] G. Coedès, who translated this inscription, thought that this Śankara was perhaps the Indian philosopher Śankarāchārya who lived in India in the late eighth and early ninth century. This philosopher of the Vedānta is known to have propagated his doctrine very widely, and his disciples made it known throughout India and even outside it.

There were other doctrines to have their adepts in Cambodia. Several inscriptions are by members of the Vishnuite sect of the Pāñcharātra. Yajñavarāha was also one "of the first in the knowledge" of various philosophical doctrines and had even studied the doctrine of the Buddha.

Indian literature was widely known in Cambodia, and it was highly appreciated. The author of the stele of Prāsāt Khna speaks of the pleasure to be enjoyed by listening to the recitation of the Mahābhārata and the other poems, with a joy "which would not have been given him by hearing a melodious song."[111] The reliefs in Khmer temples illustrating the episodes of the Rāmāyana, of the Mahābhārata and of some Purāna are evidence that the Khmers were acquainted with Indian epic. F. Martini has shown that they even assimilated the marvelous histories to such an extent that from the twelfth century the sculptors of Angkor Wat represented scenes belonging to a Cambodian version of the Rāmāyana.[112]

Instruction

This knowledge of Indian philosophical doctrines *fig. 140* and literature could be acquired by students from masters teaching in the *āśrama* and monasteries. The way student life was organized is laid out in the regulations of the monasteries founded by Yaśovarman. "The Vishnuites who have dedicated themselves to study shall receive each day, beginning with the young, and with the old, the necessary means of subsistence. Four tooth-picks, eight arec nuts, a portion... of husked rice, sixty betel leaves... and a bundle of firewood will be given to the master and to the celibate students....The rice shall not be given in grains, but cooked. Three bowls [of grains] will make ten bowls of boiled rice. The participants [to the distribution] shall be served in order. One jug, one incense-burner, one heating stove to serve for four months, shall be given individually to the master... the couch, the razor and the scissors shall be renewed every year in each cell. Once in their cells, the Vishnuites shall be no longer under the authority of the Superior." In addition "at the annual feast, and at the Five Feasts, an extra shall be added to the food."

Monastery rules also provide for the scholar's equipment: "the virtuous scholar shall receive virgin leaves, animal black and chalk." Chou Ta-kuan gives some additional information about writing materials: "Ordinary writing, like official texts, is done on deer skins, doe skins and others dyed black. According to their dimensions in length and width, everyone cuts them as he likes. They use a powder like Chinese 'white earth' and mold it into sticks called *suo*. Holding this stick they write characters that do not wear off on the parchment. When they have finished, they put the stick over their ears. The characters enable one to tell who has written them. If one rubs with something damp, they are obliterated....They always write from left to right and not from bottom to top." G. Groslier thinks that merchants who had to do their accounts and students who had to write exercises wrote with chalk on blackened skins; this support could be reused after the text had been removed with water. However, the rules of Yaśovarman's monasteries mention leaves and not skins as writing supports. Until recently religious and literary texts in Pāli or Khmer were engraved with a point on latania or fan-palm leaves, *cadjan*, prepared for this. After the text was engraved the *cadjan* were covered with animal black which slid off the smooth surface of the leaves but filled the engraved lines. In either case the scribe did not use either ink or brush, as the Chinese chronicler noted with astonishment, observing at the same time that the engraved leaves are arranged in regular piles. On the reliefs there are figures carrying long thin leaves stacked and thonged like the engraved manuscripts on fan-palm preserved in modern monasteries and at the Buddhist Institute of Phnom Penh.

The students were able to read written texts in the temples and monasteries, but they also received oral instruction. There is often mention in the epigraphy of knowledge received directly from the mouth of the *guru*. According to the Indian method the disciple listened and learnt by heart the master's teaching in order to understand it better. An inscription of 1041 A.D. recounts how a learned Brahman by the name of Chāla was charged by king Sūryavarman I to teach treatises of grammar to students in a monastery at the east of the capital. "Mounting to a raised seat he broadly dispensed instruction to his pupils every day, like the sun [calling out each day] by its light [the flowering] of the lotus." Hearing the explanations, superior to those of the other (teachers), that he gave of the texts of the treatises, the grammar students thought: "only the author [of this treatise] would be able to explain it like this."[113] The students had to learn conscientiously what the master said, but discussion was not forbidden and those who were "troubled by a dubious point" could turn to this *guru* who dissipated their doubts. "If the problem had not yet been resolved, this intelligent man, invited by the parents of the students, gave the solution straight away. Churned by the multitude of the learned, with the mountain of a great problem, the ocean of milk of his intelligence gave the sought-after meaning that had not yet been found."

Instruction was not reserved for men alone. The queen Indradevī is known to have surpassed "by her knowledge the knowledge of the philosophers... appointed Instructress in chief by the king, she always distributed instruction to the crowd of women. Established in the domain called Narendrāśrama, seductive by the studies [that were zealously followed there by] the king's wives; she shone there, surrounded by the constant respect of her pupils, beneficent for them, like Sarasvatī incarnate."[114]

Numerous Indian texts are mentioned in the epigraphy as being well known in Cambodia, but little is said about local literature. There was however some local writing, certainly in Sanskrit and possibly in Old Khmer as well. The epigraphic texts are the only Angkorian writings to come down to us; they are generally written in perfectly correct classical Sanskrit. The reliefs of Angkor Wat studied by F. Martini prove that by this time the Khmers had composed their own version of the Rāmāyana. An inscription at Banteay Srei recounts how Yajñavarāha

140 A spiritual advisor receives a layman, the Bayon, inner gallery (late twelfth-early thirteenth century). In the gallery of a monastery a *guru* receives a prince or noble. With his hands joined in a posture of respect, the latter listens to the Master's advice. This great Brahman seems to wear a case over his ascetic's top-knot; he is attended by several monks.

"encouraged the writing of little stories, he who knew the different languages and writings and wrote theatrical plays....By his poems and his fine actions he aroused the envy of the wise and noble living on other continents."[115] There was certainly a dramatic literature. Plays were performed on certain feast days; thus Jayarājadevī, the first wife of Jayavarman VII, commissioned her own dancers to act and give performances of scenes from the Jātaka. Dancers seem to have been already miming the marvels of legend at this period. The royal ballets of modern Cambodia inherited this tradition.

THE TEMPLE AS A REFUGE FOR THE UNFORTUNATE AND THE SICK

fig. 141 The god's dwelling should be open to all who suffer and come to ask for help. Temples are places of asylum for humans and also for animals: "If the innocent come trembling to seek refuge here they shall not be delivered over to their persecutors, and these shall not be allowed to seize them. Neither by deed, thought or word shall any one here be made to perish; nor shall anyone be pointed out to another who is pursuing him, either in or outside the hermitage. Of all inoffensive creatures, none shall be killed in the neighborhood of this hermitage, nor on the banks of this pool of Yaśodhara." The right of asylum is not only to be granted to the innocent, but sometimes to the guilty as well: "Even if they are guilty of repeated offences, the inhabitants of this place are not to be punished; but those who are pleased to hurt living beings are to be punished without mercy."

The sick must be able to seek succour at these holy places. Jayavarman VII was concerned with founding 102 hospitals in his kingdom to receive and treat the sick. On some of the sites where these hospitals stood have been discovered the steles bearing the foundation inscriptions of these charitable works. The texts of the different stelae are almost identical. The hospital is inseparable from a shrine in which is honored a Buddha from a world different from ours, Bhaishajyaguru who shines with the "brilliance of the beryl." When he was still a *Bodhisattva*, the future Bhaishajyaguru desired to become brilliant as a beryl when he attained the Supreme Awakening; he also made a wish that simply by invocation of his name the sick should be given back their health. The image of this Buddha, sometimes called the "Buddha of medicine," is carved on the pediments of the little shrines attached to hospitals.

The texts of the hospital stelae define the organization of each of these establishments. We will quote from the stele of Say-feng[116] which is close to Vientiane in Laos, and one of the northernmost points reached by the Angkorian kingdom. The text of this inscription mentions the persons employed by the hospital: nursing staff and servants. The hospital is open to the four castes. Two doctors are to attend to each caste; they are assisted by a man and two women "with a right to lodging." The personnel also includes: "two dispensers responsible for the distribution of remedies, receiving the measures of rice. Two cooks, with a right to fuel and water, who have to tend the flowers and the lawn, and to clean the temple... fourteen hospital warders, entrusted with the administration of the remedies... two women to grind the rice." As the hospital is a religious foundation, "two sacrificers and one astrologer, all three pious, are to be named by the Superior of the royal monastery. Every year each of them shall be provided with the following: three coats and three lengths of cloth, fifteen pairs of garments, three pewter vases." In addition they were to receive paddy, wax and pepper. The sick are to be fed with "the rice forming part of the oblation to the deities [fixed] at one bushel a day" and with the remains of the sacrifices.

The text next gives a long list of the medicaments placed by the king at the disposition of the sick: honey, sesame, clarified butter, a mixture of pepper, cumin and rottleria tinctoria, musk, asafoetida, camphor, sugar, "aquatic animals," turpentine, sandal-

wood, coriander, cardamum, ginger, kakola, origano, mustard seed, senna, curcuma aromatica of two kinds, etc.

The sites of most of the hospitals have been lost. At Angkor, the shrines built beside two of these establishments are still standing, Ta Prohm Kel, south of Phnom Bakheng and near Angkor Wat, and the Hospital Chapel beside the temple of Ta Keo.

All these Cambodian religious foundations, whether Brahman or Buddhist, were thought of as beneficent for their donors and for the kingdom. In one of the final stanzas of the hospital stele of Say-feng, Jaya-varman VII expresses the hope that his posterity will not abandon this pious work and will acquire the merits of it: "Filled with extreme sympathy for the good of the world, the king, furthermore, expressed this wish: all the beings plunged in the ocean of existences, may I draw them from it by virtue of this good work! May the kings of Cambodia, devoted to the good, who protect this foundation, attain, with their posterity, their wives, their mandarins, their friends, the abode of deliverance, where there is no more sickness! May they, with heavenly women, who arouse the pleasure of love, who abound in divine delights, disport themselves, clothed in a divine body, in all corners of space...." Note that this abode of delights promised to the kings is not *nirvāna* but one of the heavenly dwellings where those reside who are reborn among the gods.

141 Suppliant, Angkor Thom, Royal Terrace, relief of the five-headed horse (late twelfth-early thirteenth century). Monasteries were obliged to receive all the destitute who came and asked for asylum. This person imploring the protection of the warriors of the Five-headed Horse is in the likeness of the unfortunate who came for help to the monks. Hardly defining the body of this suppliant figure, the sculptor has concentrated all the interest on the expression of the face, with its asymmetrical eyes, lips half open, and the protruding tongue of a man dying of thirst.

THE FEASTS OF THE YEAR

There is very little to be learnt from the epigraphy about the feasts that punctuated the year's course. Fortunately Chou Ta-kuan is more explicit. Nowadays the Cambodian New Year is fixed in the middle of the month of April, but in the thirteenth century the first Khmer month corresponded to the tenth Chinese month, so it was in October–November. The beginning of the New Year was a time of great rejoicing: "In front of the palace they set up a great platform to hold more than a thousand people. It is entirely covered with garlands and flowers. Opposite, about twenty *chang* away, they heap up wooden uprights and assemble them into high scaffolding, like the masts for building *stūpas* and more than twenty *chang* high. Every night they built three or four, or five or six. At the top they put rockets and fire crackers. This expense is borne by the provinces and noble houses. When night falls the sovereign is requested to come and watch the show. They let off the rockets and bangers. The rockets can be seen for more than a hundred *li;* the squibs are as big as perriers, and they shake the whole town when they go off. The mandarins and nobles take part in the festivities with candles and betel nut; they spend a great deal. The sovereign also invites foreign ambassadors to the show. This goes on for two weeks, then everything stops." Such celebrations have not survived into the modern tradition. It is true that children used to let off crackers, but most of the festivities went on in the palace. Among the royal ceremonies marking the beginning of a new year one of the most important was certainly the baptism or dousing of the king. Chou Ta-kuan knows nothing about what went on in the pal-

ace. He attaches so much importance to the fireworks because he could see them. What he reports about other festivities is even less complete, but with such poor documentation as we have we must value what he can tell us. "Every month there is a feast. In the fourth month they 'throw the ball.' In the ninth, it is the *ya-lie;* the *ya-lie* consists in assembling the whole population of the kingdom in the city and passing it in review in front of the palace. In the fifth month they 'fetch the water of the Buddhas'; they collect the Buddhas together from everywhere in the kingdom, bring water, and wash them in the presence of the king. They 'sail boats on dry land'; the prince goes up into a belvedere to watch the festivity. In the seventh month they 'burn the rice.' At this time the new rice is ripe, they fetch it outside the south gate and burn it in honor of the Buddha. Innumerable women go to this ceremony in carriages or on elephants, but the king does not go. On the eighth month there is the *ai-lan; ai-lan* is to dance. They choose talented musicians who come to the palace every day to do the *ai-lan;* there are also pig and elephant fights. The prince invites the foreign ambas-

142 The Great Square of Angkor Thom. It is impossible to take a complete picture of the whole immense Square of Angkor Thom. It is bounded on the west by the Palace and the Baphuon, on the south by the Bayon, on the east by the Preah Pithu and the Towers of the Tightrope Walkers, prolonged by a long avenue as far as the North Gate. In the foreground rise the *nāga* of the terrace of Preah Pithu. The Towers of the Tightrope Walkers are strange oblong-plan buildings which are not shrines. According to Chou Ta-kuan it was here that litigants came to wait for a kind of Trial by Ordeal.

143 Polo players, Angkor Thom, Royal Terrace (late twelfth-early thirteenth century). On the north end of the terrace a large relief shows the different competitions associated with royal festivities. There are wrestlers, and polo players who brandish curved sticks and gallop on horses with bells jingling on the breastplate. Although the stone is eroded, the relief is still vigorous. The movements of horses and riders have rarely been so truthfully rendered.

sadors to watch. The feast lasts ten days. I don't remember what happens in the other months."

"Burning the rice" was an agricultural feast which we have already described. It is likely that the great feasts connected with agriculture were the occasion for royal ceremonies. Thus until a recent period the feast of "burning the paddy" was celebrated in the Royal Palace of Phnom Penh. The ceremony described by E. Porée-Maspéro is certainly a survival of the Angkorian feast. As in the thirteenth century, it was not presided over by the king. A Brahman took the sovereign's place; he was given the title "King of Makh," from the name of the month in which the feast was celebrated. "The Brahman went to the hall of public ceremony where he was formally doused with water 'to take misfortune upon himself.' He then mounted his elephant and the procession reformed, this time larger since it included the carts of the 'paddy processions' and a ballet troupe that mimed the harvest. Three times more they went round the paddy, then the temporary king was taken home. Two days later the King of Makh set fire to the paddy dolls; then they threw water to put it out. The grains of paddy thus grilled and 'refreshed' were distributed to the provincial governors who gave them to the sowers to mix with their seed. Some of this grain was put in the paddy of the royal granary that was trampled by the King of Makh. On that night, he abdicated."[117]

The ceremony of dousing images of the Buddha has remained; it is celebrated during the festivities of the New Year, not only in Cambodia, but throughout southeast Asia. It leads on, especially in Laos, to a dousing of monks and even to a general sprinkling of the whole population, in the midst of the public festivities.

Festivals were a pretext for all kinds of entertainments. On the north outer gallery of the Bayon a relief takes us into the midst of attractions like a real fair ground: processions of strange animals, jugglers, musicians. The only thing missing is the cock and boar fights that are carved on the south wall of the same gallery. On the right, a row of people is seated along a tribune watching a procession of animals among which can be made out deer, a rhinoceros, an ox carrying an ox-pecker bird on its back, a stilt bird, a water buffalo or perhaps a gaur. Other animals follow, in cages or held on leashes: a hare, a

fig. 143

fig. 97

little feline—tiger or panther—a large bird and lastly a monkey whose master is holding it with a belt. Is this a menagerie passing by the tribune? In some Indian ceremonies they used to make animals pass in procession. It is possible that the artist intended to show here one of these processions.

In the left part of the relief the atmosphere is that of a fair day. In the lower register two orchestras hem in the clowns; a harpist twangs the strings of his instrument, others bang cymbals, others clap their hands to mark the rhythm of a song; in each group one musician is playing a monocord with a double gourd rather similar to an Indian *vīnā*. In the center of the same register a man is lying on his back with his legs in the air turning a wheel with his feet; beside him another acrobat is holding three little men on his head and hands. The upper register is unfinished. On the left can be made out a group of wrestlers with bulging muscles: some are about to grapple, others are already in a clinch, while some have already bitten the dust. On the right a fencing duel is in progress. Between these two groups are tightrope walkers. This part of the relief is only sketched out, but one tight-

rope walker is recognizable carrying a yoke with two bundles hanging from it, to serve as a balancing pole.

The acrobats must have been performing on the *fig. 144* public square. In the palaces and temple enclosures women dancers mimed the sacred legends. On public holidays these more refined entertainments were probably also offered to the people at large, so that humble folk had a chance to watch and admire the sinuous girations of the richly decked ballerinas. Until quite recently the performances of the royal ballet at Phnom Penh were still highly prestigious. It was no rare occurrence for audiences to forsake the modern theater to watch the legendary wonders of the Rāmāyana brought back to life in an atmosphere of magic and dreams.

144 Dancers and musicians, the Bayon, outer south gallery (late twelfth-early thirteenth century). An orchestra accompanies an acrobatic dancer. He is raising one leg vertically and dancing with a pole in his hands. In the orchestra can be identified a harpist and a player on a calabash gourd monochord, rather similar to the Indian *vīnā*.

145 Statuette of a wrestler, National Museum, Phnom Penh. This little bronze, clearly later than the art of the Bayon, is of a surprising realism. The image has no unnecessary detail. The artist has rendered the effort and determination of the wrestler by depicting his wide eyes, swollen chest, clenched fists and elbows drawn back.

146   Angkor Wat, view on the three upper enceintes (first half of the twelfth century). The delicate silhouettes of a few sugar palm trees still rise near the cruciform terrace preceding the access to the gallery with the reliefs. The three upper surrounding walls are piled up in steps on the high base. The horizontal lines of the galleries contrast with the verticals of the shrines. The superstructures of these towers owe their characteristic "obus" shape to the large number of stories, tapering as they rise, and to the multiplication of indentations that break up the angles.

ROYAL CEREMONIAL

No yearly festival can have compared with the great royal ceremonies that celebrated the accession or demise of a sovereign, or again when the king had triumphed over his enemies and marched through his capital in a victory parade.

Royal Sacring

Virtually nothing is known about the procedure of a sacring ceremony. To this date the Cambodian epigraphy and Chinese texts alike have been consulted in vain. The only rite to be clearly mentioned is the *abhisheka*, the dousing with water. This act is certainly the most important of the whole ceremony, for the term by itself is used to describe royal consecration. The inscription of Pre Rup twice refers to this rite in its description of the sacring of Rājendravarman; "Consecrated [king] by the sprinkling of his head... he led the army of Kambu spread out in space like Kārttikeya leading the army of the gods"; and further on, alluding to the coolness of the king's body, the text mentions the same rite: "Just as the water of the *tīrtha* which adhered to his body at the time of the celebration of his sacring was reluctant to dry..." This last phrase confirms that the dousing water was drawn from a *tīrtha*, a holy basin; but which pool or which river was thus privileged we do not know. It might have been the river of Siem Reap which had been sanctified by flowing over the *lingam* carved in its bed. A pre-Angkorian sculpture, the lintel of Wat Eng Khna, depicts the *abhisheka* of a king. The sovereign, seated European style on a dais,

receives the water that is poured on his head by one Brahman after another. The Indian texts consider the *abhisheka* as the essential rite of sacring and mention that the queen may be associated in this ceremony. Now the Great Stele of the Phimeanakas makes clear that Queen Indradevī "received the king's sacring." The Sanskrit text shows clearly that this sacring was a dousing, since the term used is *abhisheka*.

It is very likely that the sacring also consisted of coronation, a mounting of the throne, and a procession, which are all ceremonies that survived until the end of the Khmer monarchy. Here again the text of the stele of Pre Rup provides a few indications. It describes the king "installed on the lion throne"; immediately after the sacring it presents him "advancing in the directions of the four points of the compass." Lastly, another stanza of the same inscription might be an allusion to a coronation: "the disk of the young sun became the jewel in the hair of this lord and illuminated his head with light."[118] This last text gives the king the name *īśvara* which normally refers to Śiva. In fact, by initiation, *dīkshā*, the king became Śiva himself.

Royal Funerals

Our sources are little more explicit in their mentions of royal funerals. It is known that after his death the king receives a posthumous name that sanctifies his identification with his chosen deity, but the texts never describe any funeral rite. Was the king cremated? G. Coedès pointed out that the Terrace of the Leper-King is situated to the north of the Royal Palace of Angkor, just as the royal cremation place of Phnom Penh is north of the modern palace; that the Terrace of the Leper-King was the Angkorian site for the funeral pyre of kings can hardly be proved from such a slender piece of evidence.

One Bayon relief certainly represents a grand cremation. It is worth noting that the scene as figured there is already the same as the one to be seen in the paintings of the Silver Pagoda of Phnom Penh, dating from the early twentieth century. The arrangements of the ceremony hardly differ from those made at the cremation of the body of king Suramarit in 1960. The pyre was prepared under a large pavilion; the urn containing the body was placed to one side, under a shelter annexed to the central pavilion. In the modern ceremony the body of the deceased king is placed in an urn, bent into the foetal position. This urn is first exhibited in the central pavilion, then set down in a secondary pavilion while the palace servants prepare the pyre in the central pavilion. This pyre is surmounted by a baldaquin, exactly as we see it in the Bayon relief. For as long as the body remains unburnt, the palace staff comes each day to place food offerings beside the urn; in the Bayon relief there are figures carrying a kind of tray on their heads, climbing the steps going up to the pavilions. It would seem that we are in the presence of the cremation of a king or prince.

It is not certain, however, that all Khmer kings were cremated. The arrangements in several Khmer temples suggest that they were funerary monuments, in the opinion of some scholars. The temple of Angkor Wat, for example, is oriented to the west, the cardinal point of the dead; to follow the sequence of the scenes carved on the large reliefs, the monument has to be gone round keeping it on the left, which is the direction of the funeral procession. Then again, at Angkor Wat and in other shrines such as Baksei Chamkrong, a well was dug beneath the central sanctuary. Faced with this evidence, G. Coedès asked whether some Khmer temples were not tombs.

J. Filliozat has since pointed out that in India the devotees of Śiva who had received the *dīkṣā* during their lifetime, the initiation identifying them with Śiva, were not cremated.[119] There are Indian texts recommending that they be buried under a stepped pyramid, surmounted by a *lingam* or even by a shrine. These are precisely the arrangements of several Khmer temples built on a high supporting base. It can therefore be said without doubt that these monuments were intended as funerary.

A note by Chou Ta-kuan is thus confirmed: "the sovereign is buried in a tower, but I do not know if they bury his body or only his bones." The chronicler also recounts a tradition according to which Angkor Wat was a tomb.

Royal Processions

"If the king goes somewhere nearby, he only uses a gold palanquin, carried by four girls of the palace. Usually when he goes out he goes to see a little golden pagoda. Those who see the king must prostrate themselves and touch the ground with their foreheads.…If not, they are seized by the masters of the ceremonies who do not let them go without making them suffer for it."

When the king went out on ceremonial occasions, however, the retinue was more imposing. The relief in the Historical Gallery parades before our eyes the great military procession of the victorious king. At the head advances a detachment of Siamese with plumes in their hair, with long skirts overhung with pendants; behind them the warriors with strange helmets crested with animals' heads. Then come clowns, standard bearers, and musicians at the head of a group of the Brahmans who are carrying the sacred fire on a shield, ringing little bells or escorting the aged Sacrificer seated on his palanquin. Behind this group of priests parade the war chiefs, each one standing on his elephant, surrounded by his horsemen and infantry; the parasols, fans and fly whisks held up round them show their rank. Among them, his head encircled in a diadem and his top knot encased in fine metalwork ornament, king Sūryavarman II advances amid his escort of troops. His jewels, his

147 Angkor Wat, central shrine (first half of the twelfth century). Dominating the whole temple, the central shrine rises to a height of 65 m. Sūryavarman II dedicated the central shrine to Vishnu, but no image of the god has been found there. In the post-Angkorian period the shrine was walled in with partitions bearing stucco images of the Buddha. It has now been opened up on the west, and in 1934 excavations were undertaken to clear the central well. Pillaging had long been going on, and the precious deposit under the pedestal removed; but at 23 m. depth another deposit was discovered, which must have been the foundation deposit: two thin gold disks, 18 cm. in diameter.

noble posture and the fifteen parasols held behind him single him out for the admiration of his subjects.

The royal procession described by Chou Ta-kuan is a court parade: "When the prince goes out, cavalry leads the escort; then come the standards, the pennons and the band. Palace girls, between three hundred and five hundred of them, wearing flowered cloths and with flowers in their hair hold great candles and form a troop; their candles are lit, even in full daylight. Then come palace girls carrying the royal utensils of gold and silver and the whole series of ornaments, all of different shapes and for what use I do not know. Then there are palace girls holding lance and buckler who are the prince's private guard: they too form a troop. Next follow the goat carts and horse carriages, all decorated with gold. The ministers and princes ride on elephants, looking into the distance as they go forward; their red parasols are numberless. After them come the wives and the concubines of the king, on palanquins, in carriages, on elephants. They certainly have more than a hundred parasols decorated with gold. Behind them comes the prince, standing on an elephant and holding the precious sword in his hand. The elephant's tusks are cased in gold. There are more than twenty white parasols decorated with gold and with solid gold handles. Numbers of elephants press round him, and cavalry guards him."

The description by the Chinese chronicler calls to mind the parade at Angkor Wat, though there is no sign on the reliefs of a female guard armed with lance and buckler; nor is there any representation of goat carts. It is interesting, however, to be told the color of the parasols; at the court of Phnom Penh the parasols that shaded the king or the queen were white and fringed with gold. The utensils of gold and silver and the ornaments whose use Chou Ta-kuan did not know are presumably the regalia which had to be carried behind the king and queen by members of the female court. Perhaps these royal utensils already included a service for betel, such as is seen on a sixteenth century relief at Angkor Wat.

Having seen king Sūryavarman II reigning on his throne in the midst of his court, and moving in the midst of a brilliant military parade, after reading once more the admiring account of the Chinese chronicler, we can conclude with him that the Khmers were not unaware "of what it is to be a prince."

THE REVIVAL OF ANGKOR IN THE SIXTEENTH CENTURY

The thirteenth and fourteenth centuries saw the decline of the power of Angkor. The creation of the Thai kingdoms of Sukhodaya and then Ayudhyā made Angkor a peripheral capital, ceaselessly threatened by these young states. The kings resigned themselves to abandoning Angkor and going to reside in the Mekong plain. Having interpreted anew the Chinese and Khmer sources, the American historian O.W. Wolters has decided that the first abandon of Angkor happened in 1370. However, even after this date kings returned to the old capital, which was not finally forsaken until 1431. J. Boisselier thinks that, when the Thais invaded in 1431, Angkor was despoiled of all its royal attributes which were carried off with the images that protect the monarchy; the king of Ayudhyā probably destroyed the arrangements laid out by Jayavarman VII to ensure the invulnerability of his kingdom.[120] It was probably then that breaches were opened in dike of Neak Pean so as to deprive the Khmer sovereign of the possession of Lake Anavatapta so that he could no longer be a *chakravartin* monarch, which was the title now claimed by the king of Ayudhyā.

The Khmer king went to reside at Phnom Penh, then at Srei Santhor, and finally at Lovek. Yaśodharapura was abandoned to the forest. Since Cambodia had adopted Theravāda Buddhism, the Brahman and Mahāyāna Buddhist cults ceased in their temples. However, at Angkor Wat, where images of the Buddha had been placed in the central shrine by Theravādin Buddhists, the temple was not abandoned. Monks had installed themselves inside the enclosure of the ancient temple of Sūryavarman II. A Cambodian prince even came to reside there during military operations. More than that, the king in 1546 decided to have the carving completed of the sculpture of the two large reliefs in the northeast quadrant of Angkot Wat which had only been sketched out in the time of Sūryavarman II.[121] So, in the mid-sixteenth century, a Khmer king came to Angkor and discovered the dead city. This king was certainly Ang Chan I who restored for a time the power of Cambodia. He it was who gave the order to finish the reliefs of Angkor Wat. We are indebted to the Portuguese Diego do Couto for an account of this discovery: "Just round the years 1550 or 1551, as the King of Camboja was out hunting elephants in the thickest forests there are in the whole kingdom his [people] while beating the bush came upon some imposing constructions entirely overgrown inside with undergrowth so thick that they could not beat it down to get in. This having been reported to the king, he went to this place, and seeing the extent and the height of the outer walls and desirous of seeing inside, he ordered that it [the brushwood] should all be immediately cut down and burnt. And he stayed there beside a fine river while this work was done by

fig. 149

fig. 148

148 The *Asura* Bāna, Angkor Wat, north gallery III (sixteenth century). The carving of the reliefs in the northeast gallery was not completed in the time of Sūryavarman II. In the sixteenth century King Ang Chan, whose reign saw a renaissance of Khmer power, undertook their completion. The relief in the north gallery shows Krishna's battle against the *asura* Bāna. The crowd of figures is carved without much skill, but the principal figures are very fine. This image of Bāna is one of the most remarkable.

five or six thousand men, who soon finished this task and cleared the whole city... of this bush of the thickest kind and tall timber that had covered it for years. And after it was all carefully cleared the King went inside, and having been all round it was struck with admiration at the extent of these buildings. And for this reason he decided immediately to move his court there."[122]

It appears that the Khmer kings kept their capital at Lovek, but Angkor was for them a holy city which it pleased them to stay in. The grandson of Ang Chan I, Satha I, who became king in 1576, resided for quite a time at Angkor where he received the Portuguese and Spanish missionaries. The traces of this renewed royal occupation are clearly apparent at Angkor Thom; carvings were done at this time on the north of the Royal Terrace, on Monument No. 486 and in one of the Preah Pithu. In 1579 the king started on a restoration of Angkor Wat, where he had the wall of the enceinte repaired "stone by stone, rebuilt the roof with its steeple of nine points and embellished this steeple with a sheath of gold."

Once again Angkor Wat became the scene of great royal solemnities. The inscription of 1579 commemorates the celebrations at the birth of a son to Satha. "By the ardent potency of the great beneficence of the merits of His Majesty the great *upāsak*, great sovereign, who leans entirely and without failing on the august Triple Jewel, a god descended on earth to take flesh in the womb of Her Majesty the blessed queen, in the form of a prince endowed with characteristic sublime marks. This birth was placed under the fortunate sign of Wednesday, 14th day of the waning moon of *āsādh*, in the year of the Hare, 1501 *śaka*....Twelve days later, on a Sunday, were gathered together Her Majesty the queen, the *rājaguru*, the astrologer and the Brahman teachers, for the purpose of the ceremony of the name-giving. His Majesty deigned to confer on his royal child the beneficent name of Brah Paramarājādhirāj. Then he took him to the Brah Bisnulok which is the meeting place of the *mahākṣetr* gods, of the great all-powerful *brahmarṣi*, and of the protective deities and the troops of the Fathers, and in devotion presented him as a precious *upāsak* to the august Triple Jewel. He had

offerings prepared, those for the end of the rains." Eight noble priests, the *rājaguru* and the teachers were invited to "accomplish" the rites of libation to the Spirits of the Dead. "They offered them at the same time divers fruits, flowers, perfumes, food from the five sacrifices according to the prescribed rules."[123]

The temple of Angkor Wat is here given its Brahmanic name: Brah Bhisnulok, "World of Vishnu." The child was considered to be an exceptional being, since he was the reincarnation of a god and bore on his body the auspicious marks, doubtless those that must appear on the body of a *chakravartin* monarch. The destiny of this young prince was not to fulfill the hopes raised by his birth. The reign of Satha I ended in disaster. In 1594 the king of Ayudhyā, Nareśvara, seized Lovek. The Khmers never recovered.

Forest engulfed Angkor Thom once more, but Angkor Wat remained the shrine revered by all Khmers, the symbol of the city that had been, for all the peoples of southeast Asia, the City of the gods, the city of Indra. From all parts of Cambodia pilgrims continued to come to the old sanctuary. Inscriptions carved on the pillars of the temple commemorate some of these pilgrimages, listing the gifts that were brought and the rewards hoped for from them in return. These requests seem at times somewhat lacking in spirituality: "May he be reborn into a family noble as to its blood, its glory and its supremacy, possess the best of elephants, the best thoroughbred horses, precious stones of all the best kinds, divine food and fine cloths, beautiful and fringed, which he can wind three times round his thighs." It is of course true that reincarnation into a rich family frees a man from material worries and allows him to seek the Path of Salvation. The text of another inscription has a pathos that is profoundly touching. It is by someone whose wife has died: "Yet, when I recall this life, I have to think that it was rather strange for us both! We could not lead it as we wished, and we have had to endure a heart-rending separation. May at least in all our future lives the slightest separation be spared us! May fatal destiny spare us, after this life that has treated us so cruelly, so repeatedly, without respite!...May Lady Pen be my wife in my future lives... following me in each existence!... I ask to

246

149 Preah Pean, Angkor Wat. Buddha images of many different periods have been assembled in the south gallery of the Cruciform Court. In the foreground are deposited a number of Buddhist stelae. Against the gallery wall the standing Buddhas all make the gesture of "reassurance." Angkor Wat has never been abandoned by the faithful throughout the centuries, and pilgrims from all parts of Cambodia have set up images of the Blessed One in the shrine which still remains holy.

see her if I am reborn in heaven. May she be with me if I return to this world!"

At times of pilgrimage the old temple would be enlivened by festivals. "They also organized fireworks, suns and other pieces lit up in the form of mice and mango [flowers] which made the fortress of Brah Bisnulok of the ancient Cambuja in its entirety shine out with brilliance to the four cardinal points. The ceremonies came to an end with a sermon on the Law, on Sunday." The pilgrims returned to their homes. In the temple a few incense sticks still burn before the wooden images of the Blessed One, and priests in saffron robes climb the worn steps of the staircases to meditate alone.

CONCLUSION

Angkorian civilization as we find it in our chosen period at the beginning of the thirteenth century already has a long history behind it. For more than a thousand years influences from India have been bringing Indian culture to this country. As time went on the political, administrative, social and even religious structures became highly complex, as the new systems were superimposed on the old without destroying them. The heritage of previous generations did not disappear, and for this reason daily life evolved very slowly. The Cambodians remained attached to their traditions, expressed in a love of simple life, of the joyous atmosphere of religious festivals, of work done without haste with tools made like little works of art. Peasant or townsman, rich or poor, the Khmer is always something of an artist. A sense of beauty is one of the Cambodian traditions.

When he reconstructed Angkor at the end of the twelfth century, Jayavarman VII was careful to respect the works of his predecessors. The ramparts of Angkor Thom delimit a holy city, since they form the enclosing wall of the temple of the Bayon. South of Angkor Thom the area of the first Yaśodharapura was probably still inhabited, for it was much more extensive than that of Angkor Thom. The priests

150   Ta Prohm, gallery overgrown with bombax (late twelfth-early thirteenth century). A bombax (silk-cotton) tree has grown over this gallery of Ta Prohm, and its roots have enveloped it like tentacles, creeping over the vaults and stretching along the pillars. If this tree fell it would drag down the whole gallery, for the roots have become inextricably mingled with the stones, twining into the joints and coiling round the blocks.

continued to celebrate the cult at Phnom Bakheng, which Yaśovarman had made into an authentic Mount Meru; at Baksei Chamkrong, which had the light of the Kailāsa; and at Angkor Wat, dedicated to the cult of Vishnu into whom Sūryavarman II had desired to be absorbed. In the old city, south of Phnom Bakheng, Jayavarman VII built a hospital whose chapel, though ruined now, still preserves on its pediments the images of the Buddha Bhaishajya-guru "who has the brilliance of the beryl" and who heals the sick.

Jayavarman VII wished to make Angkor Thom into a reflection of the city of the thirty-three gods which crowns Mount Meru. In order not to deprive his predecessors of the fruits of their pious works, he included their foundations in the new city. While the Bayon, designated the assembly hall of the gods, was built at the center of Angkor Thom; the king preserved the Royal Palace built by Rājendravarman in the tenth century as the palace of Indra; but in front of this palace he constructed the Royal Terrace and the Terrace of the Leper-King. Having made his capital into a City of the gods, surrounded by holy places, among them Lake Anavatapta, which will not dry out before the end of the present cosmic period; Jayavarman VII thought he had ensured the permanent survival of his capital and of Angkorian civilization. Two hundred years later, however, the city was despoiled of all that was to have made it indestructible, and reduced to bondage by the Thai kingdom of Ayudhyā.

Of the Angkor of seven centuries ago, all that remains are a few religious buildings, more or less   *fig. 150* ruined. The royal palaces built of perishable materials have totally disappeared, no less than the houses of the ordinary folk. With their long avenues of giants, and surmounted by the four heads of the Kings of the Four Points of the Compass, the gates of Angkor Thom now only give access to a dead city, overrun by vegetation. Has Angkorian civilization then perished with the desertion of the city?

In writing this book we set out to collect evidence, from the abandoned temples and from contemporary documents, of what it had been. By examining the reliefs carved in the sanctuaries, in bending over the texts of the inscriptions, we have sought to learn how the Khmers of Angkor lived, how they were governed and what were their spiritual aspirations. The reliefs, in pride of place those of Angkor Wat and the Bayon, have displayed to our eyes the Khmers of the twelfth century from every walk of life, and engaged in the most varied activities: peasants with their cattle, craftsmen in their workshops, aristocrats receiving their friends, princes and kings giving audience. We have seen grave magistrates pronouncing judgments and women bending tenderly over their children, soldiers helping wounded companions, relatives nursing the sick. We have divined the joyous exuberance of some and the affliction of those raising a hand to wipe away a tear. We have looked and looked again at these reliefs without tiring of them; even after many hours of study they have more details to reveal at each new examination. Innumerable aspects of Angkorian civilization are illustrated there in stone. The epigraphical texts introduce us too to genealogies, the rise of certain families, and to their litigations and the outcome of certain suits.

After seeing these ancient scenes fixed in stone we have visited the villages, country towns and the capital of modern Cambodia; there we have time and again come upon the scenes that caught our attention as we examined the reliefs. Angkorian civilization still survives in the peaceful life of the countryside, in the patient work of the craftsmen, in the poetry and humor of the storyteller as he sits of an evening in the village, recounting the wonderful exploits of Rāma or some other hero.

The beauty of the Khmer monuments is moving testimony to the greatness and grandeur of Angkorian civilization. The wonderful harmony of the composition of the temple of Angkor Wat is surely an expression of the aspiration of the devotee to surpass and identify himself with his chosen deity. The strange arrangement of the Bayon, the plan of its central shrine in the form of a lotus and the multiplicity of the towers with faces could only have been imagined by one possessed of great knowledge of the Buddhist texts, and at the same time an artist enamoured of poetry and the miraculous. Architectural conceptions such as these could only germinate in a deeply spiritual atmosphere. For as long as the Khmer monuments remain standing, even ruined as they are, and the divine images remain absorbed in their blissful meditations; Khmer civilization will not perish. May the prayer of Jayavarman VII be thus granted, and this testimony of Khmer civilization survive until the end of the time of our *kalpa*.

151 Avalokiteśvara, Angkor Thom, Gate of the Dead (late twelfth-early thirteenth century). This statue is one of the loveliest in Bayon art. The smooth brow, the barely salient eyebrows, the slightly hollowed temples, and the nearly parted lips are modeled with extreme sensitivity. Under its image of Amitābha carved at the front of the top knot, the face with its closed eyes, deep in meditation, mirrors inexpressible gentleness.

FOOTNOTES

1. Diego do Couto, *Cinco livros da Duodecima Decada da Asiae*, chap. 6 quoted by Bernard-Philippe Groslier, *Angkor et le Cambodge au XVIᵉ siècle: D'après les sources portugaises et espagnoles*, (Paris, 1958) p. 68.

2. George Coedès, *Inscriptions du Cambodge*, 8 vols. (Publication of the Ecole Française d'Extrême-Orient, Hanoi, Paris, 1937–66) 2: 177, s.v. "Grande stèle du Phimeanakas." (hereafter cited as *I.C.*).

3. Tchéou Ta-kouan, "Mémoires sur les coutumes du Cambodge," trans. Paul Pelliot, *Bulletin de l'Ecole Française d'Extrême-Orient* (Hanoi, Saigon and Paris, 1902) 2: 123 (hereafter cited as *BEFEO*). Chou Ta-kuan's account is of primary importance for this study; the numerous extracts from this chronicle which we shall have occasion to quote in the following pages will appear henceforth without references.

4. On the reliefs the men all have very short hair, which appears to be straight; in the modern period, however, many Cambodians have curly hair.

5. Ma Touan-lin, *Ethnographie des peuples étrangers à la Chine*, trans. Hervey de Saint-Denys, vol. 2 (Geneva, 1876–83) pp. 477–81.

6. Ibid.

7. This quotation from Chou Ta-kuan follows a discussion by the chronicler of the behavior of Cambodian women. Cf. J. Moura, *Le Royaume du Cambodge*, vol. 1 (Paris, 1883) p. 330, who refutes Chou Ta-kuan on this matter.

8. Paul Pelliot, "Le Fou-nan," *BEFEO* (1903) 3: 279.

9. There were representations of Balarāma in the pre-Angkorian period.

10. Cf. Appendix p. 000.

11. George Coedès and Pierre Dupont, "Les stèles de Sdok Kak Thom, Phnom Sandak et Prah Vihear," *BEFEO* (1943–46) 43: 101.

12. J. Moura, p. 62.

13. The scene takes place on the lower part of a relief showing a forest inhabited by hermits.

14. Paul Pelliot, *BEFEO* (1902) 2: 44, n. 3.

15. J. Moura, p. 66.

16. Diego do Couto, in Bernard-Philippe Groslier, p. 74.

17. Etienne Lunet de Lajonquière, *Inventaire descriptif des monuments du Cambodge*, 3 vols. (Paris, 1902–1911) 1: 203. This monument is inventoried as Prāsāt Kuk Nokor, no. 147, figs. 118–119.

18. Ibid., 2: 88 s.v. "East Sneng," no. 866; "West Sneng," no. 876, fig. 115.

19. George Coedès and Pierre Dupont, *BEFEO* (1943–46) 43: 147.

20. Cf. Commission des Moeurs et Coutumes du Cambodge, pub. *Cérémonies des douze mois, fêtes annuelles cambodgiennes*, (Phnom Penh, n.d.) p. 81.

21. George Coedès, *Les Etats hindouisé d'Indochine et d'Indonésie*, (Paris, 1948) p. 205.

22. George Coedès, *I.C.*, 3: 163, s.v. "Stèle de Kdei Ang."

23. George Coedès and Pierre Dupont, *BEFEO* (1943–46) 43: 94ff.

24. George Coedès, *I.C.*, 5: 90, s.v. "Un piédroit de Prâsât Kûk Pradak."

25. George Coedès, *I.C.*, 3: 3, s.v. "Inscription de Vat Basset."

26. George Coedès, *I.C.*, 2: 97, s.v. "Inscription de Tûol Prâsât."

27. George Coedès, "La stèle de Prah Khan d'Angkor," *BEFEO* (1941) 41: 296.

28. M. Déricourt, "Observations archéologiques aériennes," *BEFEO* 50: 519.

29. Georges Groslier, *Recherches sur les Cambodgiens*, (Paris, 1921) p. 97.

30. Paul Pelliot, "Le Fou-nan," *BEFEO* 3: 262.

31. P. Paris, "Les bateaux des bas-reliefs khmers," *BEFEO* (1941) 41: 335ff.

32. George Coedès and Pierre Dupont, *BEFEO* (1943–46) 43: 147.

33. George Coedès, "Les gîtes d'étape," *BEFEO* (1940) 40: 347.

34. Etienne Lunet de Lajonquière, 1: 92, no. 85; Henri Parmentier, "Le temple de Vat Phu," *BEFEO* (1914) 14: 1ff.; Louis Finot, "Vat Phou," *BEFEO* (1902) 2: 24ff.

35. Etienne Lunet de Lajonquière, 1: 92, no. 85; Henri Parmentier, *BEFEO* (1914) 164: 1ff.

36. Etienne Lunet de Lajonquière, 1: 16, no. 23; H. Mauger, "Phnom Cisor," *BEFEO* (1938) 38: 620ff.

37. Udong is known especially as the royal burial place, but vestiges of the eighth and ninth centuries are to be seen on the ground or reused in the structures of modern pagodas.

38. Etienne Lunet de Lajonquière, 1: 78, no. 78.

39. The temple of Kompong Preah is not included in La-

jonquière's inventory. It consists of two interesting shrines and has given its name to one style of pre-Angkorian art.

40. ETIENNE LUNET DE LAJONQUIÈRE, 3: 439, no. 865.

41. Ibid., 3: 427, no. 861.

42. Ibid., 3: 391, no. 816.

43. Ibid., 2: 324, no. 466. The architecture and images of Lopburi constitute a Khmer art in Thailand which has its own characteristics.

44. Ibid., 2: 278, no. 447; ERIK SEIDENFADEN, "An Excursion to Phimai," *Journal of the Siam Society* (Bangkok) 171: 1 ff.

45. ETIENNE LUNET DE LAJONQUIÈRE, 2: 173, no. 398.

46. Ibid., 1: 366 ff., nos. 275–83; GEORGE COEDÈS, "La date de Koh Ker," *BEFEO* (1931) 31.

47. ETIENNE LUNET DE LAJONQUIÈRE, 1: 242, no. 173; H. MAUGER, "Le Prah Khan de Kompong Svay," *BEFEO* (1939) 39: 197 ff.

48. PHILIPPE STERN, *Les monuments du style du Bayon et Jayavarman VII*, (Paris, 1965) pp. 97–98.

49. ETIENNE LUNET DE LAJONQUIÈRE, 1: 283, no. 214: J. DE MECQUENEM, "Les bâtiments annexes de Beng Mealea," *BEFEO* (1913) 132: 1 ff.; JEAN BOISSELIER, "Ben Mealea et la chronologie des monuments du style d'Angkor Vat," *BEFEO* (1954) 46: 187 ff.

50. PHILIPPE STERN, "Le style du Kulen," *BEFEO* (1938) 38: 111 ff.; PIERRE DUPONT, "Les monuments du Phnom Kulen," *BEFEO* (1938) 38: 199 ff.; idem, "Recherches archéologiques sur le Phnom Kulen," *BEFEO* (1938) 38: 426 ff.

51. JEAN BOULBET, "La Rivière aux mille 'linga'," *Nokor Khmer*, no. 2 (Phnom Penh, 1970).

52. BERNARD-PHILIPPE GROSLIER, pp. 69–70.

53. GEORGE COEDÈS, "A la recherche du Yaçodharâçrama," *BEFEO* (1932) 32: 84 ff.

54. Chankarâchârya, a Vedantic philosopher, was born on the Malabar coast in the late eighth century. He is said to have lived from 778 to 820. His principle work was a commentary on the Brahmasūtra. Unlike other Vedantic philosophers, who admit the duality of the Brahman, the supreme Self; and the Atman, the individual Self; he affirmed that the Brahman is the only reality and denied the reality of the existence of the universe.

55. GEORGE COEDÈS, "Stèle de Prâsât Komnap: st. XVIII," *BEFEO* (1932) 32.

56. JEAN FILLIOZAT, "Le symbolisme du monument du Phnom Bakheng," *BEFEO* (1954) 44: 527 ff.

57. GEORGE COEDÈS, "Stèle de Prâsât Komnap: st. XXIII," *BEFEO* (1932).

58. GEORGE COEDÈS, "Les inscriptions de Bat Chum," *Journal Asiatique*, (Paris, 1908) p. 239.

59. The father of Rājendravarman was king of Bhavapura, the center of the original Chenla. Rājendravarman completed the unification of Cambodia begun by Jayavarman II.

60. AUGUSTE BARTH, *Inscriptions sanskrits du Cambodge*, (Paris, 1885) p. 139.

61. FRANÇOIS MARTINI, "En marge du Râmayâna Cambodgien," *Journal Asiatique*, (Paris, 1950) pp. 81 ff.; idem, "Quelques notes sur le Râmker," *Artibus Asiae*, vol. 24³/₄ (Ascona, Switzerland, 1959) pp. 351 ff.

62. The monument of Nakorn Luong, built by King Prāsāt Thong, repeats with considerable modifications certain architectural elements of Angkor Wat, such as windows with balusters.

63. The Battle of Kurukshetra, the last combat of the Mahābhārata, during which the two armies of the Pāndava and the Kaurava annihilated each other.

64. The Battle of Lanka, the last combat of the Rāmayāna, during which Rāma killed the king of the *rākshasa*, Rāvana.

65. JEAN FILLIOZAT, "Le temple de Hari dans le Harivarsa," *Arts Asiatiques*, (1961) 8₃: 195 ff.

66. LOUIS DELAPORTE, *Voyage en Cambodge*, (Paris, 1880) p. 166.

67. GEORGE COEDÈS, "La stèle de Ta Prohm," *BEFEO* (1907) 7: 38.

68. GEORGE COEDÈS, "La stèle de Prah Khan," *BEFEO* (1941) 41: 288.

69. MAURICE GLAIZE, *Les monuments du groupe d'Angkor*, (Saigon, 1948²) p. 220.

70. GEORGE COEDÈS, "La stèle de Prah Khan," *BEFEO* (1941) 41: 285.

71. Ibid., p. 302.

72. LOUIS FINOT and VICTOR GOLOUBEW, "Le symbolisme de Neak Pean," *BEFEO* (1923) 23: 401 ff.; JEAN BOISSELIER, "Pouvoir royal et symbolisme architectural: Neak Pean et son importance pour la royauté angkorienne," *Arts Asiatiques*, (1970) 21: 91 ff.

73. BERNARD-PHILIPPE GROSLIER, pp. 101 ff.

74. Ibid., p. 71.

75. The Mahārājikka are the four great kings ruling the four points of the compass.

76. MADELEINE GITEAU, "Le barattage de l'Océan dans l'ancien Cambodge," *Bulletin de la Société des Etudes Indochinoises* (Saigon, 1951) 26₂: 156.

77. GEORGE COEDÈS, *I.C.*, 4: 250, s.v. "Stèles des Prâsât Chrun d'Angkor Thom."

78. ETIENNE AYMONIER, *Le Cambodge*, 3 vols. (Paris, 1901–1903) 3: 533.

79. GEORGE COEDÈS, *I.C.*, 1: 141, s.v. "La stèle de Prè Rup."

80. Ibid., p. 142.

81. GEORGE COEDÈS, "Stèle de Prâsât Komnap: st. XXII," *BEFEO* (1932).

82. GEORGE COEDÈS, "La stèle de Ta Prohm," *BEFEO* (1907) 7: 114.

83. GEORGE COEDÈS, *I.C.*, 1: 114, s.v. "La stèle de Prè Rup."

84. GEORGE COEDÈS, *I.C.*, 1: 11, s.v. "La stèle de Tang Krang."

85. GEORGES GROSLIER, p. 131.

86. Ibid., p. 90.

87. GEORGE COEDÈS, "L'inscription de Ban That," *BEFEO* (1912) 122: 27.

88. It is interesting to see that the text is unable to castigate Dharanindravarman I, the legitimate king, who appears there as an obstacle to the unity of the kingdom.

89. GEORGE COEDÈS, "La stèle de Prah Khan," *BEFEO* (1941) 41: 286.

90. Sadāśiva Jayendrapandita, whose family had charge of *devarāja* ritual, quit monastic life to marry a sister-in-law of King Sūryavarman I. On this occasion, the stele of Sdok Kak Thom was inscribed with a history of the family of Sadāśiva and at the same time, a history of the Khmer kings since Jayavarman II.

91. GEORGE COEDÈS and PIERRE DUPONT, *BEFEO* (1943–46) 43: 101.

92. GEORGE COEDÈS, *I.C.*, 1: 219, s.v. "Nouvelles inscriptions de Prâsât Khna."

93. GEORGE COEDÈS, *I.C.*, 3: 209, s.v. "Inscription du *gopura* oriental du Phimeanakas"; S. SAHAI, *Les institutions politiques et l'organisation administrative du Cambodge ancien*, (Publication of the École Française d'Extrême-Orient, Hanoi, Saigon and Paris, n.d.) 75: 54.

94. GEORGE COEDÈS, *I.C.*, 1: 248, s.v. "La stèle du Prâsât Tor."

95. GEORGE COEDÈS, *I.C.*, 1: 25, s.v. "La stèle de Prah Ko."

96. GEORGE COEDÈS, *I.C.*, 2: 180, s.v. "La Grande stèle du Phimeanakas."

97. Ibid., p. 180, "St. XCVIII."

98. GEORGE COEDÈS, *I.C.*, 2: 31, s.v. "Inscription de Kuk Trapeang Srok."

99. LOUIS FINOT, "L'inscription de Ban That," *BEFEO* (1912) 12₂: 26.

100. When the *asura* attacked Mount Meru, Indra and the gods were forced at first to retreat. As they fled they met a troop of young *garuda* who were in danger of being crushed by the army of gods. Out of compassion for the *garuda*, Indra turned and faced the *asura*, who were completely worsted this time.

101. The *chakravartin* monarch is the universal monarch, he whose chariot wheels can turn everywhere without meeting any obstacle. The *chakravartin* monarch *par excellence* is Vishnu, who conquered the world in three steps.

102. The principal entrance to a Khmer temple is generally on the east. Angkor Wat is orientated to the west, the cardinal point of the dead. The moat surrounding it is only crossed by a roadway on the west.

103. The name of Rājendrabhadreśvara, Rājendravarman's favorite deity, contains the name of the god of Wat Phu, Bhadreśvara.

104. GEORGE COEDÈS, "La stèle de Ta Prohm," *BEFEO* (1907) 7: 32.

105. GEORGE COEDÈS, *I.C.*, 1: 153, s.v. "Nouvelles inscriptions de Banteay Srei."

106. GEORGE COEDÈS, "Stèle de Prâsât Komnap." *BEFEO* (1932).

107. GEORGE COEDÈS, *I.C.*, 3: 92, s.v. "Inscription de Prâsât Ta Kam."

108. GEORGE COEDÈS, *I.C.*, 1: 259, s.v. "Nouvelles inscriptions du Phnom Bayang."

109. GEORGE COEDÈS, *I.C.*, 1: 153, s.v. "Nouvelles inscriptions de Banteay Srei."

110. Chankarāchārya, cf. n. 54.

111. GEORGE COEDÈS, *I.C.*, 1: 217, s.v. "Deux nouvelles inscriptions de Prâsât Khna."

112. In particular the representation of the *svayamvara* of Sītā in the northwest pavilion of Angkor Wat. Cf. n. 61.

113. GEORGE COEDÈS, *I.C.*, 1: 217, s.v. "Deux nouvelles inscriptions de Prâsât Khna."

114. GEORGE COEDÈS, *I.C.*, 2: 216, s.v. "La Grande stèle du Phimeanakas."

115. GEORGE COEDÈS, *I.C.*, 1: 153, s.v. "Nouvelles inscriptions de Banteay Srei."

116. LOUIS FINOT, "Inscription sanscrite de Say-fong," *BEFEO* (1903) 3: 18.

117. COMMISSION DES MOEURS ET COUTUMES DU CAMBODGE, pub. *Cérémonies des douze mois, fêtes annuelles cambodgiennes*, (Phnom Penh, n.d.) pp. 79–81.

118. GEORGE COEDÈS, *I.C.*, 1: 111, s.v. "La stèle de Prè Rup."

119. JEAN FILLIOZAT, *Kailâsaparamparâ*, Felicitation volume to H.H. Prince Dhaninivat, 2: 245.

120. JEAN BOISSELIER, "Pouvoir royal et symbolisme architectural," *Arts Asiatiques*, (Paris, 1971) 21: 21.

121. GEORGE COEDÈS, "La date d'exécution des deux bas-reliefs tardifs d'Angkor Vat," *Journal Asiatique*, (Paris, 1962).

122. BERNARD-PHILIPPE GROSLIER, p. 69.

123. SAVEROS LEWITZ, "Textes en khmer moyen," *BEFEO* (1907) 7: 114–116.

APPENDIXES

BRAHMAN AND BUDDHIST ICONOGRAPHY

The Khmers of the Angkorian period had all listened time and again to the tales of wonder that were illustrated before their eyes in the carvings on the pediments, lintels or mural reliefs of the temples. We have thought it useful to give here brief summaries of some of the myths that inspired the Khmer artists. We shall be able to do no more than skim the surface in these few pages. There is no question of describing all the manifestations of Śiva or all the *avātar* of Vishnu, or giving a detailed account of the most recent life of the Buddha and his former existences, or of the interventions of the *Bodhisattva* in the affairs of our earth. We can do no more than mention the myths most often carved on the walls of the sanctuaries, some from Brahman and some from Buddhist iconography.

ŚIVA

The Trimūrti

Apart from Angkor Wat, the great Brahman temples of the Khmers were dedicated to Śiva. There are nonetheless numerous Vishnuite myths on the walls of the shrines. It is noticeable in fact that the Khmer artists illustrated only a restricted number of the manifestations of Śiva. For the Śivaites all is Śiva, and some representations of the Trimūrti are an expression of this conception, uniting Śiva, Vishnu and Brahma. In a group carved in the round now deposited with Angkor Conservation, Śiva is seated in the center and the busts of the two other deities emerge from his thighs, Brahma on his right and Vishnu on his left.

Śiva

Śiva is generally represented in his shrines symbolically, as the *lingam*, though sometimes he is worshiped as an anthropomorphic statue, in the aspect of a god wearing the hairknot of the ascetics, sometimes decorated with a crescent; his brow is engraved with a third eye; his two hands generally hold the trident, *triśula*, and rosary.

Dancing Śiva

Exceptionally, especially on bronze reliefs and small bronze images, the god has five heads and ten arms. There is only one example in Khmer territory of a dancing Śiva with five heads and ten arms; this is the colossal statue of the Prāsāt Kraham of Koh Ker. Nearly all the other images of Śiva dancing are carved in relief. When Śiva dances the *tāndava*, he tramples a demon underfoot. This dance is the source of the five cosmic powers: creation, preservation, destruction, incarnation and liberation or salvation. There are however other manifestations of the dance of Śiva; some texts describe 108 of them. A pediment on the East Gopura I of Banteay Srei shows a totally joyous choreography. The god here has only one head; he is smiling as he dances with his ten arms spread. Two figures, seated in the lower angles of the pediment, beat time for his movements: a drummer and a cymbalist who is the female Śivaite saint, Karikalammeyar, her body emaciated from excessive austerities.

Śiva and His Consort

The Khmer artists enjoyed showing Śiva with his wife at his side, Parvatī, the "Daughter of the Mountains," who is also called Umā. A delightful group at Banteay Srei shows the god embracing his consort, who is seated, small and smiling graciously on his knee. Sometimes the couple sits on the back of Nandin, the bull which is Śiva's mount. *fig. 117* *fig. 10*
Texts of inscriptions often allude to the descent of the Ganges on earth. The river, falling from the sky, was about to cause a tremendous cataclysm. Śiva, out of compassion for earth's creatures, caught it in his hair, so as to dispel the violence of the shock before allowing it to flow out over the earth. This is why the goddess Gangā is sometimes seen in India sitting in Śiva's hair. At the temple of Bakong at Roluos, one group *fig. 6* represents Śiva "surrounded by the liana creeper of the arms of Umā and Gangā," with each goddess holding a hand on one of Śiva's thighs. They surround the god and appear to be on good terms with each other, although the Indian treatises on iconography state that when he spreads out his hair to receive Gangā, Śiva bends tenderly towards Umā who is showing her jealousy with an angry look.

Manifestations of Śiva Granting Favors (anugrahamūrti)

Śiva is "The propitious One"; he grants gifts to gods and men if they have merited his favors by their devotion. Thus he gave Vishnu the *chakra*, the disk which will be in his hand a terrible weapon against the *asura*, the enemies of the gods. In the terrestial world Śiva assists heroes against their adversaries. Khmer artists recounted several times how Arjuna, a hero ally of Krishna, obtained from Śiva the gift of a miraculous weapon, *pāśupatāstra*. To earn the gift of this weapon Arjuna retired into the Himalaya where he underwent such excessive asceticism that the hermits of the mountain were alarmed. To bring Arjuna's austerities to an end Śiva approached him in the guise of a hunter. Just at that moment an *asura*, who had changed himself into the likeness of a boar, charged at Arjuna to kill him. Thereupon both Śiva and Arjuna each let fly an arrow at the animal and struck him. Angered against each other, the two archers rushed forward to fight. Arjuna was only human and had no strength against a god; he was vanquished and swooned. When he came round he recognized Śiva and prostrated himself before him. The god thus gratified gave him the desired weapon. At the Baphuon, at Prāsāt Sen Keo, at Angkor Wat and even at the Bayon is a carving of the scene with Śiva and Arjuna each shooting his arrow at the boar placed between them.

The gifts of Śiva sometimes go to less attractive characters, such as Rāvana, king of the *rākshasa* demons of Lanka (Ceylon), the enemy of Rāma. As he was returning to Lanka, Rāvana passed the Kailāsa, the mountain on which Śiva reigns in company with Parvatī. Now Śiva had forbidden access to the mountain. Rāvana was furious and behaved like a boor. He shouted abuse at the monkey-headed guardian, who cursed him and predicted that his power would be destroyed by monkeys. Finally in order to attract Śiva's attention, Rāvana raised up the base of the Kailāsa and shook the mountain, much to the consternation of the hermits and animals living on its slopes. Parvatī was terrified and hid herself in Śiva's bosom. The god merely pressed on the mountain with one toe so that its whole weight bore down on the *rākshasa*. Crushed under the mass of the mountain, Rāvana groaned, cried out in pain and, understanding the power of Śiva, began to sing his praises. He suffered, prayed and sang for a thousand years; then Śiva set him free and gave him a sword. He was still under the curse of the monkey-faced guardian, however. The Rāmāyana gives an account of how this curse was carried out. The shaking of the Kailāsa by Rāvana is often represented in Khmer art. The Museums of Battambang have two pictures on lintels of the tenth century. The myth is also splendidly illustrated at Banteay Srei, at Angkor Wat, at the Bayon, to quote only the best known examples. The silhouette of Rāvana with his ten heads and twenty arms is included in decorative compositions. The effort of Rāvana, the panic of the inhabitants of the Kailāsa and even the fright of Parvatī contrast with the majestic serenity of Śiva.

Śiva in His Terrible Aspect

Because he is benevolent, Śiva is the enemy of all who upset the order of the world, so he has to fight the adversaries of the gods and heroes. The Khmers only illustrated a few of these ferocious manifestations. To our knowledge there are no representations of Śiva dancing on the skin of the elephant whose form an *asura* had assumed; nor do they seem to have illustrated the god coming out of a *lingam* and upsetting Yāma, god of death, with a kick, when he wanted to carry off one of Śiva's worshipers. But on the other hand on a lintel in the Museum of Wat Po Veal in Battambang, decorated with Śivaite themes, the sculptor has given a very naive illustration of the Tripurāntakamūrti, the manifestation of Śiva, destroyer of the three cities. Three *asura*, three brothers had each built a city, one of iron on the earth, one of silver in the air, and the third of gold in the sky. They had obtained from Brahma a promise that these three cities could only be destroyed by a single arrow. From these fortresses that they thought impregnable, the *asura* never ceased attacking the gods. The gods went to ask Śiva for help. To defeat them, Śiva gave each god half his own strength, then he mounted a chariot which Brahma agreed to drive. He also agreed to find the arrow which could shoot through the three cities. Then Vishnu took on the aspect of a miraculous arrow which, when shot by Śiva, destroyed the *asura* and their fortresses. On the relief in the Battambang Museum, Śiva stands in a chariot driven by Brahma and lets fly an arrow. The cities, shown as three *prāsāt*, are tipping over without collapsing, and falling head first, with their masters.

One cannot but rejoice at the defeat of the *asura* and the rout of Yāma, but it is not without regret that we hear the story of the death of Kāma, the god of Love; Śiva seems to have regretted it himself. The myth more than once provided inspiration for the Khmer sculptors. Śiva retired to the Himalayas to devote himself to rigorous austerities. He is indeed the Mahāyogin, the greatest of all ascetics. The daughter of Himavan, the god of the Himalaya, in whom the consort of Śiva had manifested herself, was disappointed to see the god so absorbed in his asceticism that he paid her no attention. Now at this time an *asura*, Tāraka, was tormenting the gods, and they knew that only a child born of Śiva would be able to put their enemy to death. They went to Kāma, the god of Love, to ask him to distract Śiva from his meditation and cast his eyes upon Parvatī. Taking the heart of the Mahāyogin as his target, Kāma let fly one of his flowery arrows. The first reaction of Śiva was terrible. Indignant at being troubled, he shot forth a fiery ray from his frontal eye, and Kāma was reduced to ashes. In doing this he had interrupted his meditation. Casting his eyes on Parvatī he was enamoured of her beauty. Their marriage was celebrated and from this union was born Skanda, the god of youth and battle, who later killed Tārakāsura.

Śiva caused the god of Love to be reborn in the aspect of Pradyumna, son of Krishna. At Banteay Srei, Angkor Wat, Banteay Samre and the Bayon the sculptors have shown Śiva as a bearded hermit sitting on the mountain sometimes represented as a stepped pyramid. In the lower part of the composition, Kāma is drawing his bow and aiming at Śiva's heart.

The Bhikshātanamūrti

The *bhikshātanamūrti*, the manifestation of Śiva in the aspect of a mendicant ascetic, begins with a terrifying scene. Śiva knew that Brahma, who then had five heads, had it in mind to commit incest with one of his daughters. In his indignation he cut off Brahma's top head. Though his anger was justified he had nonetheless committed a crime against the first of the Brahmans, and was obliged to expiate his fault. He needed to purify himself by going to Vārānasi (Benares) and bathing in the Ganges. During his long pilgrimage he went through the forest of Devadāruvana where there were hermits living in company with their wives. The god evidently intended to have some fun at the expense of these hermits, for the grave tone of the beginning of this story changes into the easy atmosphere of "Śiva's tricks."

The *rishi* of Devadāruvana were rather too imbued with a sense of their moral worth. They had addressed themselves to rigorous asceticism and considered themselves to be definitively engaged in the path of the *dharma*. Śiva undertook to show them that their serenity was not unshakeable, and their detachment from all passion more apparent than real. He took on the guise of a handsome and young hermit, "dressed in air." At the sight of him all the hermits' wives fell madly in love with him. They followed him, surrounded him and, losing all restraint, began to undress. Such behavior on the part of their spouses aroused the rage of the *rishi* who started cursing the divine ascetic. They set an antelope on the god, who took hold of him. In some pictures of the scene Śiva holds the creature in one hand, while in the other he is shown keeping as an attribute the axe reddened in the fire thrown at him by the *rishi*. At these manifestations of his power the *rishi* recognized Śiva. They became aware how far they were from that perfect Serenity they had thought in their vanity to have achieved. In this myth Śiva made game of the *rishi* and their wives in order to make them understand that renunciation of all passion is the first stage in the achievement of perfection.

We have been able to identify a representation of the *bhikshātanamūrti* in a relief of the southwest pavilion of the third enceinte of Angkor Wat. Śiva appears at the top of the composition as a handsome hermit wearing a little *sampot*, for the nude is strictly forbidden in Khmer art. The wives of the *rishi* are gathered round him, some trying to touch him while others are decking themselves to appear more attractive and a few are even beginning to untie their skirts. At the bottom of the scene the *rishi* are shown in front of their caves, depicted in a stylized manner; the little old men are talking together and pointing at the scene above. The grotesquery of the jealousy of these old greybeards is cruelly underlined by the sculptor.

The Lingodbhavamūrti

We have already said that Śiva is generally adored in the sanctuaries in his phallic aspect as a *lingam*. The first meaning of *lingam* is "mark," "sign," "emblem," and only secondarily "phallus." In Śivaite thought it is not an erotic image. The legend of its origin, the *lingodbhavamūrti*, is closely linked with the cosmic myth of Creation.

Between two *kalpa*, Vishnu was resting on the primordial ocean. At the beginning of a new cosmic period Brahma appeared on a lotus growing out of Vishnu's navel. The two gods began to quarrel, each claiming that he was the creator of the universe. There suddenly appeared between them a flaming pillar, neither of whose ends they could see. Brahma took the form of a bird and flew off to try to reach the top of the pillar while Vishnu, becoming a Boar, tried to discover its base. They continued their search for thousands of years, but in vain; the pillar had no end. Confronted with this prodigy they each decided to return to the point of departure. Understanding that the pillar was a manifestation that surpassed them they paid it homage. Then the pillar opened and Śiva appeared, revealing to them that it was he who was the Creator.

While Brahma was flying towards the top of the hill, however, he saw a *ketaki* flower which had fallen from the top of the hill. He asked it to bear witness before Vishnu that his flight had led him to the top of the miraculous apparition. As a punishment for this deception Brahma was condemned never to have shrines of his own, but only chapels in the temples dedicated to Śiva and Vishnu. The *ketaki* flower was forbidden by Śiva ever to form part of the offerings brought to him by his worshipers.

Representations of the *lingodbhavamūrti* are very rare in Cambodia, but the myth was certainly portrayed once, on a lintel at Wat Eng Khna, now in the Museum of Phnom Penh. The main scene on the lintel figures the *abhisheka* of a prince, but on the arch framing this composition one can clearly make out a *lingam* bearing a head of Śiva being adored on one side by a bird and on the other by a boar.

Harihara

Harihara is an image combining the two deities: Śiva (Hara) and Vishnu (Hari) in one. The right hand side of the body is Śiva's, his hands generally holding the rosary and the trident; the other half of the body is Vishnu's who has the disk and the club as attributes. The hair of this composite divinity is raised into a high knot on the right and covered with a tiara on the left; on its brow is engraved the half of Śiva's middle eye. In the pre-Angkorian period large numbers of Harihara statues were carved, one of the most remarkable being the Harihara of Prāsāt Andet. It should be remembered that the capital before Angkor was Hariharālaya. The Khmers seem to have had a particular veneration for this manifestation of the unity of the two gods, Śiva existing in the form of Vishnu and Vishnu in that of Śiva: for they said "Hari is in the heart of Hara as sweetness in sugar."

Ardhanarīśvara

In another hybrid manifestation of Śiva the left part of the god's body is female and the right remains male. Existing by himself, Śiva combines in himself the two principles, the male and the female. In some traditions the female principle may be identified with Vishnu. It may, on the other hand, be considered that it represents his *shaktī*, his energy personified in his consort. From the seventh century, the epigraphy shows the Khmers as thinking that the feminine half of Ardhanarīśvara was Umā. The inscription of Tūol Kok Preah begins thus: "Victorious is He who, though possessing half of the body of Umā, is the first of the ascetics." Khmer representations of Ardhanarīśvara are few. The finest is a statue in the Museum of Wat Po Veal in Battambang, but only the torso survives.

Durgā

We have described the *shaktī* of Śiva, the consort who personifies his energy, under the name of Umā "the Favorable"; she is equally Durgā "The Inaccessible," Gaurī "The Blonde," Parvatī "Daughter of the Mountain," Kāli "The Dark." She appears with Śiva in groups known as Umāmaheśvara of which images, often riding the bull Nandin, are numerous in Khmer art, especially on temple pediments and lintels. Two famous full relief sculptures represent Umā seated on Śiva's knee: one, from Banteay Srei, is preserved in the National Museum of Phnom Penh; the other is in the Depot of the Angkor Conservation. She is invoked at the same time as her husband: "May the Shaktī, daughter of the mountain [Himalaya], the ardent and faithful wife, closely united with Śiva, contribute to the fortune of creatures."

In Cambodia, Durgā was often shown in her fight against the *asura* Mahisha, who took the form of a buffalo. Several pre-Angkorian statues show Durgā standing on a pedestal decorated with the head of the buffalo. On Angkorian reliefs she appears riding a lion, fighting Mahisha. On the base of a pilaster in Banteay Samre the goddess leans lightly with her hand on the lion's head and faces the buffalo, while, supple as a dancer, she prepares to transfix the enemy of the gods. In this aspect of destroyer of *asura*, Durgā is sometimes considered as the sister of Vishnu and like him holds in her hands the disk and the conch. These attributes were said to have been given her by the god to help her fight against Mahisha.

Skanda

Skanda was born from the union of Śiva and Parvatī, the eternally young leader of the army of the gods. In India representations of Skanda are extremely varied. In Cambodia the god generally has two arms and rides a peacock; when he does not wear the royal tiara his hair is divided into three large locks, knotted on the top of his head; this is the characteristic hair arrangement of very young men and children.

A pre-Angkorian statue carved in the round shows Skanda seated astride a peacock whose tail forms a kind of support or backing for the image. The loveliest depiction of Skanda is carved in low relief in the gallery of the third enceinte of Angkor Wat. The god is shown as a magnificent archer, sumptuously adorned, riding a peacock; there are few such elegant images of Skanda. According to one legend, Skanda's arrow came from the sun. The brightness of Sūrya, the Sun, was threatening to burn up the world. To save beings from this peril Viśvakarman, the architect of the gods, managed to extract some of the sun's heat and with this energy he made an arrow that he gave to Skanda.

Ganeśa

Ganeśa, "Lord of the *gana*," little spirits of the Kailāsa, is also Vishneśvara, the "Lord of the obstacles" that he is able to overcome for his worshipers or raise up against his enemies. He is the elephant-headed god; said to have been born from the union of Śiva and Parvatī who, wishing to imitate the sport of a pair of elephants in the forest, gave birth to a son with an elephant's head. Other legends recount that he was born with a human head, but did not keep it. According to one tradition, this head was burnt to ashes by the glance of Sani (Saturn) to whom Śiva gave the order to give to Ganeśa the head of the first living creature lying to the north, that he came across; this was an elephant.

The Śiva Purāna says that Ganeśa was born from the sweat of Parvatī; the goddess wanted a child who would be entirely devoted to her. She immediately ordered him to forbid access to any who came to his dwelling. Śiva came to see his wife and was refused admittance also. He was furious and called Vishnu, Skanda and other deities to his aid; during the battle which followed, he cut off the young man's head. Then Parvatī appeared and in her distress and anger caused a thousand divine warriors to appear who sorely pressed the troop of gods. To put an end to this horrible confusion, Śiva ordered the gods to take the head of the first living creature they met to put on the shoulders of Parvatī's creature; they found an elephant. After appeasing Parvatī in this way, Śiva entrusted the new god with the command of the *gana*.

Ganeśa never has more than one tusk; the other was broken during a fight and in Cambodian images he holds it in his hand. Sometimes he has two arms, sometimes four. His most characteristic attributes are the *ankusa*, the elephant hook, and the noose. Whether seated or standing Ganeśa is always shown with an obese body.

The Cambodian images of Ganeśa belong to the different periods of Khmer art and some very pretty statuettes have been found of this god in bronze. Ganeśa was not often carved on the reliefs, however; he occasionally appears as an onlooker in Śivaite scenes.

The Importance of Śivaite Iconography in Cambodia

Although it has given rise to a smaller number of representations than the Vishnuite myths, Śivaite iconography plays a very important part in Khmer art. It emphasizes the importance of certain essential manifestations of the god to whom the majority of Brahman temples in Cambodia were dedicated when two Śivaite sects, the Śaiva and the Pāśupata, were being established. In these temples a *lingam* is erected inside the shrine, but the lintels, pediments and even the outer surfaces of the walls often carry reliefs of scenes of Vishnuite myth. We should not be surprised, for to Śivaites all is Śiva.

VISHNU

In Khmer shrines, statues represent the god standing, with four arms, wearing the royal tiara, for Vishnu is the universal monarch. In the pre-Angkorian period this headdress had the form of a cylindrical miter sometimes decorated; in the Angkorian images it comprises a diadem and a casing for the top-knot, sometimes a cover for the nape as well. In his upper hands Vishnu holds the disk and the conch; in his lower, the club and the earth shown as a ball. Some images of Vishnu have eight hands and hold attributes belonging to other deities: fire, flask, antelope skin, thunderbolt.

fig. 139

Vishnu Riding on Garuda

Vishnu's mount is the bird Garuda. In Khmer art Garuda has bulging eyes and a thick curved beak; his torso is human but wings sprout behind his shoulders. In the art of the Baphuon, however, he has no arms. The lower part of his body is covered with feathers and his feet have sharp claws. Garuda is richly bejeweled and, like his master, wears the diadem and top-knot case of worked metal.

Carved in the round, Vishnu is rarely shown riding Garuda; but this aspect of the god is common on the reliefs, and on little bronze statuettes Vishnu is nearly always shown standing on the shoulders of his mount.

Śrīdevī and Bhūmidevī

Vishnu's consort is Lakshmī, goddess of Beauty, also called Śrī, "Fortune." She is shown as a very beautiful young woman, holding a lotus in each of her two hands.

Sometimes there is a second wife with Vishnu. This is Bhūmidevī, the "Earth," whom Vishnu went to seek at the bottom of the Ocean at the time of his *avātar* as the boar.

Vishnu Reclining

The largest image of Vishnu known in Cambodia is the reclining Vishnu of the Western Mebon of which unfortunately only the bust and a few fragments have been recovered. This representation was only rarely rendered in the round, but it often appears in the reliefs on lintels and historiated pediments, and on pilaster bases as well.

fig. 69

The meaning of the cosmic myth referred to by this image explains the great favor it enjoyed in Khmer art. Between two cosmic periods, while all is sunk in darkness, Vishnu rests on a snake floating on the primordial waters; and meditates on the world. This serpent, a thousand-headed *nāga*, is Ananta, "He who has no end," or Chesha, "He who remains" when all is destroyed. Often the goddess Śrī sits at the feet of her spouse; sometimes Śrī and Bhūmidevī are both represented together. In Khmer art Vishnu is shown stretched out in a posture of rest, but not of sleep; his chest is raised and supported on his right elbow. When a new cosmic period is about to begin, a golden lotus grows out of Vishnu's navel; it opens and Brahma appears on the flower. He will preside over the new creation.

fig. 53

The representations of the recumbent Vishnu are among the loveliest sculptures on the Khmer reliefs. The silhouette of the god resting on the snake is well suited to the rectangular frame of a lintel. When Brahma appears on the lotus issuing from Vishnu's navel, the scene fits perfectly into the triangular composition of a pediment. The Khmers liked to see Vishnu represented reclining, it spoke to them of serenity and the hope of a new world, promised by the apparition of Brahma.

The Avātar

Each time the world is imperiled, Vishnu takes on an incarnation as a man or an animal in order to restore the *dharma*. A list of ten of these *avātar*, or "descents" of Vishna into the world brings together the principle incarnations of the god. Not all *avātar* are illustrated in Khmer art; for instance in the iconography that concerns us we very rarely see the *avātar* of the fish who saved the human race and animal species from the deluge. There are also only a very few images in which it might be possible to recognize the sixth *avātar*, Paraśurāma, who delivered the earth from the oppression of the *kshatriya*. The penultimate *avātar* bears the name of Buddha, a strange incarnation which borrows some characteristics from the historic Buddha. To our knowledge there is not a single example in Khmer Vishnuite iconography that can be identified with this Buddhāvatāra.

It cannot, however, be categorically maintained that there is no example in Cambodia of representations of Kalkin, the future *avātar* of Vishnu that will occur at the end of our era. Then all will be plunged in barbarism. The Kalkyāvatāra has a messianic aspect. In the midst of this horrifying confusion Vishnu will manifest himself in the form of Kalkin, a man with a horse's head or riding a horse. Brandishing a flaming sword he will destroy all those responsible for this decline; he will reestablish the *dharma;* and after ensuring a new happy age for the world, will return to heaven. On a lintel at Banteay Srei the sculptor has carved a figure with horse's head, holding in his upper hands the disk and the conch and in his lower the heads of two demons. It is quite likely that this figure represents Kalkin.

The other *avātara* of Vishnu can be more certainly identified; some are human, some animal; there are even some hybrid ones, but all are manifestations of the god's power and of his care for living beings.

The Avātar of the Tortoise and the Churning of the Ocean of Milk

Exhausted by fighting against the *asura*, the *deva* (the gods) took Indra's advice and went to implore the help of Vishnu. Vishnu told them to make a temporary truce with the *asura* and to cooperate with them in churning the Ocean of Milk to extract from it *amrita*, the elixir of immortality. To make the churn they needed a pivot, with a rope to turn it. Mount Mandara was uprooted to form the pivot. With the promise of a share of the *amrita*, the *nāga* Vāsuki agreed to act as the rope and curled himself round the mountain. Then the *deva* and *asura* began pulling on the *nāga*, alternatively in one direction and in the other. The operation was not without difficulties. First of all Mount Mandara sank into the Ocean. At this point Vishnu took on the form of a huge tortoise and supported the mountain on his back. Meanwhile poor Vāsuki, tugged this way and that, was overcome with nausea and vomited a hideous poison, *hālāhala*, that threatened to destroy all living things.

fig. 42

Fortunately Śiva in his mercy took up the *hālāhala* in the hollow of his hand and drank it; but the poison was so violent that it burnt his throat, and since that time Śiva is called Nīlakantha, the god "with the blue throat."

The churned Ocean gave forth all kinds of wonders: the elephant Airāvata which Indra chose as his mount, the *apsarā*, celestial dancers, the goddess Śrī, and, at last, the elixir of immortality. The *asura* fell upon the *amrita*, but Vishnu was watching. Using his magic power he took on the appearance of a woman so beautiful that the *asura* were bewitched and gave up the *amrita* to her. Vishnu immediately gave it to the gods to drink. As it was being handed out a demon-like creature called Rāhu, the eighth planet, slipped in among the *deva* to make off with some of the *amrita*. The Sun and Moon saw him and denounced him, and just as Rāhu was taking a sip of the ambrosia Vishnu threw his disk and cut off his head before he had been able to swallow a single drop. Only his head was made immortal. In his resentment Rāhu tries to swallow the Sun and the Moon during eclipses. Since he no longer has a body he is unable to swallow them up, and they only pass through his mouth.

In Khmer iconography Mount Mandara is shown as a column resting on the back of the Tortoise. Its summit spreads out into a lotus on which Vishnu sometimes appears, holding the mountain. Quite often there is contamination from the images of the reclining Vishnu, and the column ends in a lotus supporting Brahma, who should not really be involved in the Churning. Vishnu is generally figured a third time in the center of the composition, beating time for the heaves of the gods and *asura*.

Representations of this myth abound in Khmer art, on lintels, pediments and even pilaster bases. There is a lovely relief of it at the Bayon, though unfortunately it is very mutilated. But the most beautiful of all is carved on a huge relief in the east gallery of Angkor Wat. Above the two long lines of *deva* and *asura* is a broad frieze of *apsarā* dancing in the air. In the Ocean are fish and strange sea creatures which in the center of the composition are torn to shreds by the violence of the whirlpool. The mountain has not been finished, but Vishnu appears as a magnificent tortoise whose shell is covered with carved flowers.

The Boar Avātar

Hiranyāksha, the "golden-eyed" *asura*, held Earth prisoner beneath the waters. To free her Vishnu took the body of a boar, "shaking his mane, bristling with sharp hairs, treading the clouds underfoot, showing his white tusks, his eyes blazing" as he is described in the Bhāgavata Purāna. He dived to the bottom of the Ocean, killed Hiranyāksha and brought the goddess of the Earth, leaning against one of his tusks, up to the surface.

There are not many illustrations of Varāhāvātara in Cambodia, though the epigraphy gives evidence of its importance there. The National Museum of Phnom Penh has a diademed head of a boar which presumably belonged to a statue of this *avātar* of Vishnu. Several stelae show the god with a boar's head and a human body.

Nārasimha, the "Man-Lion"

The brother of Hiranyāksha, Hiranyākaśipu, "with the golden garment" had obtained from Brahma a promise that he would not be killed either by day or by night, by god or man or animal. He oppressed the gods and men, even threatening his own son Prahlāda, a devotee of Vishnu. One evening as he was tormenting his son, he dared to defy Vishnu, saying that if the god was everywhere he should equally well be in one of the columns of his palace. Saying this he struck his fist against one of the pillars in the hall. There was a terrible roaring and Vishnu appeared in the aspect of a lion-headed man who threw himself upon the impious *asura* and tore out his entrails. The promise of Brahma had not been violated. Vishnu-Nārasimha was neither completely god nor man, nor animal; and the murder of Hiranyākaśipu happened neither by day nor by night, but at dusk.

Images of Nārasimha appear on lintels and pediments in Khmer art. There are many from the tenth century. The god is shown with a monstrous head which was used on conventional representations of lions at this period. A lion-headed statue in the Bayon style, preserved in the National Museum of Phnom Penh, may have been an image of Nārasimha that was worshiped in a shrine.

The Avātar of the Dwarf Brahman and the Conquest of the World in Three Steps

Bali, the grandson of Prahlāda, and thus a descendent of Hiranyākaśipu was a just person, even though he was an *asura*. By asceticism he acquired such powers that the gods were alarmed. They asked Vishnu to intervene. As Bali was going to carry out the horse sacrifice, Vishnu came to him in the likeness of a dwarf Brahman and asked him for the gift of as much ground as he could cover in three steps. Bali agreed. According to Indian custom he solemnly granted this request by pouring water over his hand. Immediately the dwarf, who was Vishnu himself, took on gigantic stature.

"Adorned with a plume, with bracelets and ear pendants, in the form of sparkling fish, wearing the Śrīvatsa [chest ornament], precious jewels, a belt and [rich] garments ringed with a garland of wood flowers such as the bees love, Bhagavat stood resplendent, the God of the long steps. In one step he covered the earth possessed by Bali, filling the atmosphere with his body, and touching the points of the horizon with his arms; in a second step he covered the sky; with his third step there remained not an atom to occupy."

Bali now possessed only the subterranean worlds. *Asura* are generally presented as arrogant, brutal, at times coarse beings; but Bali is a really noble figure. In one tradition his spiritual advisor had put him on his guard against the request of the dwarf Brahman; but he, though he was aware of the consequences of his act, was unwilling to refuse the request of a Brahman and granted the gift that would dispossess him. In modern Cambodia Bali remains a divinity of the earth and the underworld. There are many ceremonies in which the faithful make prayers and offerings to Krung Bali, King Bali.

Khmer epigraphy often refers to this myth of the Trivikrama;

for Vishnu, conqueror of the world in three steps is the *chakravartin* monarch *par excellence*, the model for all sovereigns. The Angkorian renderings of the Trivikrama are original. Vishnu, in an attitude of majesty, balances one foot on the earth and places the other on a lotus flower that rises from the water and is offered by a woman. K. Bhattacharya considers that this lotus, risen from the primordial Ocean and held by Lakshmī, "Mother of the World," symbolizes the universe. The same author also refers to an inscription mentioning that the foot of Trivikrama is "lifted by the Gangā." We must remember that a single image often refers to two aspects of a myth. This scene is illustrated in the central shrine of Prāsāt Kravan; we find it again in reliefs at the Baphuon and on pediments on various buildings.

Rāma

Vishnu became incarnate in Rāma to end the tyrannical dominion of Rāvana and the *rākshasa* over the island of Lanka (Ceylon). Rāma was one of the four sons that the king of Ayodhyā, Daśaratha, had begotten from his wives. Him it was that the ageing king destined for the throne. When everything was ready for the sacring of Rāma, one of Daśaratha's wives reminded the king that he had once promised to grant her a wish, and demanded that her son Bharata receive the sacring while Rāma be sent into exile for twelve years. Despite the sorrow of all Ayodhyā and the protestations of Bharata himself, Rāma went off into the forest, accompanied by his wife Sītā and his brother Lakshmana who insisted on following him. When after the death of Daśaratha, Bharata came to beg him to return to Ayodhyā and reign there, Rāma remained true to the promise made to his father and refused to return from exile. Several Angkorian reliefs illustrate scenes from the life of Rāma, Sītā and Lakshmana in the forest. On a pediment and a lintel of Banteay Srei we see the horrible demon Viradha carrying off Sītā. Luckily Rāma and Lakshmana were on guard; they shot Viradha down with an arrow. But unfortunately they were unable to prevent Rāvana carrying off the young woman. To gain his ends Rāvana tried to separate Sītā from her companions. He sent the *rākshasa* Marīcha towards them in the form of a golden hind to which Rāma gave chase at the request of Sītā. Hit by an arrow, the dying *rākshasa* imitated the voice of Rāma calling his brother to his help. Urged on by the entreaties and even the reproaches of Sītā, Lakshmana went off to find his brother. Rāvana was watching for this moment to seize the young woman and carry her off against her will to his palace on Lanka.

After this the Rāmāyana recounts the long struggle of Rāma against Rāvana to overcome him and recover his wife. First he allies with Sugrīva, the prince of the monkeys, who is pursued by his brother Valin. In the fight to the death between Valin and Sugrīva, Rāma intervenes in support of his ally and shoots down Valin with an arrow. With Sugrīva and his army Rāma and Lakshmana prepare to invade Lanka while Hanuman, a hero among monkeys, slips into Lanka and enters the palace to give Rāma's ring to Sītā and promise her that her deliverance is near. The fight against the *rākshasa* goes on with varying fortunes. A combat takes place between the two

fig. 26

fig. 68

fig. 42

brothers and Indrajit, the son of Rāvana. The latter owns some arrows with the power to turn into snakes and wind like ropes round Rāma and Lakshmana. The two princes were on the point of stifling when Garuda, mortal enemy of all snakes, intervened and delivered them. Several eleventh and twelfth century reliefs illustrate this episode.

Finally the epic battle of Lanka begins. A relief illustrating it covers the whole wall of one western gallery at Angkor Wat. Soon Rāma and Rāvana are face to face, and Rāma kills his enemy with an arrow. Sītā is free, but Rāma refuses to take her back as his wife because she has lived in Rāvana's house. She then agrees to undergo an ordeal by fire to prove her innocence. Later on Rāma's jealousy returns and causes Sītā to be exiled; then the king regrets his injustice and comes to her, but she invokes the Earth who opens up to receive her.

fig. 45

Krishna

Krishna is the major *avatar* of Vishnu, for "only Krishna is Bhagavat entirely" [Bhagavata Purāna]. Vishnu became incarnate in him to make the cruel king of Mathura, Kamsa, perish. A sage had predicted that Kamsa would be put to death by one of his nephews; he therefore had all his sister's children put to death as soon as they were born. Two of them escaped this massacre, however: the seventh, Balarāma and the eighth, Krishna, who was saved by substituting a changeling. In his place a girl was killed by Kamsa but she, appearing in the sky, announced the death of her murderer in a terrifying voice.

Meanwhile Krishna was growing up in a village with a foster-mother. One day when she had left him alone he stole some butter. When she got back the young woman was annoyed and attached the child to a heavy stone mortar. Krishna however had divine strength. Crawling on all fours he dragged the mortar behind him and it hit and uprooted two trees in its path, thus liberating two people who had been imprisoned by a curse. The exploits of the child Krishna are each more extraordinary than the next. One after another he strangled the snake Kalya that tried to suffocate him, then killed two *asura* who had taken, one the form of a buffalo and the other of a horse. Illustrations of these combats appear in Khmer art; but the legend that most inspired the Angkorian artists was that of Krishna lifting up Mount Govardhana so as to protect the villagers. They had provoked Indra's anger, and he sent a terrible thunderstorm against them. Krishna, who was the true cause of the god's annoyance, intervened in favor of the villagers and "lifting up Mount Govardhana from its base in one hand, he held it in the air as easily as small child holds a mushroom." He told the shepherds and shepherdesses to come and take shelter with their flocks. "Insensible to the pangs of hunger and thirst and indifferent to his own comfort, he held up the mountain for seven days." The oldest Khmer images of Krishna supporting Mount Govardhana go back to pre-Angkorian art; but the scene appears too on most of the eleventh and twelfth century monuments.

In the end Krishna revenged himself on his uncle. He came to Mathura killed Kamsa in his palace, and became king. Even a life of luxury amid his 16,000 wives could not retain Krishna

fig. 13

fig. 125

fig. 20 for long. He joined with Balarāma at the side of the five Pāndava princes in their fight against their cousins the Kaurava. This war is the main subject of the Mahābhārata. On the eve of the final battle Krishna revealed to Arjuna, one of the Pāndava, in the long poem of the Bhagavadgītā, that all deeds should be done with perfect detachment and preached *bhakti*, devotion, to him.

fig. 120 The battle of Kurukshetra was atrocious. It is shown in the great south relief of the western gallery of Angkor Wat. Krishna's life ended in tragedy. A war broke out within his clan and Balarāma perished. Krishna then retired into the forest and there was killed by a hunter, who mistook him for an antelope and letting fly an arrow, hit him in the heel—the only part of his body that was vulnerable, as with Achilles. Thus the last *avātar* of Vishnu end in an atmosphere of sorrow. They probably record heroes who gained fame in the internecine wars of the Indian principalities. More human than the other *avātar* they met a tragic fate.

BRAHMA

The third god of the Trimūrti is not as vigorous a character as Śiva and Vishnu. Brahma is the Brahman god *par excellence*.

Brahma is represented with four faces. Each of his mouths has revealed one of the Veda. His mount is the swan, the *hamsa*.

The legends about Brahma are cruel. It is told how he pursued one of his daughters to commit incest with her, until Śiva cut off his fifth head. The legend of the lingodbhavamūrti presents him as boastful and even as a liar. Vishnuite myths are more favorable to him. Enthroned on the lotus issuing from the navel of Vishnu, he participates in the new creation of the world, at the dawn of a cosmic era.

BUDDHIST ICONOGRAPHY

The pre-Angkorian period has left us quite a number of statues of Buddha of high quality both as to craftsmanship and as to the postures and expression of the faces. In the first two centuries of Angkorian art, Buddha images become rare; but after the middle of the eleventh century, Khmer Buddhist art became widespread. The iconography of the Angkorian images is primarily Mahāyānist. In shrines and on reliefs we find images of the Buddha and the *Bodhisattvas*. Only at the temple of Preah Palilay, built to the north of the Royal Palace of Angkor Thom, are there nothing but scenes from the life of the Buddha in a perspective which is that of the ancient Buddhism often called the "Lesser Vehicle."

Buddha and Bodhisattva

The Buddha, the "Enlightened One," is also the "Blessed," *fig. 149* Bhagavat, or the "Conqueror," Jina. But the historic Buddha is not the only one. During past cosmic periods there were multitudes of Buddhas. Some of these attained Enlightenment and were freed from the bond of rebirth, but they kept this wisdom for themselves and did not preach a doctrine. These are the *pratyeka buddha*, the Buddhas for themselves. They were able to achieve this state even outside Buddhist religion. It is possible that they are represented in the innumerable Buddha images carved in little arcades, on friezes, on the walls of shrines or on the cresting along the tops of walls or roof ridges.

Only "perfectly enlightened" Buddhas reveal the Buddhist Law to the world. This Law that they have discovered through Enlightenment offers to all living things the way to achieve liberation from reincarnation. All perfectly enlightened Buddhas have had the same career. Each moment in the life of the historical Buddha had been lived in the same way by all the past Buddhas, his predecessors; and the life of the Maitreya, the Buddha of future, will take the same course. In consequence it may not be easy to recognize in a temple relief whether some episode depicted there refers to the life of Śākyamuni or to that of a Buddha of the past.

There are lists of past Buddhas, lists that vary according to the schools and texts. One of the most famous of these Buddhas is Dipankara who, during a past era, announced to a young ascetic, Sumedha, that, as he desired, he would achieve the state of Buddhahood. After a considerable number of rebirths he who had been the ascetic Sumedha was reincarnated to become the historical Buddha. Dipankara was represented in the pre-Angkorian period, making the gesture of presentation with his right hand. A statue of Sumedha has been found, later than the art of the Bayon, showing the hermit stretched out at full length to make his body into a passage for Dipankara so that he should not soil his feet. The present cosmic era, or *kalpa*, is to be honored with the apparition of five Buddhas. Three of them preceded Śākyamuni. The fifth, Maitreya, will only be born once more among men in order to achieve complete Enlightenment and Buddhahood. While waiting for this ultimate rebirth he resides in an upper heaven, that of the Tushita gods, gods "who are satisfied."

Mahāyāna and Hināyāna

From a very early date, the teaching of the Buddha was interpreted and commented by different schools of philosophy. In spite of their divergences, the early schools did not deviate much from the original Buddhism. But the speculations of these schools prepared the way for a new tendency which gradually developed the Mahāyāna doctrine, that of the "Greater Vehicle" or better the "Great means of progression" towards salvation, the "Great ferry" across the ocean of existences. Considering their doctrine as a superior mode of progression towards salvation, the adepts of the Mahāyāna dubbed the old Buddhism Hināyāna, "Lesser Vehicle," "Small means of progression" towards salvation, or even "Small ferry." Among the sects of the earlier Buddhism the Theravāda, the "doctrine of the Ancients" developed in Ceylon and then in southeast Asia, and after the end of the thirteenth century it became the chief religion of Cambodia.

Mahāyāna Buddhism, starting out from speculations on the

nature of the Buddhas and *Bodhisattvas*, has become a religion of salvation. During their previous lives the *Bodhisattvas* accumulated merit which destined them for the state of Buddhahood; but out of compassion for all creatures they delay their entry into *nirvāna*, which is ultimate extinction, liberation from all material life. By a transfer of the merits acquired by the Buddhas and *Bodhisattvas*, their worshipers can achieve their own salvation. Late Mahāyāna Buddhism recognizes the existence of five transcendent Buddhas or Jina who are above human Buddhas. Western writing often refers to them as "Buddhas of Meditation," but this term does not appear in ancient Buddhist texts. Each of these Jina is localized in the cosmos: Vairochana at the zenith, Akshobhya to the east, Ratnasambhava to the south, Amitābha to the west and Amoghasiddhi to the north. Ancient Mahāyānist texts sometimes substitute Bhaishajyaguru for Akshobhya. He is the "Master of Remedies" to whom are dedicated the hospital chapels founded by Jayavarman VII. Above the five Jina is the Adi Buddha, the primordial Buddha.

To these five Jina correspond five human Buddhas and five *Bodhisattvas*. The historical Buddha, Śākyamuni, corresponds to Amitābha. The *Bodhisattvas* most often represented in Angkorian art, Avalokiteśvara and Vajrapāni, correspond respectively to Amitābha and Akshobhya. Further, each Jina possesses an energy, a *shaktī*, personified as a goddess. Among these goddesses Tarā is the most frequently met with. She is associated with Avalokiteśvara in the ancient Mahāyānist texts. Tarā is the "Star," or "She who takes across," consequently "She who saves." The Mahāyānist pantheon comprises many other gods, some of whom are Brahman in origin. Among the *figs. 11, 138* gods we should quote Hevajra and Trailokavijaya, "Who is victorious over the three worlds." Lastly Prajñāpāramitā, "Perfection of wisdom," is a female deity personifying texts, the sutra of the Prajñāpāramitā.

The Life of the Buddha

For one acquainted with the altar statues and paintings of the modern shrines of southeast Asia, Angkorian Buddhist iconography may seem somewhat monotonous, in spite of its high quality as sculpture. The images carved in the round only show the Blessed One in very few poses, and the carvings on the pediments repeat again and again the images of the Buddha being worshiped by assembled figures often in princely costume. Then again the images of the Buddha have been mutilated on many of the reliefs, the result of some iconoclastic movement at present only explained by hypotheses. Only the temple of Preah Palilay shows more varied iconography, in the direction of the ancient Buddhism.

Except at a late date, there is no known image of the birth of prince Siddhārtha, the future Buddha. Scenes of his life start with the Great Departure, when he decides to leave his father's palace to live a monk's life. Still wearing his royal decorations, he leaves at night on horseback, accompanied only by his groom; but the gods give him escort while the Mahārājikka, the great kings of the four points of the compass, hold the hoofs of his horse so that their galloping does not awaken the sleeping occupants of the palace. At the Bayon, Ta Prohm,

Neak Pean and even Wat Nokor of Kompong Cham the miraculous scene is inscribed like a triumphal march within the approximate triangle of the tympana.

After leaving Kapilavastu, the capital of his father, the king of the Śākya, prince Siddārtha dismounts from his horse who will shortly die of sorrow. He removes his princely garb which he hands to his groom; then, drawing his sword, he cuts off his long hair. The "Cutting of the hair" is shown at the Bayon; it occurs again on a pilaster of Ta Prohm on which certain historiated scrolls frame scenes from the life of the Buddha. The most moving representation however dates from the reoccupation of Angkor in the sixteenth century. A pediment oj Preah Pithu shows the *Bodhisattva* cutting off his hair while, on the lower register, his groom, overcome with grief and leaning his head on the dying horse, is weeping.

There is no example, that we know of, of the time when the Blessed One, having become the hermit of the Śākya family, Śākyamuni, sought in vain through a variety of religious experiences, to find the way of Deliverance.

The height of Buddha's career was the acquisition of Enlightenment, the *Bodhi*. The Buddha seated in meditation with crossed legs and his hands in his lap was represented time and again both in the round and in relief, and some of these images are among the masterpieces of Khmer art. The sculptors represented several episodes of this climactic moment, and especially the fight against Māra. Māra appears as a demon; he is in fact king of a class of deities of very high rank who "dispose of the phantasms of others" and who would be frustrated if universal respect for Buddhist Law led to total renunciation by all beings. Māra thus does all in his power to prevent the achievement of Enlightenment. He tried to frighten the Buddha with a monstrous army; then, disputing his merits, set about persuading him that he must leave the diamond throne that had miraculously risen up from the ground. The Buddha then took the Earth to witness to the merit he had acquired by multitudes of gifts in the course of his previous existences. According to Indian custom a donor must always pour water over the hands of the recipient of the gift. In his previous lives the *Bodhisattva* had made thousands of gifts, and each time he had poured water over the hands of those he had gratified. The Earth had received this water and had kept it. When asked to bear witness she appeared in the aspect of a young goddess, Brah Dharani, and began to wring out her hair. Now all the water previously poured by the Blessed One each time he had made a gift flowed out of the Earth's hair, in a torrent which swept away the monstrous army. After trying without success to seduce the Buddha through his daughters, Māra submitted. The future Buddha was at last able to absorb himself in meditation and achieve complete Enlightenment. During this meditation, realizing the incessant repetition of sufferings from one life to the next, he became aware of the path to be followed to escape from the wheel of rebirth.

The victory over Māra is illustrated on pediments at the Bayon, at Preah Palilay and at Beng Mealea; the two former are badly damaged and the third is partly unfinished. A relief on a wall at Ta Prohm shows the same scene; it is a large composition in which can be made out the assault of Māra and the figure of the Earth, standing near the Buddha. Victorious over Māra, the Buddha is still in the posture of Taking the Earth as Witness: touching the edge of his seat, the diamond throne, with the tips of the fingers of his right hand.

The Buddha's meditation continued for seven weeks according to the Theravāda; for only four, in the Mahāyāna tradition. Angkorian iconography has stressed one incident that occurred during this period. While the Blessed One was meditating more and more deeply on the truths he had discovered during his Enlightenment, a diluvian rain began to pour. A *nāga*, Muchilinda, came to him to shelter him. The coils of his body formed a seat for the Buddha whose head he protected with his unfurled hoods. Khmer art multiplied with great success the images of the Buddha seated in meditation on the *nāga*.

There are many pediments on which the Buddha is seated among worshipers who are doubtless receiving instruction. It is unfortunately not easy to identify the sermons precisely. We are not even able to recognize the first sermon during which the Buddha set in motion the Wheel of the Law, nor the sermon in Trayastrimsa, the heaven of the thirty-three gods on the summit of Mount Meru, where the Buddha preached his doctrine to his mother. After her death on earth, she had been reborn in a higher heaven; she came down now among the gods, over whom Indra throned, to listen to the sermon of the Blessed One. After teaching them for three months, the Buddha returned to earth on a triple staircase, accompanied by Brahma and Indra. The other episodes of the Buddha's life, founding a community of monks, visiting monasteries, occur but seldom; there is however a pediment at Preah Palilay illustrating the episode of the raging elephant. The Buddha was at Rājagriha, a royal city near the place of his Enlightenment. His jealous cousin Devadatta set a raging elephant at him, but in his presence the elephant became quiet and knelt at his feet. The Preah Palilay pediment translates the scene into one of great serenity, both in the benevolent posture of the Buddha and in the submission of the elephant.

Mahāparinirvāna, the entry into total extinction, was not often shown in Angkorian art. The Buddha, sick and very old, was at Kuśinagara. He gave his last advice to the monks who attended him, then lay down on his right side and left this life, never to be reborn. Images of the Mahāparinirvāna are mostly in the Theravāda tradition. One of the finest sculptures is a statue deposited in the Preah Pean of Angkor Wat. It is unusual in showing the Buddha lying on his left side. The Buddha is alone. Only in modern iconography do the artists show the disciples round him, demonstrating their distress at the disappearance of their master.

The Previous Lives of the Buddha

After being told by the Buddha Dipankara that he would one day attain Buddhahood, the young hermit Sumedha went through an incalculable number of reincarnations. When he became the Buddha Śākyamuni he remembered his previous existences and revealed some of them to his disciples. They form the sequence of the 547 canonical *jātakas*.

The favorite subjects of the artists were the ten existences preceding the final incarnation of the Blessed One. Here and there in Angkorian iconography one can identify episodes belonging to these previous lives On one pediment two figures brandishing their weapons are trying to frighten the young prince Temiya. Temiya, an incarnation of the future Buddha, seeing his father inflicting harsh punishments on the guilty, decided to renounce the throne; he feared that the exercise of power would bring him to carry out acts of violence such as this. Henceforth he adopted the behavior of an imbecile, insensible to everything. His father tried in vain to draw him from his inertia with promises of pleasure or with threats; to no avail. In despair the father decided to put him to death. When a palace servant took him into the forest to execute the sentence, the young man came out of his apathy and showed himself with his full strength and intelligence. The king hastened to him, called by the servant; but prince Temiya had already taken vows that he would lead a hermit's life.

Most of the other *jātakas* cannot be identified on the partially damaged reliefs. The only one that can be recognized with certainty is the last one, the *jātaka* of prince Vessantara. While he was still very young Vessantara was already inexhaustibly charitable. His father's kingdom possessed a miraculous elephant whose presence was sufficient to make the rain fall where the elephant stood. The neighboring kingdom was suffering fearful drought, and the people of this land came to ask Vessantara for the gift of this elephant, and obtained it; but in the kingdom which had lost the elephant that ensured its prosperity, the people began to murmur and the king had to exile his son.

The prince, accompanied by his wife Maddī and their two children, went off to the forest on a wagon; but on the way, beggars asked them first for the horses, then for the wagon. Vessantara gave them away. At that time there lived nearby a Brahman called Jūjaka. He was old and ugly and madly enamoured of his young wife. She was mocked by the other women of the village for the trouble she took with her old husband. One day, having had enough of this, she asked Jūjaka to find her some servants and suggested he ask Vessantara for his children as slaves. The old Brahman went off to find the prince and found him alone, for the gods had arranged to keep Maddī delayed in the forest. Vessantara, being unable to refuse to give when asked, handed over his children who were taken off by Jūjaka. Returning to the hermitage and hearing the hideous news, Maddī fainted. Meanwhile Jūjaka took the children to the court of their grandparents, hoping to sell them at a high price; this he obtained and had such a celebration with the money that he died of it.

The gods made one more test of the charity of Vessantara. In the guise of a Brahman, black and emaciated, Indra came to ask him for Maddī herself; the prince consented. Then Indra, revealing his divinity, reunited the pair; and the king and queen with their grand-children came in a great procession to find Vessantara and Maddī.

Representations of the *Vessantarajātaka* exist in various Angkorian temples, primarily at the Bayon and at Thommanon. A small relief in the National Museum of Phnom Penh figures, in three tableaux, the three essential gifts: the elephant, the children and Maddī. The carving is skillful, the silhouettes elegant. The three scenes take place in a serene atmosphere that neglects

266

the dramatic character of the series of gifts in order to stress the merits acquired by Vessantara and, perhaps against their will, by his family.

Avalokitesvara

Pediments, lintels, and mural reliefs as well, show large numbers of images of the *Bodhisattva* whose statues were often set up in the shrines. For the *Bodhisattva* are eminently compassionate and can receive the prayers of the faithful. They are exceptional beings, destined for Enlightenment, who voluntarily defer their entry into *nirvāna* in order to lead all that lives towards salvation.

Of all the *Bodhisattva*, Avalokitesvara was by far the most widely revered in Cambodia. His name is generally interpreted as "Lord who looks down from on high," [in compassion]. He is also Lokesvara, "Lord of the worlds" [which he protects], or again Padmapāni, "He who holds the lotus in his hand." To him is addressed the famous *Om mani padme hūm*, "Om! the jewel in the lotus, hūm!" This formula does not seem to occur earlier than the eleventh century.

Avalokitesvara appears in the form of a young man with four arms. On his head, in front of the hair bun, he wears the image *fig. 88* of Buddha Amitābha. He holds in his hands the lotus, rosary, book and ambrosia flask. His palace, Potalaka, rises in the Himalaya, on a mountain bearing the same name.

Avalokitesvara can be invoked to obtain salvation and also for protection against earthly perils: illness, damage by water or fire. Lokesvara is powerful on behalf of his devotees, and much superior to the gods who rule our universe. Even Śiva, though first among the gods of the terrestial world, needed to resort to him. Together with his wife Umā, he begged Lokesvara to let him achieve Buddhahood; and the *Bodhisattva* promised the two deities that they would see their wish realized. The scene is carved on a wall of the west gallery of Banteay Chhmar. The long relief in this gallery presents a series of large compositions illustrating various manifestations of Avalokitesvara, in the manner of the invocations of a litany.

There is a group in the reservoir of Neak Pean representing Avalokitesvara in the aspect of the Horse Balāha. Some merchants had been shipwrecked near an island populated by ogresses. These ladies were in the habit of attracting shipwrecked mariners, marrying them and then devouring them once a newly wrecked ship provided them with a new cargo of husbands. The leader of these unfortunates quickly realized the fate in store for his companions and himself. He made an ardent prayer to Lokesvara. The merciful *Bodhisattva* came to him in the guise of a miraculous horse, Balāha, and told the *fig. 90* mariners to hold on to him. Then the horse plunged into the sea and carried the mariners home. One *jātaka* tells the same story but attributes the miraculous intervention to the future historical Buddha. However, it is not only material salvation that is brought by Balāha to those who pray to him, but spiritual salvation, by liberation from the cycle of rebirth.

Khmer art has bequeathed some wonderful Buddhist images to us. With their eyes closed, and only the vestige of a smile, Buddha and *Bodhisattva* concentrate their spirits in blissful *fig. 151* meditation. Yet they lean slightly forward to show their compassion for all those who invoke them.

GLOSSARY

Abbreviations: Kh. = Khmer
Skt. = Sanskrit

Abhisheka – skt.   Ritual ablution. Royal sacring by dousing or sprinkling with water

Amrita – skt.   Ambrosia. Elixir of immortality

Añjali – skt.   Posture of homage, with the hands joined

Apsarā – skt.   Female deity; celestial dancer

Āśrama – skt.   Hermitage

Asura – skt.   Demon heroes, enemies of the gods

Avātar – skt.   A human or animal incarnation of the god Vishnu, descending into the world to deliver it from some peril

Baray – kh.   Artificial lake, of religious significance

Beng – kh.   Pool, marsh

Bhikshu – skt.   Mendicant monk

Chakra – skt.   Disk. In Brahmanic iconography the *chakra* is among the attributes of Vishnu; in Buddhist iconography it is the wheel, symbol of the Buddhist Law

Chakravartin – skt.   Universal monarch

Devarāja – skt.   Śivaite ritual on which, since the ninth century, the foundations of the Khmer monarchy were based

Devatā – skt.   Deity. A name given to the female figures carved on temple walls

Dharma – skt.   Right. Law founded on religious and moral rule

Dharmaśāstra – skt.   Juridical treatise

Garuda – skt.   Mythical bird, enemy of snakes, the mount of Vishnu

Gopura – skt.   The entrance pavilion to a temple; gate house

Guru – skt.   Spiritual advisor, master

Hamsa – skt.   Wild goose or swan, the mount of Brahma

Kalpa – skt.   Cosmic period

Kinnarī – skt.   Mythical being with the bust of a woman and a bird's body; harpy

Lingam – skt.   Sign, emblem, phallus. Symbol of the creative power of Śiva

Makara – skt. Mythical marine monster with teeth and sometimes a proboscis. Sometimes identified with the crocodile

Mandala – skt.   Symbolic diagram arranged in a circle

Mandapa – skt.   Pavilion. In a temple, a hall, generally resting on columns; the hall built in front of a shrine

Nāga (fem. *Nāgī*) – skt.   Snake, generally many-headed. A water deity. Guardian of treasure

Pradakshina – skt.   Rite of circumambulation round a cult object or a monument in the auspicious direction, i.e. keeping it on the right

Prāsāt – kh. (skt. *Prāsāda*)   Terraced palace, temple, tower-shrine

Prasavya – skt.   Rite of circumambulation round a cult object or a monument in the inauspicious direction, i.e. keeping it on the left

Pūjā – skt.   Rite of homage to a god manifest in an image

Rākshasa (fem. rākshasī) – skt.   Demon beings, inhabiting Lanka (Ceylon) with Rāvana as their king

Rishi – skt.   Ascetic, hermit

Sampot – kh.   Lower garment of the Cambodians, which is draped round the hips and knotted in front; the ends of the cloth, passed between the legs, are attached to the belt at the back

Samrit – kh.   Bronze whose alloy contains some gold and silver

Sarong – kh.   Lower garment worn as a skirt. In Angkorian art it is the female garment

Śivakshetra – skt.   Area consecrated to Śiva

Stūpa – skt.   Buddhist monument in the form of a dome which holds relics or commemorates a religious event

Tīrtha – skt.   Sacred ford, sacred basin

Trapeang – kh.   Pool, pond

Triśūla – skt.   Trident, attribute of Śiva

Upayuvarāja – skt.   Princely title generally borne by a king who has abdicated

Vīnā – skt.   Indian stringed musical instrument

Yuvarāja – skt.   Princely title, generally borne by the heir apparent

MAPS AND PLANS

MAP OF CAMBODIA

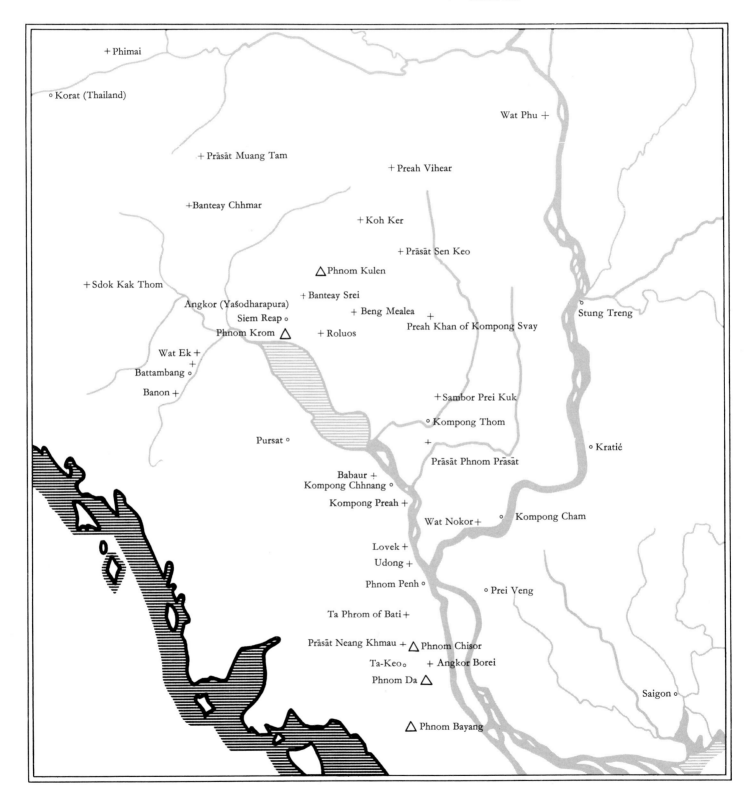

△ = monuments situated on a hill or mountain (= *phnom*)
o = modern cities
+ = ancient sites

+ Phimai

o Korat (Thailand)

Wat Phu +

+ Prāsāt Muang Tam

+ Preah Vihear

+Banteay Chhmar

+ Koh Ker

+ Prāsāt Sen Keo

+ Sdok Kak Thom

△ Phnom Kulen

+ Banteay Srei

Angkor (Yaśodharapura)
Siem Reap o
Phnom Krom △

+ Beng Mealea

+
Preah Khan of Kompong Svay

Stung Treng

+ Roluos

Wat Ek +
+
Battambang o

Banon +

+Sambor Prei Kuk

o Kompong Thom

Pursat o

+
Prāsāt Phnom Prāsāt

o Kratié

Babaur +
Kompong Chhnang o

Kompong Preah +

Wat Nokor+   o Kompong Cham

Lovek +

Udong +

Phnom Penh o

o Prei Veng

Ta Phrom of Bati +

Prāsāt Neang Khmau + △ Phnom Chisor

Ta-Keo o   + Angkor Borei

Phnom Da △

Saigon o

△ Phnom Bayang

PLAN OF THE GREAT SQUARE OF ANGKOR THOM

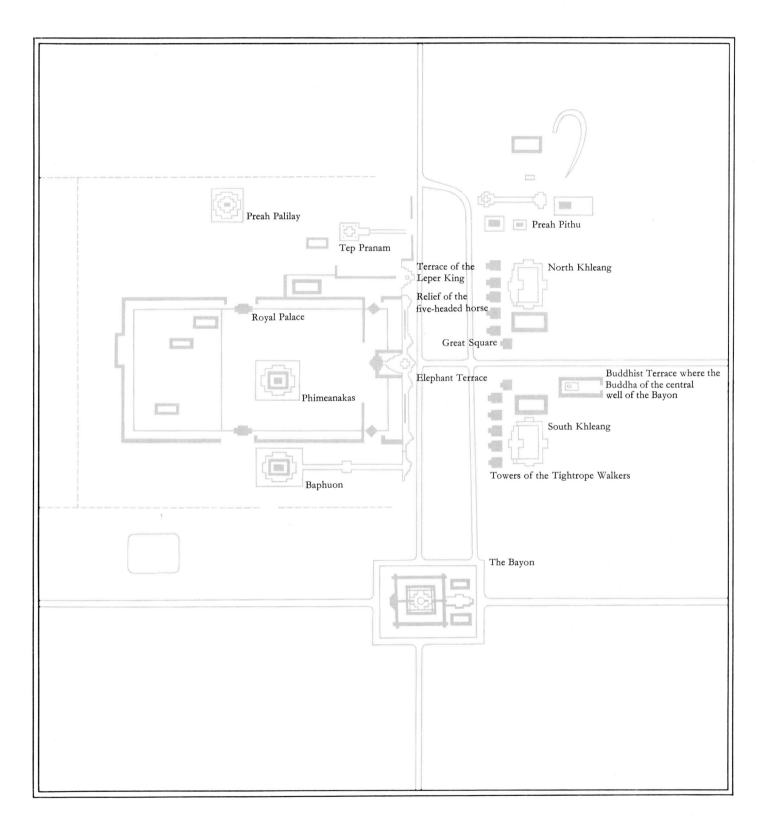

Preah Palilay

Tep Pranam

Terrace of the
Leper King

Relief of the
five-headed horse

Royal Palace

Great Square

Phimeanakas

Elephant Terrace

Baphuon

Preah Pithu

North Khleang

Buddhist Terrace where the
Buddha of the central
well of the Bayon

South Khleang

Towers of the Tightrope Walkers

The Bayon

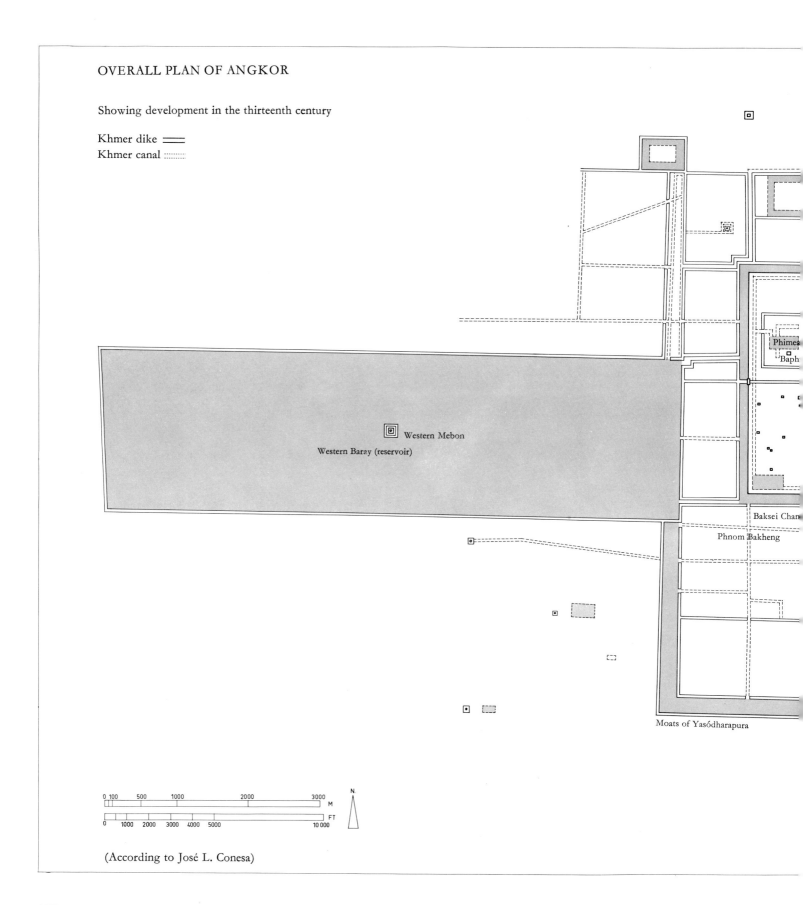

OVERALL PLAN OF ANGKOR

Showing development in the thirteenth century

Khmer dike ═══
Khmer canal ┄┄┄

Phimea
Baph

Western Mebon

Western Baray (reservoir)

Baksei Chan

Phnom Bakheng

Moats of Yasódharapura

0 100 500 1000   2000   3000
                                    M

0   1000 2000 3000 4000 5000   10 000

FT

N.

(According to José L. Conesa)

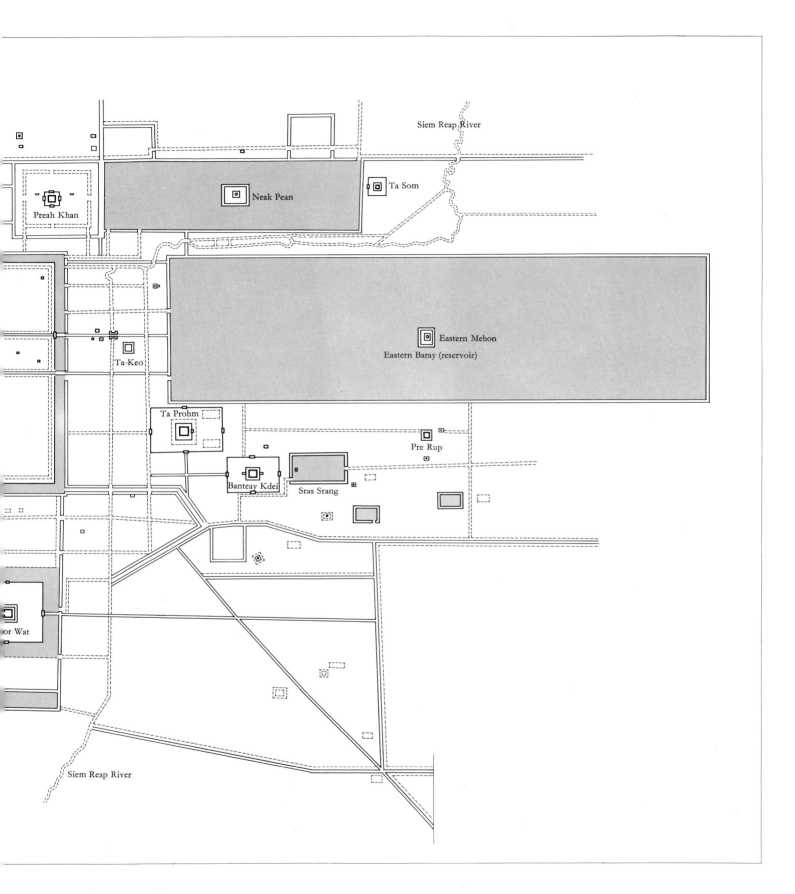

Siem Reap River

Ta Som

Neak Pean

Preah Khan

Eastern Mebon

Eastern Baray (reservoir)

Ta-Keo

Ta Prohm

Pre Rup

Banteay Kdei

Sras Srang

or Wat

Siem Reap River

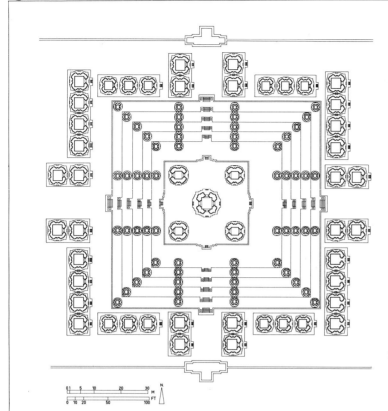

PHNOM BAKHENG, ANGKOR

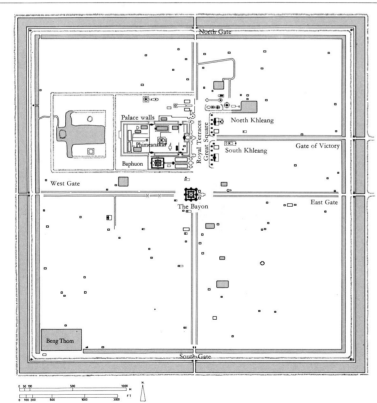

ANGKOR THOM: map of the city

North Gate

Palace walls

North Khleang

Phimeanakas

Gate of Victory

South Khleang

Baphuon

West Gate

The Bayon

East Gate

Beng Thom

South Gate

Royal Terraces

Great Square

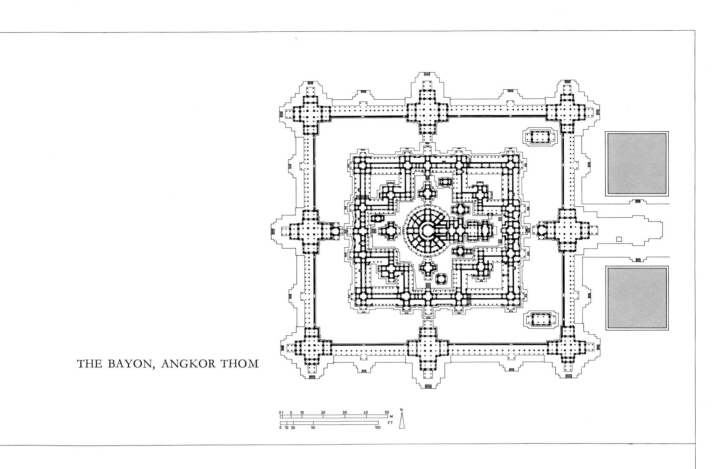

THE BAYON, ANGKOR THOM

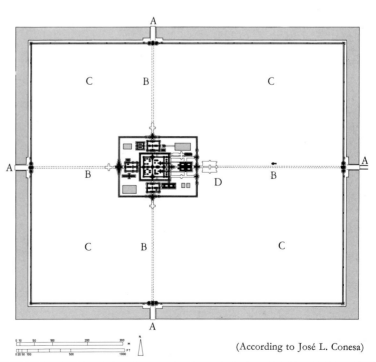

EAH KHAN, ANGKOR:

Roadways on the dikes across the moat   C Quadrants occupied by the city
Axial causeways   D Dance platform in front of the temple

(According to José L. Conesa)

BIBLIOGRAPHY

ABBREVIATIONS

Art. As.	*Artibus Asiae*; Ascona, Switzerland
BCAI	*Bulletin de la commission archéologique de l'Indochine*; Paris
BEFEO	*Bulletin de l'Ecole Française d'Extrême-Orient*; Hanoi, Saigon, Paris
Publ. EFEO	Publications de l'Ecole d'Extrême-Orient; Paris and Saigon

AYMONIER, ETIENNE. *Le Cambodge*. 3 vols. Paris, 1901–1903.

BHATTACHARYA, KAMALESWAR. *Les religions brahmaniques dans l'ancien Cambodge, d'après l'épigraphie et l'iconographie*. vol. XLIX. Paris, 1961.

BOISSELIER, JEAN. *La statuaire khmère et son évolution*. vol. XXXVIII. Paris and Saigon, 1955.

—"*Tendances de l'Art Khmer*." In *Annales du Musée Guimet*. Paris, 1956.

—"Asie du Sud-Est: le Cambodge." In *Manuel d'archéologie d'Extrême-Orient*. Paris, 1966.

—"Note sur l'art du bronze dans l'ancien Cambodge." In *Art. As.* vol. XXIX. Ascona, 1968.

BOISSELIER, JEAN and BEURDELEY, JEAN-MICHEL. *The Heritage of Thai Sculpture*. trans. by James Emmons. New York and Tokyo, 1975.

BRIGGS, LAURENCE-PALMER. *The Ancient Khmer Empire*. Philadelphia, 1951.

COEDÈS, GEORGE. "Les bas-reliefs d'Angkor-Vat." In *BCAI*. Paris, 1911.

—"Bronzes khmers." In *Ars Asiatica*. vol. V. Paris and Brussels, 1923.

—*Pour mieux comprendre Angkor*. 2nd ed. Paris, 1947.

—"Les Etats hindouisés d'Indochine et d'Indonésie." In *Histoire du Monde*. vol. VIII. Paris, 1948.

—*Inscriptions du Cambodge*. 8 vols. Publ. EFEO. Hanoi then Paris, 1937–1966.

—*Les peuples de la péninsule indochinoise*. Paris, 1962.

DAUPHIN-MEUNIER, ACHILLE. *Histoire du Cambodge*. Paris, 1961.

DELVERT, JEAN. *Le Paysan cambodgien*. Paris-La Haye, 1961.

DUPONT, PIERRE. "Les débuts de la royauté angkorienne." In *BEFEO*. vol. XLVI. Paris and Saigon, pp. 119ff.

—*La statuaire préangkorienne*. In *Art. As. Supplementum XV*, Ascona, 1955.

FILLIOZAT, JEAN. "Le symbolisme du monument du Phnom Bakheng." In *BEFEO*. vol. XLIV. Paris and Saigon, pp. 527ff.

GITEAU, MADELEINE. *Histoire du Cambodge*. Paris, 1957.

—*Khmer Sculpture and the Angkor Civilization*. trans. by Diana Imber. New York, 1965.

—*Histoire d'Angkor*. Paris, 1974.

—*Iconographie du Cambodge post-angkorien*. Publ. EFEO. vol. C. Paris, 1975.

GLAIZE, MAURICE. *Les Monuments du Groupe d'Angkor*. Saigon, 1948.

LUNET DE LAJONQUIÈRE, ETIENNE. *Inventaire descriptif des monuments du Cambodge*. 3 vols. Paris, 1902–1911.

MARCHAL, HENRI. *L'architecture comparée dans l'Inde et l'Extrême-Orient*. Paris, 1944.

—*Le décor et la sculpture khmers*. Paris, 1951.

—*Les temples d'Angkor*. Paris, 1955.

MARTINI, FRANÇOIS. "En marge du Râmâyana cambodgien." In *BEFEO*. vol. XXXVIII. Paris and Saigon, pp. 285ff.

PARMENTIER, HENRI. *Art khmer classique*. Publ. EFEO. vol. XXIX. Paris, 1939.

PORÉE-MASPÉRO, EVELYNE. *Etude sur les rites agraires des Cambodgiens*. Paris and The Hague, 1962.

STERN, PHILIPPE. "Diversité et rythme des fondations royales khmères." In *BEFEO*. vol. XLIV. Paris and Saigon, pp. 649ff.

—*Les monuments khmers du style du Bayon et Jayavarman VII*. Paris, 1965.

TCHÉOU TA-KOUAN. *Mémoires sur les coutumes du Cambodge*. trans. and annotated by P. Pelliot. In *BEFEO*. vol. II. Paris and Saigon, pp. 123ff. New edition with notice by G. Coedès and P. Demiéville. Paris, 1951.

THIERRY, SOLANGE. *Les Khmers*. Paris, 1964.

INDEX

The numbers in italics refer to illustrations

Agni *9, 25*

Amitābha 224; *88, 151*

Ananta 82; *53, 69*

Anavatapta (Lake) 146, 213, 214, 245; *89*

Ang Chan I 246; *148*

Ang Duong 46

Angkor Thom 10, 14, 20, 50, 61, 86, 99, 118, 130, 146, 147, 148, 173, 176, 179, 186, 213, 246, 249, 250; *31, 54, 56, 67, 78, 106, 108, 109, 110, 111, 112, 113, 114, 115, 141, 142, 143, 151*

Angkor Wat 9, 10, 20, 33, 34, 47, 55, 61, 74, 75, 94, 118, 122, 124, 126, 128, 159, 165, 194, 195, 200, 201, 219, 222, 232, 241, 242, 243, 245, 246, 250; *5, 14, 22, 26, 36, 70, 72, 73, 74, 75, 76, 77, 94, 99, 102, 103, 119, 120, 124, 131, 146, 147, 148*

Angkor Wat (style) 94; *52*

Arjuna *24*

Avalokiteśvara 26, 86, 142; *40, 44, 90, 151*

Ayudhyā 118, 245, 246, 249

Bakong 99, 108, 118; *6*

Baksei Chamkrong 106, 242, 249; *58*

Balāha 142, 144; *90*

Balarāma 16, 46; *20*

Banon 18, 84; *40, 43, 127*

Banteay Chhmar 35, 52, 61, 75, 76, 86; *2, 15, 23, 44, 45, 46*

Banteay Kdei 44, 136; *11, 81, 82, 84*

Banteay Samre 33, 118; *13, 25, 71*

Banteay Srei 16, 46, 55, 108, 161, 212, 222, 232; *9, 20, 21, 61, 62, 63, 64, 65, 105, 117, 125, 128, 129*

Ban Thalat 71

Baphuon 36, 55, 115, 116, 222; *67, 68, 135, 142*

Baray, East 108, 118, 146; *47*

Baray, West 102, 120, 146

Battambang 62, 82, 222; *40, 136*

Bayon 9, 16, 26, 31, 35, 38, 52, 56, 61, 72, 75, 76, 78, 79, 86, 94, 130, 142, 147, 154, 161, 162, 169, 173, 176, 194, 195, 200, 201, 206, 213, 222, 238, 242, 249, 250; *3, 7, 16, 17, 19, 27, 28, 29, 32, 34, 35, 37, 38, 46, 78, 79, 80, 91, 92, 93, 97, 98, 100, 101, 107, 118, 121, 122, 133, 140, 142, 144*

Beng Mealea 71, 94; *52*

Bhadraśvara 78, 81; *50*

Bhārata-Rāhu 22; *46*

Bodhisattva 26, 84, 142, 219, 220, 234; *40, 44, 88*

Brahma 22, 50, 95, 102, 126, 144, 230, 238; *8*

Buddha 26, 72, 81, 82, 84, 89, 95, 104, 118, 126, 130, 138, 146, 158, 201, 203, 214, 219, 222, 231, 234, 236, 238; *12, 18, 33, 81, 130, 147, 149*

Champassak 71, 81; *139*

Chau Say Tevoda 118; *70*

Dharanīndravarman I 192, 195, 212

Dharanīndravarman II 138; *87, 88*

Divākarapandita 62, 78, 196, 212

Durgā 228

Gangā 204, 206; *6*

Garuda 56, 81, 138, 195, 228; *95*

Hanuman 84, 195; *42*

Hariharālaya 20, 99, 100; *6, 55, 57*

Harśavarman I 104, 106, 192, 193, 212

Harśavarman II 224

Harśavarman III 192, 196, 212

Hevajra *11, 138*

Hinayāna 14, 219

Indra 176, 192, 201, 211, 213, 249; *18, 20, 108*

Indradevī 205, 206, 232, 241

Indravarman 20, 99, 108, 118, 191, 201

Jayarājadevī 203, 206, 233; *126*

Jayavarman II 20, 66, 68, 78, 101, 196, 212

Jayavarman III 52, 66, 101

Jayavarman IV 20, 92, 192, 106; *51*

Jayavarman V 20, 108, 114, 212

Jayavarman VI 212

Jayavarman VII 10, 20, 22, 26, 46, 80, 82, 86, 89, 91, 94, 95,

101, 128, 130, 136, 138, 144, 148, 173, 176, 179, 191, 192, 196, 201, 203, 206, 212, 213, 216, 219, 224, 237, 249; *46, 80, 82, 83, 88, 123, 126, 137*
Jayavīravarman 20, 69, 114, 192

Kailāsa (Mount) 106, 249; *58, 65*
Kalya 56
Kāma 100
Kamsa *125*
Kāvindrārimathana 108, 196
Khleang, North and South 114, 130, 182
Koh Ker 20, 71, 92, 224; *51*
Kompong Kdei 71; *33*
Kompong Preah 82
Korat 89
Krishna 16, 26, 33, 47, 56, 82, 126, 161, 219; *13, 20, 125, 148*
Krol Romeas 94; *123*
Kuk Nokor *30*
Kurukshetra (battle) 122, 195; *120*

Lakshmana 222; *26, 68*
Lakshmī 198
Lanka (battle) 122, 195, 219; *45*
Lingaparvata 81, 82
Lokeśvara 84, 142; *40, 88*
Lolei 23, 100
Lopburi 89
Lovek, 245, 246

Mahābhārata 23, 116, 231; *20, 24*
Mahārājikka 176, 211, 213
Mahāyāna 14, 26, 118, 219
Mandara (Mount) *42*
Marīcha 56; *26*
Mebon, East 23, 106, 108, 196, 219; *59*
Mebon, West 118; *69*
Meru (Mount) 102, 104, 201, 211, 213, 249; *57, 59, 73*
Muang Tam *10, 47*
Muchilinda 56; *12, 130*

Nandin 197; *10, 53*
Neak Pean 142, 144, 146, 213, 245; *89, 90*
Norodom 65, 189

Parvatī 89
Phimai 71, 80, 89, 94
Phimeanakas 108, 179, 182, 203, 216, 241; *116*
Phnom Bakheng 20, 100, 102, 104, 108, 114, 130, 173, 213, 235, 249
Phnom Basset 82
Phnom Chisor 71, 82
Phnom Kulen 20, 50, 78, 95, 100, 104, 146, 201, 222, 223
Phnom Penh 31, 76, 186, 232, 239, 243; *33*

Phnom Penh National Museum *11, 18, 95, 96, 117, 123, 138, 145*
Phnom Sandok 62
Phum Bavel *136*
Prajñāpāramitā 136
Prāsāt Damrei Krap 95
Prāsāt Komnap 192, 227
Prāsāt Komphus 226, 228
Prāsāt Kravan 106
Prāsāt Sen Keo 24, *135*
Prāsāt Suor Prat 130; *142*
Prāsāt Thom 92; *51*
Prāsāt Trapeang Totung Thngay *104*
Preah Khan of Angkor 71, 80, 86, 92, 130, 134, 138, 142, 146, 219, 222; *85, 86, 87, 88, 126, 134, 137*
Preah Khan of Kompong Svay 71, 92, 94; *123*
Preah Ko 100; *55*
Preah Palilay 118
Preah Pean of Angkor Wat *149*
Preah Pithu 246; *8, 142*
Preah Vihear 78, 91, 92, 211; *49, 50*
Pre Rup 108, 191, 224, 241

Rāhu 22
Rājendravarman II 20, 23, 106, 108, 152, 191, 192, 196, 212, 219, 224, 228, 241, 249; *51, 58, 59, 60*
Rāma 26, 58, 126, 222; *26, 42, 45, 68*
Rāmāyana 26, 58, 231, 232, 239
Rāvana 22; *26, 42, 45, 65, 68*
Roluos 20, 99, 108, 118

Sadāśiva 66
Sambor Prei Kuk 71
Samrong Sen 36
Satha I 246
Say-feng 235
Sdok Kat Thom 47, 66, 78
Siem Reap (River) 71, 100, 104, 146, 159, 166, 241; *33, 53*
Sitā 84; *26, 42, 68*
Śiva 22, 23, 79, 81, 84, 89, 92, 95, 102, 104, 106, 219, 222, 224, 228, 241, 242; *6, 8, 10, 49, 50, 53, 58, 65, 117, 136*
Śivakaivalya, 66, 201, 212
Skanda 50
Sneng 62
Spean Praptos 71; *33*
Srah Srang 44; *84*
Srei Santhor 245
Sugrīva *68*
Sukhodaya 89, 245; *85*
Sūrya 50
Sūryavarman I 20, 66, 82, 92, 115, 182, 192, 196, 198, 219, 232
Sūryavarman II 20, 62, 75, 118, 159, 192, 194, 195, 200, 201, 212, 219, 243, 245, 251

Ta-Keo 115, 235; *66*

278

Tang Kauk 62; *30*
Ta Prohm 34, 134, 136, 196, 222, 225; *83, 86, 137, 150*
Ta Som 132; *1*
Tep Pranam 104
Theravāda-Buddhism 14, 219, 245; *40*
Thommanon 118; *70*
Trailokyavijaya 91
Trāyastrimsa 213
Trimūrti 23; *8*
Tūol Prāsāt 68

Udayādityavarman I 22, 192
Udayādityavarman II 115, 118, 146, 212; *67*
Udong 82, 152
Umā 50, 106, 224; *6, 10, 53, 65, 117*

Vajradhara 91
Valin *68*

Vāmaśiva 66, 100, 102
Vessantara 222; *18*
Viśvakarman 124
Vīralakshmī 66, 192
Vishnu 16, 23, 33, 50, 79, 81, 82, 92, 95, 106, 118, 124, 126, 195, 219, 224, 227; *8, 20, 38, 42, 53, 69, 139, 147*

Wat Baset 68
Wat Ek Phnom 18, 84; *42*
Wat Nokor 82; *41*
Wat Phu 71, 79, 81, 82, 92, 94, 108, 212, 230; *39, 50, 60, 139*

Yajñavarāha 108, 114, 192, 212, 213, 230, 231, 232; *61*
Yāma *124, 131*
Yaśodharapura 176, 213, 245, 249; *51, 57*
Yaśovarman I 9, 20, 23, 66, 92, 100, 102, 104, 106, 108, 146, 148, 173, 191, 212, 213, 230, 231, 232, 249; *57, 59*
Yaśovarman II 22, 192, 213; *46*

PHOTO CREDITS

Raymond Cauchetier: 1, 5, 7, 41, 52, 71, 73, 84, 85, 99, 101

Yves Coffin: 3, 10, 21, 42, 48, 51, 53, 61, 65, 66, 67, 80, 81, 89, 103, 110, 111, 119, 130, 135, 141, 149, 151

Ecole Française d'Extrême-Orient: 22, 26, 36, 124, 131

Madeleine Giteau: 17, 30, 33, 35, 39, 46, 47, 60, 64, 72, 76, 79, 91, 113, 139, 143

Hans Hinz: 2, 6, 8, 9, 11, 12, 13, 14, 15, 18, 20, 23, 25, 31, 34, 40, 43, 44, 45, 54, 55, 56, 58, 63, 68, 69, 70, 77, 82, 83, 87, 88, 90, 94, 95, 96, 98, 100, 102, 104, 106, 109, 116, 117, 118, 120, 123, 125, 126, 127, 128, 134, 136, 138, 142, 145, 148

M. Ordonnaud: 49, 50

Henri Stierlin: 4, 16, 19, 21, 27, 28, 29, 32, 37, 38, 57, 62, 74, 75, 78, 86, 92, 93, 97, 105, 107, 108, 112, 115, 121, 122, 129, 132, 133, 137, 140, 144, 146, 147

(The numbers refer to the captions.)

This book was printed on the presses of Schüler S.A., Arts Graphiques, Bienne, in September, 1976. Photoengraving: E. Kreienbühl & Co. AG, Lucerne. Binding: H. & J. Schumacher S.A., Berne/Schmitten. Designers: André Rosselet and Yves Buchheim. Editorial: Barbara Perroud. Production: Yves Buchheim.

Printed in Switzerland